Mometrix
TEST PREPARATION

MACE®

Secrets Study Guide

DEAR FUTURE EXAM SUCCESS STORY

First of all, **THANK YOU** for purchasing Mometrix study materials!

Second, congratulations! You are one of the few determined test-takers who are committed to doing whatever it takes to excel on your exam. **You have come to the right place.** We developed these study materials with one goal in mind: to deliver you the information you need in a format that's concise and easy to use.

In addition to optimizing your guide for the content of the test, we've outlined our recommended steps for breaking down the preparation process into small, attainable goals so you can make sure you stay on track.

We've also analyzed the entire test-taking process, identifying the most common pitfalls and showing how you can overcome them and be ready for any curveball the test throws you.

Standardized testing is one of the biggest obstacles on your road to success, which only increases the importance of doing well in the high-pressure, high-stakes environment of test day. Your results on this test could have a significant impact on your future, and this guide provides the information and practical advice to help you achieve your full potential on test day.

Your success is our success

We would love to hear from you! If you would like to share the story of your exam success or if you have any questions or comments in regard to our products, please contact us at **800-673-8175** or **support@mometrix.com**.

Thanks again for your business and we wish you continued success!

Sincerely,
The Mometrix Test Preparation Team

Need more help? Check out our flashcards at:
http://mometrixflashcards.com/MACE

Written and edited by the Mometrix Exam Secrets Test Prep Team
Printed in the United States of America

Table of Contents

Introduction

Thank you for purchasing this resource! You have made the choice to prepare yourself for a test that could have a huge impact on your future, and this guide is designed to help you be fully ready for test day. Obviously, it's important to have a solid understanding of the test material, but you also need to be prepared for the unique environment and stressors of the test, so that you can perform to the best of your abilities.

For this purpose, the first section that appears in this guide is the **Secret Keys**. We've devoted countless hours to meticulously researching what works and what doesn't, and we've boiled down our findings to the five most impactful steps you can take to improve your performance on the test. We start at the beginning with study planning and move through the preparation process, all the way to the testing strategies that will help you get the most out of what you know when you're finally sitting in front of the test.

We recommend that you start preparing for your test as far in advance as possible. However, if you've bought this guide as a last-minute study resource and only have a few days before your test, we recommend that you skip over the first two Secret Keys since they address a long-term study plan.

If you struggle with **test anxiety**, we strongly encourage you to check out our recommendations for how you can overcome it. Test anxiety is a formidable foe, but it can be beaten, and we want to make sure you have the tools you need to defeat it.

Secret Key #1 – Plan Big, Study Small

There's a lot riding on your performance. If you want to ace this test, you're going to need to keep your skills sharp and the material fresh in your mind. You need a plan that lets you review everything you need to know while still fitting in your schedule. We'll break this strategy down into three categories.

Information Organization

Start with the information you already have: the official test outline. From this, you can make a complete list of all the concepts you need to cover before the test. Organize these concepts into groups that can be studied together, and create a list of any related vocabulary you need to learn so you can brush up on any difficult terms. You'll want to keep this vocabulary list handy once you actually start studying since you may need to add to it along the way.

Time Management

Once you have your set of study concepts, decide how to spread them out over the time you have left before the test. Break your study plan into small, clear goals so you have a manageable task for each day and know exactly what you're doing. Then just focus on one small step at a time. When you manage your time this way, you don't need to spend hours at a time studying. Studying a small block of content for a short period each day helps you retain information better and avoid stressing over how much you have left to do. You can relax knowing that you have a plan to cover everything in time. In order for this strategy to be effective though, you have to start studying early and stick to your schedule. Avoid the exhaustion and futility that comes from last-minute cramming!

Study Environment

The environment you study in has a big impact on your learning. Studying in a coffee shop, while probably more enjoyable, is not likely to be as fruitful as studying in a quiet room. It's important to keep distractions to a minimum. You're only planning to study for a short block of time, so make the most of it. Don't pause to check your phone or get up to find a snack. It's also important to **avoid multitasking**. Research has consistently shown that multitasking will make your studying dramatically less effective. Your study area should also be comfortable and well-lit so you don't have the distraction of straining your eyes or sitting on an uncomfortable chair.

The time of day you study is also important. You want to be rested and alert. Don't wait until just before bedtime. Study when you'll be most likely to comprehend and remember. Even better, if you know what time of day your test will be, set that time aside for study. That way your brain will be used to working on that subject at that specific time and you'll have a better chance of recalling information.

Finally, it can be helpful to team up with others who are studying for the same test. Your actual studying should be done in as isolated an environment as possible, but the work of organizing the information and setting up the study plan can be divided up. In between study sessions, you can discuss with your teammates the concepts that you're all studying and quiz each other on the details. Just be sure that your teammates are as serious about the test as you are. If you find that your study time is being replaced with social time, you might need to find a new team.

Secret Key #2 – Make Your Studying Count

You're devoting a lot of time and effort to preparing for this test, so you want to be absolutely certain it will pay off. This means doing more than just reading the content and hoping you can remember it on test day. It's important to make every minute of study count. There are two main areas you can focus on to make your studying count.

Retention

It doesn't matter how much time you study if you can't remember the material. You need to make sure you are retaining the concepts. To check your retention of the information you're learning, try recalling it at later times with minimal prompting. Try carrying around flashcards and glance at one or two from time to time or ask a friend who's also studying for the test to quiz you.

To enhance your retention, look for ways to put the information into practice so that you can apply it rather than simply recalling it. If you're using the information in practical ways, it will be much easier to remember. Similarly, it helps to solidify a concept in your mind if you're not only reading it to yourself but also explaining it to someone else. Ask a friend to let you teach them about a concept you're a little shaky on (or speak aloud to an imaginary audience if necessary). As you try to summarize, define, give examples, and answer your friend's questions, you'll understand the concepts better and they will stay with you longer. Finally, step back for a big picture view and ask yourself how each piece of information fits with the whole subject. When you link the different concepts together and see them working together as a whole, it's easier to remember the individual components.

Finally, practice showing your work on any multi-step problems, even if you're just studying. Writing out each step you take to solve a problem will help solidify the process in your mind, and you'll be more likely to remember it during the test.

Modality

Modality simply refers to the means or method by which you study. Choosing a study modality that fits your own individual learning style is crucial. No two people learn best in exactly the same way, so it's important to know your strengths and use them to your advantage.

For example, if you learn best by visualization, focus on visualizing a concept in your mind and draw an image or a diagram. Try color-coding your notes, illustrating them, or creating symbols that will trigger your mind to recall a learned concept. If you learn best by hearing or discussing information, find a study partner who learns the same way or read aloud to yourself. Think about how to put the information in your own words. Imagine that you are giving a lecture on the topic and record yourself so you can listen to it later.

For any learning style, flashcards can be helpful. Organize the information so you can take advantage of spare moments to review. Underline key words or phrases. Use different colors for different categories. Mnemonic devices (such as creating a short list in which every item starts with the same letter) can also help with retention. Find what works best for you and use it to store the information in your mind most effectively and easily.

Secret Key #3 – Practice the Right Way

Your success on test day depends not only on how many hours you put into preparing, but also on whether you prepared the right way. It's good to check along the way to see if your studying is paying off. One of the most effective ways to do this is by taking practice tests to evaluate your progress. Practice tests are useful because they show exactly where you need to improve. Every time you take a practice test, pay special attention to these three groups of questions:

- The questions you got wrong
- The questions you had to guess on, even if you guessed right
- The questions you found difficult or slow to work through

This will show you exactly what your weak areas are, and where you need to devote more study time. Ask yourself why each of these questions gave you trouble. Was it because you didn't understand the material? Was it because you didn't remember the vocabulary? Do you need more repetitions on this type of question to build speed and confidence? Dig into those questions and figure out how you can strengthen your weak areas as you go back to review the material.

Additionally, many practice tests have a section explaining the answer choices. It can be tempting to read the explanation and think that you now have a good understanding of the concept. However, an explanation likely only covers part of the question's broader context. Even if the explanation makes perfect sense, **go back and investigate** every concept related to the question until you're positive you have a thorough understanding.

As you go along, keep in mind that the practice test is just that: practice. Memorizing these questions and answers will not be very helpful on the actual test because it is unlikely to have any of the same exact questions. If you only know the right answers to the sample questions, you won't be prepared for the real thing. **Study the concepts** until you understand them fully, and then you'll be able to answer any question that shows up on the test.

It's important to wait on the practice tests until you're ready. If you take a test on your first day of study, you may be overwhelmed by the amount of material covered and how much you need to learn. Work up to it gradually.

On test day, you'll need to be prepared for answering questions, managing your time, and using the test-taking strategies you've learned. It's a lot to balance, like a mental marathon that will have a big impact on your future. Like training for a marathon, you'll need to start slowly and work your way up. When test day arrives, you'll be ready.

Start with the strategies you've read in the first two Secret Keys—plan your course and study in the way that works best for you. If you have time, consider using multiple study resources to get different approaches to the same concepts. It can be helpful to see difficult concepts from more than one angle. Then find a good source for practice tests. Many times, the test website will suggest potential study resources or provide sample tests.

Practice Test Strategy

If you're able to find at least three practice tests, we recommend this strategy:

UNTIMED AND OPEN-BOOK PRACTICE

Take the first test with no time constraints and with your notes and study guide handy. Take your time and focus on applying the strategies you've learned.

TIMED AND OPEN-BOOK PRACTICE

Take the second practice test open-book as well, but set a timer and practice pacing yourself to finish in time.

TIMED AND CLOSED-BOOK PRACTICE

Take any other practice tests as if it were test day. Set a timer and put away your study materials. Sit at a table or desk in a quiet room, imagine yourself at the testing center, and answer questions as quickly and accurately as possible.

Keep repeating timed and closed-book tests on a regular basis until you run out of practice tests or it's time for the actual test. Your mind will be ready for the schedule and stress of test day, and you'll be able to focus on recalling the material you've learned.

Secret Key #4 – Pace Yourself

Once you're fully prepared for the material on the test, your biggest challenge on test day will be managing your time. Just knowing that the clock is ticking can make you panic even if you have plenty of time left. Work on pacing yourself so you can build confidence against the time constraints of the exam. Pacing is a difficult skill to master, especially in a high-pressure environment, so **practice is vital**.

Set time expectations for your pace based on how much time is available. For example, if a section has 60 questions and the time limit is 30 minutes, you know you have to average 30 seconds or less per question in order to answer them all. Although 30 seconds is the hard limit, set 25 seconds per question as your goal, so you reserve extra time to spend on harder questions. When you budget extra time for the harder questions, you no longer have any reason to stress when those questions take longer to answer.

Don't let this time expectation distract you from working through the test at a calm, steady pace, but keep it in mind so you don't spend too much time on any one question. Recognize that taking extra time on one question you don't understand may keep you from answering two that you do understand later in the test. If your time limit for a question is up and you're still not sure of the answer, mark it and move on, and come back to it later if the time and the test format allow. If the testing format doesn't allow you to return to earlier questions, just make an educated guess; then put it out of your mind and move on.

On the easier questions, be careful not to rush. It may seem wise to hurry through them so you have more time for the challenging ones, but it's not worth missing one if you know the concept and just didn't take the time to read the question fully. Work efficiently but make sure you understand the question and have looked at all of the answer choices, since more than one may seem right at first.

Even if you're paying attention to the time, you may find yourself a little behind at some point. You should speed up to get back on track, but do so wisely. Don't panic; just take a few seconds less on each question until you're caught up. Don't guess without thinking, but do look through the answer choices and eliminate any you know are wrong. If you can get down to two choices, it is often worthwhile to guess from those. Once you've chosen an answer, move on and don't dwell on any that you skipped or had to hurry through. If a question was taking too long, chances are it was one of the harder ones, so you weren't as likely to get it right anyway.

On the other hand, if you find yourself getting ahead of schedule, it may be beneficial to slow down a little. The more quickly you work, the more likely you are to make a careless mistake that will affect your score. You've budgeted time for each question, so don't be afraid to spend that time. Practice an efficient but careful pace to get the most out of the time you have.

Secret Key #5 – Have a Plan for Guessing

When you're taking the test, you may find yourself stuck on a question. Some of the answer choices seem better than others, but you don't see the one answer choice that is obviously correct. What do you do?

The scenario described above is very common, yet most test takers have not effectively prepared for it. Developing and practicing a plan for guessing may be one of the single most effective uses of your time as you get ready for the exam.

In developing your plan for guessing, there are three questions to address:

- When should you start the guessing process?
- How should you narrow down the choices?
- Which answer should you choose?

When to Start the Guessing Process

Unless your plan for guessing is to select C every time (which, despite its merits, is not what we recommend), you need to leave yourself enough time to apply your answer elimination strategies. Since you have a limited amount of time for each question, that means that if you're going to give yourself the best shot at guessing correctly, you have to decide quickly whether or not you will guess.

Of course, the best-case scenario is that you don't have to guess at all, so first, see if you can answer the question based on your knowledge of the subject and basic reasoning skills. Focus on the key words in the question and try to jog your memory of related topics. Give yourself a chance to bring the knowledge to mind, but once you realize that you don't have (or you can't access) the knowledge you need to answer the question, it's time to start the guessing process.

It's almost always better to start the guessing process too early than too late. It only takes a few seconds to remember something and answer the question from knowledge. Carefully eliminating wrong answer choices takes longer. Plus, going through the process of eliminating answer choices can actually help jog your memory.

Summary: Start the guessing process as soon as you decide that you can't answer the question based on your knowledge.

How to Narrow Down the Choices

The next chapter in this book (**Test-Taking Strategies**) includes a wide range of strategies for how to approach questions and how to look for answer choices to eliminate. You will definitely want to read those carefully, practice them, and figure out which ones work best for you. Here though, we're going to address a mindset rather than a particular strategy.

Your odds of guessing an answer correctly depend on how many options you are choosing from.

Number of options left	5	4	3	2	1
Odds of guessing correctly	20%	25%	33%	50%	100%

You can see from this chart just how valuable it is to be able to eliminate incorrect answers and make an educated guess, but there are two things that many test takers do that cause them to miss out on the benefits of guessing:

- Accidentally eliminating the correct answer
- Selecting an answer based on an impression

We'll look at the first one here, and the second one in the next section.

To avoid accidentally eliminating the correct answer, we recommend a thought exercise called **the $5 challenge**. In this challenge, you only eliminate an answer choice from contention if you are willing to bet $5 on it being wrong. Why $5? Five dollars is a small but not insignificant amount of money. It's an amount you could afford to lose but wouldn't want to throw away. And while losing $5 once might not hurt too much, doing it twenty times will set you back $100. In the same way, each small decision you make—eliminating a choice here, guessing on a question there—won't by itself impact your score very much, but when you put them all together, they can make a big difference. By holding each answer choice elimination decision to a higher standard, you can reduce the risk of accidentally eliminating the correct answer.

The $5 challenge can also be applied in a positive sense: If you are willing to bet $5 that an answer choice *is* correct, go ahead and mark it as correct.

Summary: Only eliminate an answer choice if you are willing to bet $5 that it is wrong.

Which Answer to Choose

You're taking the test. You've run into a hard question and decided you'll have to guess. You've eliminated all the answer choices you're willing to bet $5 on. Now you have to pick an answer. Why do we even need to talk about this? Why can't you just pick whichever one you feel like when the time comes?

The answer to these questions is that if you don't come into the test with a plan, you'll rely on your impression to select an answer choice, and if you do that, you risk falling into a trap. The test writers know that everyone who takes their test will be guessing on some of the questions, so they intentionally write wrong answer choices to seem plausible. You still have to pick an answer though, and if the wrong answer choices are designed to look right, how can you ever be sure that you're not falling for their trap? The best solution we've found to this dilemma is to take the decision out of your hands entirely. Here is the process we recommend:

Once you've eliminated any choices that you are confident (willing to bet $5) are wrong, select the first remaining choice as your answer.

Whether you choose to select the first remaining choice, the second, or the last, the important thing is that you use some preselected standard. Using this approach guarantees that you will not be enticed into selecting an answer choice that looks right, because you are not basing your decision on how the answer choices look.

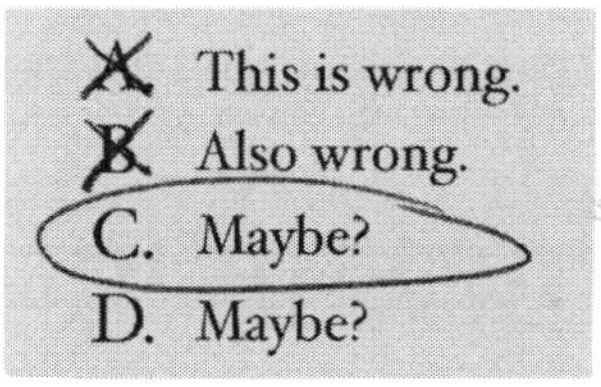

This is not meant to make you question your knowledge. Instead, it is to help you recognize the difference between your knowledge and your impressions. There's a huge difference between thinking an answer is right because of what you know, and thinking an answer is right because it looks or sounds like it should be right.

Summary: To ensure that your selection is appropriately random, make a predetermined selection from among all answer choices you have not eliminated.

Test-Taking Strategies

This section contains a list of test-taking strategies that you may find helpful as you work through the test. By taking what you know and applying logical thought, you can maximize your chances of answering any question correctly!

It is very important to realize that every question is different and every person is different: no single strategy will work on every question, and no single strategy will work for every person. That's why we've included all of them here, so you can try them out and determine which ones work best for different types of questions and which ones work best for you.

Question Strategies

✓ Read Carefully

Read the question and the answer choices carefully. Don't miss the question because you misread the terms. You have plenty of time to read each question thoroughly and make sure you understand what is being asked. Yet a happy medium must be attained, so don't waste too much time. You must read carefully and efficiently.

✓ Contextual Clues

Look for contextual clues. If the question includes a word you are not familiar with, look at the immediate context for some indication of what the word might mean. Contextual clues can often give you all the information you need to decipher the meaning of an unfamiliar word. Even if you can't determine the meaning, you may be able to narrow down the possibilities enough to make a solid guess at the answer to the question.

✓ Prefixes

If you're having trouble with a word in the question or answer choices, try dissecting it. Take advantage of every clue that the word might include. Prefixes can be a huge help. Usually, they allow you to determine a basic meaning. *Pre-* means before, *post-* means after, *pro-* is positive, *de-* is negative. From prefixes, you can get an idea of the general meaning of the word and try to put it into context.

✓ Hedge Words

Watch out for critical hedge words, such as *likely, may, can, often, almost, mostly, usually, generally, rarely*, and *sometimes*. Question writers insert these hedge phrases to cover every possibility. Often an answer choice will be wrong simply because it leaves no room for exception. Be on guard for answer choices that have definitive words such as *exactly* and *always.*

✓ Switchback Words

Stay alert for *switchbacks*. These are the words and phrases frequently used to alert you to shifts in thought. The most common switchback words are *but, although*, and *however*. Others include *nevertheless, on the other hand, even though, while, in spite of, despite*, and *regardless of*. Switchback words are important to catch because they can change the direction of the question or an answer choice.

⊘ FACE VALUE

When in doubt, use common sense. Accept the situation in the problem at face value. Don't read too much into it. These problems will not require you to make wild assumptions. If you have to go beyond creativity and warp time or space in order to have an answer choice fit the question, then you should move on and consider the other answer choices. These are normal problems rooted in reality. The applicable relationship or explanation may not be readily apparent, but it is there for you to figure out. Use your common sense to interpret anything that isn't clear.

Answer Choice Strategies

⊘ ANSWER SELECTION

The most thorough way to pick an answer choice is to identify and eliminate wrong answers until only one is left, then confirm it is the correct answer. Sometimes an answer choice may immediately seem right, but be careful. The test writers will usually put more than one reasonable answer choice on each question, so take a second to read all of them and make sure that the other choices are not equally obvious. As long as you have time left, it is better to read every answer choice than to pick the first one that looks right without checking the others.

⊘ ANSWER CHOICE FAMILIES

An answer choice family consists of two (in rare cases, three) answer choices that are very similar in construction and cannot all be true at the same time. If you see two answer choices that are direct opposites or parallels, one of them is usually the correct answer. For instance, if one answer choice says that quantity *x* increases and another either says that quantity *x* decreases (opposite) or says that quantity *y* increases (parallel), then those answer choices would fall into the same family. An answer choice that doesn't match the construction of the answer choice family is more likely to be incorrect. Most questions will not have answer choice families, but when they do appear, you should be prepared to recognize them.

⊘ ELIMINATE ANSWERS

Eliminate answer choices as soon as you realize they are wrong, but make sure you consider all possibilities. If you are eliminating answer choices and realize that the last one you are left with is also wrong, don't panic. Start over and consider each choice again. There may be something you missed the first time that you will realize on the second pass.

⊘ AVOID FACT TRAPS

Don't be distracted by an answer choice that is factually true but doesn't answer the question. You are looking for the choice that answers the question. Stay focused on what the question is asking for so you don't accidentally pick an answer that is true but incorrect. Always go back to the question and make sure the answer choice you've selected actually answers the question and is not merely a true statement.

⊘ EXTREME STATEMENTS

In general, you should avoid answers that put forth extreme actions as standard practice or proclaim controversial ideas as established fact. An answer choice that states the "process should be used in certain situations, if..." is much more likely to be correct than one that states the "process should be discontinued completely." The first is a calm rational statement and doesn't even make a definitive, uncompromising stance, using a hedge word *if* to provide wiggle room, whereas the second choice is far more extreme.

⊘ Benchmark

As you read through the answer choices and you come across one that seems to answer the question well, mentally select that answer choice. This is not your final answer, but it's the one that will help you evaluate the other answer choices. The one that you selected is your benchmark or standard for judging each of the other answer choices. Every other answer choice must be compared to your benchmark. That choice is correct until proven otherwise by another answer choice beating it. If you find a better answer, then that one becomes your new benchmark. Once you've decided that no other choice answers the question as well as your benchmark, you have your final answer.

⊘ Predict the Answer

Before you even start looking at the answer choices, it is often best to try to predict the answer. When you come up with the answer on your own, it is easier to avoid distractions and traps because you will know exactly what to look for. The right answer choice is unlikely to be word-for-word what you came up with, but it should be a close match. Even if you are confident that you have the right answer, you should still take the time to read each option before moving on.

General Strategies

⊘ Tough Questions

If you are stumped on a problem or it appears too hard or too difficult, don't waste time. Move on! Remember though, if you can quickly check for obviously incorrect answer choices, your chances of guessing correctly are greatly improved. Before you completely give up, at least try to knock out a couple of possible answers. Eliminate what you can and then guess at the remaining answer choices before moving on.

⊘ Check Your Work

Since you will probably not know every term listed and the answer to every question, it is important that you get credit for the ones that you do know. Don't miss any questions through careless mistakes. If at all possible, try to take a second to look back over your answer selection and make sure you've selected the correct answer choice and haven't made a costly careless mistake (such as marking an answer choice that you didn't mean to mark). This quick double check should more than pay for itself in caught mistakes for the time it costs.

⊘ Pace Yourself

It's easy to be overwhelmed when you're looking at a page full of questions; your mind is confused and full of random thoughts, and the clock is ticking down faster than you would like. Calm down and maintain the pace that you have set for yourself. Especially as you get down to the last few minutes of the test, don't let the small numbers on the clock make you panic. As long as you are on track by monitoring your pace, you are guaranteed to have time for each question.

⊘ Don't Rush

It is very easy to make errors when you are in a hurry. Maintaining a fast pace in answering questions is pointless if it makes you miss questions that you would have gotten right otherwise. Test writers like to include distracting information and wrong answers that seem right. Taking a little extra time to avoid careless mistakes can make all the difference in your test score. Find a pace that allows you to be confident in the answers that you select.

☑ KEEP MOVING

Panicking will not help you pass the test, so do your best to stay calm and keep moving. Taking deep breaths and going through the answer elimination steps you practiced can help to break through a stress barrier and keep your pace.

Final Notes

The combination of a solid foundation of content knowledge and the confidence that comes from practicing your plan for applying that knowledge is the key to maximizing your performance on test day. As your foundation of content knowledge is built up and strengthened, you'll find that the strategies included in this chapter become more and more effective in helping you quickly sift through the distractions and traps of the test to isolate the correct answer.

Now that you're preparing to move forward into the test content chapters of this book, be sure to keep your goal in mind. As you read, think about how you will be able to apply this information on the test. If you've already seen sample questions for the test and you have an idea of the question format and style, try to come up with questions of your own that you can answer based on what you're reading. This will give you valuable practice applying your knowledge in the same ways you can expect to on test day.

Good luck and good studying!

Authorized Duties

Building Relationships

Maintaining Good Interpersonal Relationships

Good interpersonal relationships are the key to functional team work. This is necessary in order to provide safe and comprehensive patient care. A medication aide can maintain good interpersonal relationships in a number of ways.

- Behave with a positive attitude.
- Try to avoid gossiping about coworkers and avoid openly criticizing them.
- Perform any tasks that are assigned promptly and notify the charge nurse if there are any tasks that the aide is unable to perform during the shift.
- Utilize teamwork by regularly offering to provide assistance to others and thanking them for any assistance they provided.

Components of Communication

There are five **components** that must be present in order for communication to take place.

Component	Description
Sender	The original source of the message
Message	What the sender is trying to convey
Channel	The means through which the message is being conveyed (typically either verbal or nonverbal)
Receiver	The person who is receiving the message
Feedback	The receiver's response to the original message (roles of sender and receiver may interchange over the course of a conversation)

Verbal Communication

Verbal communication is one way in which people communicate. It encompasses what is said as well as the manner in which it is said. When communicating with the patient, the medication aide should take into account the patient's language and word choice, as well as the tone of voice and the volume at which the words are spoken. When talking with a patient, it is important for the medication aide to think carefully about what they say prior to saying it, as words can often be misunderstood. It is also important to ensure that comments are appropriate to the setting and conversation.

Nonverbal Communication

Nonverbal communication is the process of sending messages using methods other than speaking. It can convey emotions and attitudes and can aid in communicating effectively with the patient. A person can communicate nonverbally using gestures, touch, or body language. A medication aide should closely monitor their own body language to make sure that it does not contradict what they are saying. For example, a medication aide who talks to the patient while frequently checking their watch is indicating that they are in a hurry. Such body language discourages open communication and should be avoided.

THERAPEUTIC COMMUNICATION

Therapeutic communication is a method of communicating with patients that encourages them to open up and provide information. Because of the level of stress involved in hospitalization, the patient often needs to communicate but is unsure how to initiate conversation with the health care staff. **Therapeutic communication** combines a variety of verbal and nonverbal communication techniques in order to encourage the patient to speak openly. By making note of the patient's body language as well as their words, the medication aide can interpret the patient's emotional state and communicate with the patient effectively.

ENCOURAGING COMMUNICATION

There are a number of steps the medication aide can take in order to encourage communication with the patient. First, the medication aide can ensure the patient is in an environment in which they can communicate freely. If the patient is comfortable, they are more likely to participate in therapeutic conversation. The medication aide should also ensure the patient's privacy during the conversation. The patient may feel embarrassed about sharing personal information in a public setting. The medication aide should make an effort to appear unhurried, encouraging the patient to talk by sitting near the patient during the conversation. The medication aide should also convey interest by facing the patient and maintaining eye contact during the conversation.

SILENCE

Silence can be an effective communication tool because it can convey a number of emotions. While communicating with the patient, **silence** can convey the sentiment of affection. This type of silence is typically accompanied by nonverbal actions, such as a hug or holding the patient's hand. Silence can also be utilized to encourage the patient to give more information. If this is done during a conversation, the patient may continue to talk to fill the silence. Silence can also give the patient time for contemplation. Care must be taken in utilizing silence as a communication tool as it can sometimes be misinterpreted as hostility or rudeness.

ASKING QUESTIONS

Asking questions can be effective in encouraging communication with the patient. There are two types of questions, open-ended and closed-ended.

- **Open-ended questions** encourage the patient to provide added detail about the subject of the conversation, while giving them more control over the conversation. Open-ended questions cannot be answered with one-word responses. "How do you feel about that?" is an example of an open-ended question.
- **Closed-ended questions** can be used to focus the conversation or get it back on track. They are typically used to elicit a one-word answer. An example of a closed-ended question is "Did you eat breakfast today?"

ACTIVE LISTENING

Active listening is the method of listening attentively to the conversation at hand. During a typical conversation, it is common for a person to not devote their full attention to what is being said. They may be thinking of other things or focusing on the work they are trying to do. When a person is **listening actively**, they are not only paying attention to the conversation, but also considering the patient's words and forming an appropriate response that will encourage further conversation. Active listening also takes into account various aspects of nonverbal communication in order to draw the appropriate conclusions from the conversation.

Reflecting

Reflecting is another method of encouraging the patient to talk about a particular subject. A medication aide **reflects a statement** by repeating all or part of the patient's original statement back to the patient. For example, the patient says, "I feel so lonely." An appropriate reflective response would be "Lonely?" Another form of reflecting is to make a statement regarding the patient's feelings. For example, the medication aide may say, "It seems like you are very happy about this." This reflects the patient's emotional state and encourages them to speak openly about what they are thinking and feeling.

General Leads and Restating

A **general lead** is a method used to encourage the patient to continue speaking about a particular subject. Examples of general leads include phrases such as "go on" or "I see." These are effective because they allow the patient to guide the conversation, giving them the opportunity to voice their thoughts and concerns. General leads also indicate that the medication aide is paying attention to what is being said.

When a medication aide **restates** something, they rephrase a comment that the patient made earlier in the conversation in order to encourage the patient to elaborate on it. For example, the medication aide might say, "So you think you have too much equipment on you?" if the patient makes a comment about all of the tubes and wires attached to them.

Empathy and Touch

Empathy is the ability to understand what the patient is feeling and to respond appropriately. Acting empathically begins by recognizing any strong emotions the patient might be having. By recognizing these emotions, the medication aide can give the patient the opportunity to talk about their feelings, as well as provide validation. Acting empathically allows the medication aide to build trust and understanding with the patient.

Using **touch** is a nonverbal method of communicating with the patient. There are times when words are not enough to provide an adequate amount of comfort. In these times, holding a hand or giving a hug can do more to encourage conversation and provide comfort. The patient's culture must be considered when considering the use of touch, as some cultures may see it as a sign of disrespect.

Providing Information and Self-Disclosing

Providing information can be an effective tool in encouraging communication. When the patient is new to the health care facility, they may feel anxious about the unfamiliar surroundings. The medication aide can help ease anxiety by providing the patient with information that is relevant to their care. However, the medication aide must be careful not to provide specific information regarding the patient's diagnosis or test and lab results, as this is not within the scope of the medication aide.

A medication aide can also encourage communication by **self-disclosing** some information about him or herself in order to ease the patient's discomfort. However, the medication aide must be careful not to dominate the conversation, as the goal of therapeutic communication is to discover what the patient is thinking and feeling.

COMMUNICATING WITH PATIENT'S FAMILY

Interaction with the **patient's family** can occur frequently during the course of patient care. The medication aide can confer with the patient's family regarding procedures that are part of the medication aide's scope of practice. When talking with the family while the patient is in the room, the medication aide should make an effort to include the patient in the conversation; it is inappropriate to talk about the patient as if he or she is not there. If any family members have a question about the patient's care, they should be referred to the nurse or charge nurse. When the medication aide is talking to the patient and/or their family, there are a number of ways that they can make sure that what they are saying is clearly communicated. The medication aide should avoid using medical terminology while talking to the patient as many find it to be confusing. The medication aide should make an effort to use words that can be understood by the layman. For example, instead of saying hypertension, the medication aide can be better understood by using the phrase high blood pressure. If a medical term must be used, the medication aide should define the term for the patient. While talking with the patient, the medication aide should speak slowly and clearly in a moderate tone of voice.

CALL LIGHTS

ANSWERING THE CALL LIGHT

The **call light** is the way in which a patient notifies the health care staff that they are in need of assistance. It should be answered promptly and courteously. If a call light is going off in a room that is not assigned to the medication aide, it is appropriate for the medication aide answer it to find out what the patient needs. If using an intercom, the medication aide should answer by asking, "May I help you?" If answering the call light personally, the medication aide should introduce oneself and inquire about the patient's needs. It is not appropriate for the medication aide to ignore a call light.

FREQUENT USE OF CALL LIGHT

Frequent use of the call bell can occur for a number of reasons. The patient may not understand how to use the call bell or may push the wrong button accidentally. If this happens, a medication aide can tape a piece of gauze over the button so that the patient can recognize the call button using their fingers. If using this method, it is important to check to make sure the call button can be pushed easily prior to leaving the room. Another reason that a patient may call frequently is that they are lonely. If this is the case, the medication aide should make an effort to stop in to see the patient as frequently as possible. This may prevent frequent calls "just to chat." One way to prevent frequent use of the call bell is to make sure the patient has all necessary items within reach prior to leaving the room. Also, ask the patient if there is anything else they might need prior to leaving the room.

COMMUNICATION BARRIERS

COMMUNICATION BLOCK

A communication block is a statement or behavior that discourages therapeutic communication. A medication aide may inadvertently use a communication block if they are hurried or uncomfortable about the conversation at hand. **Common communication blocks** include the use of sarcasm or jokes in order to deflect the situation. The medication aide may change the subject or may attempt to minimize the problem in order to ease their own discomfort. Offering false assurances or telling the patient how they should feel in a given situation may discourage the patient from communicating with the medication aide.

Communicating with Patients Who Cannot Speak English

Patients who are unable to speak English may be a challenge to communicate with. Though it is possible to ask a family member to help in translating, many facilities prefer to use an official interpreter when conveying medically related information to the patient. Whether communicating through a family member or an interpreter, the medication aide should look at the patient and address them while speaking. The aide should speak slowly and clearly, and watch the patient's body language and facial expressions closely as this can help in the communication process. Before the family leaves, the medication aide should ask them to write down a few common phrases, such as bathroom and water, to help with meeting the patient's needs.

Handling Inappropriate Comments Toward Staff

Some patients may attempt to use sexual innuendo jokingly or as a way to ease their own discomfort. However, such comments are considered to be harassment. Members of the health care staff have a right to work in an environment that is free of harassment. Some may try to diffuse the situation with a joke, but this approach is typically ineffective in halting the abusive behavior. If the patient begins making inappropriate comments, the medication aide should immediately inform the patient that their comments are unacceptable and will not be tolerated. This should be stated firmly, but politely. If the patient continues the inappropriate behavior, the charge nurse should be notified.

Inability to Communicate with Patient

Sometimes the medication aide may be unable to communicate with the patient despite his or her best efforts. If the patient is intubated or has severe aphasia, they may not be able to effectively communicate their needs. The medication aide should attempt to figure out what the patient is trying to say by running through a list of common needs, such as being thirsty, hot, cold, or in pain. If the medication aide cannot decipher what the patient is trying to say, they should tell the patient that they are unable to understand. They should not pretend to understand as this behavior can cause distress for the patient. The inability to communicate often results in frustration on the part of the patient. If this happens, the medication aide should provide appropriate reassurance and emotional support.

Delegation

DELEGATION

Delegation refers to assigning a task to another person. It is within the nurse's scope of practice to assign tasks to the medication aide, nurse aide, and LPN; however, it is not within the medication aide's scope of practice to assign tasks to others. Though the medication aide is responsible for performing the task, it is the responsibility of the nurse to make sure that it is done properly and in a timely manner. When assigned a task, the medication aide should make sure they understand how to perform that task. If they do not know how to do it, the medication aide should either ask for instructions in order to perform the task safely or decline the assignment.

FIVE RIGHTS OF DELEGATION

It is important for a medication aide to understand how a task is delegated in order to know if it is being delegated appropriately. The five rights of delegation can be utilized to determine if the assignment is appropriate.

- The first right refers to the task: whether the task can be delegated to another person or if it is more appropriate for it to be performed by the nurse.
- The second right refers to the circumstance; the medication aide should ask herself if the patient is stable enough for the task to be safely performed.
- The third right refers to the right person. The medication aide should ask herself if she feels she is able to perform the task appropriately.
- The fourth right refers to directions. The medication aide should ask herself if she received adequate instructions regarding the assignment.
- The final right refers to supervision. The medication aide should ask herself if she is going to have an appropriate amount of supervision while performing the task.

Role of the MA-C

Medication Aide-Certified

Role and Requirements for Certification

A medication aide is a valuable member of the health care team, particularly in environments with limited registered nurses. The primary **role** of the medication aide is to assist the nurse in providing care for the patient, with the added responsibility of medication administration and monitoring patients for adverse reactions to medications.

The **requirements to become certified as a medication aide** vary depending upon the state, and not all states offer medication aide certification. One must already have certification as a nurse aide and then obtain additional training (mandated by the state) prior to siting for the medication aide certification exam. For nurse aide certification, most states require a minimum of 75 hours of training, including classroom instruction and review of basic skills. After the training has been completed, a nurse aide must undergo the state certification exam in order to be qualified to provide care to patients. Additional training in medication administration is then required per state regulations, prior to sitting for the medication aide examination.

Scope of Practice

Scope of practice is a list of tasks that a medication aide is allowed to perform as determined by the state certification board. It is the responsibility of the medication aide to be aware of what tasks they can and cannot perform. Any activity that does not appear on the list falls outside the medication aide's scope of practice. If the medication aide is caught performing an activity that is not on the list, they run the risk of losing certification. The medication aide is liable for any harm that comes to the patient as a result of them performing an activity that is outside their scope of practice.

Tasks Outside of the Medication Aide's Scope of Practice

There are a number of tasks that **fall outside the medication aide's scope of practice**. A medication aide is not allowed to receive orders from a doctor; only a nurse can receive these orders. A medication aide may not insert or remove devices from a patient's body, such as indwelling catheters, IVs, or rectal tubes. Also, a medication aide may not perform any sort of sterile procedure. The medication aide may only assist in medication administration after receiving special training and may only assist in administering certain types of medication.

Legal and Ethical Issues

HIPAA

The Health Insurance Portability and Accountability Act (HIPAA) and state laws govern **who may receive healthcare information** about a person, how permission is to be obtained, how the information may be shared, and patients' rights concerning personal information. HIPAA strives to protect the **privacy** of an individual's healthcare information. Facilities must prevent this information from being accessed by unauthorized personnel. Healthcare information is required to be protected on the **administrative**, **physical**, and **technical** levels. The patient must sign a release form to allow any sharing of patient information. There are stiff penalties for violation of these laws, ranging from $100 for an unintentional violation to $50,000 for a willful violation. Facilities that violate HIPAA may also be subject to corrective actions. Penalties are governed by the Department of Health and Human Services' Office for Civil Right and the state attorneys general.

Application of HIPAA to Practice

As an integral member of the health care team, the medication aide must always be aware of HIPAA regulations and apply this knowledge to practice. The medication aide is responsible for the following efforts to protect and maintain patient privacy:

- The medication aide must read and follow facility policies regarding the transfer of patient data.
- Communication between health care personnel about a patient should always be in a private place so that this information is not overheard by those who do not have the right to share the information.
- Access to charts must be restricted to only those health care team members involved in that patient's care.
- Patient care information for unlicensed workers cannot be posted at the bedside, but must be on a care plan or the patient chart in a protected area.
- The medication aide must not give information casually to anyone (e.g., visitors or family members) unless it is confirmed that they have the right to have that information.
- Family members must not be relied upon to interpret for the patient; an interpreter must be obtained to protect patient privacy.
- Computers with patient information must have passwords and safeguards to prevent unauthorized access of patient information.
- The medication aide should not leave voicemail messages containing protected healthcare information for a patient but should instead ask the patient to call back.

Review Video: HIPAA
Visit mometrix.com/academy and enter code: 412009

OSHA

The **Occupational Safety and Health Act (OSHA)** seeks to keep workers safe and healthy while on the job. OSHA mandates that employers maintain a safe environment, workers are made fully aware of any hazards, and that access to personal protective gear is made available to workers who come into contact with hazardous materials. By following these regulations, an employer keeps injury and illness of workers to an absolute minimum. This fosters productivity, since workers are not absent due to illness or injury, employee health costs are contained, and the turnover rate is decreased, saving money spent on hiring and training new employees. OSHA is concerned about healthcare employee exposure to radiation, as well as chemical and biological agents, when caring for patients. Information is available to help hospitals and other facilities write plans that comply with best practices to deal with this and other threats to employees. Cleaning procedures, decontamination, and hazardous waste disposal are all covered by OSHA and apply to everyday hospital operation as well as disaster situations.

Review Video: Intro to OSHA
Visit mometrix.com/academy and enter code: 913559

CMS

The **Centers for Medicare and Medicaid (CMS)**, part of the U.S. Department of Health and Human Service department, see to it that healthcare regulations are observed by healthcare facilities that receive federal reimbursement. They reimburse facilities for care given to Medicare, Medicaid, and the state Children's Health Insurance Program (CHIP) recipients. They also monitor adherence to HIPAA regulations concerning healthcare information portability and confidentiality. CMS examines documentation of patient care when deciding to reimburse for care given. CMS has regulations for all types of medical facilities, and these regulations have profoundly impacted nursing practice because nurses must ensure that they comply with regulations related to the quality of patient care and concerns regarding cost-containment. Each facility should provide guidelines to assist nursing staff in meeting the specific documentation requirements of CMS.

OBRA 1987

The **Omnibus Budget Reconciliation Act of 1987 (OBRA 1987)**, also known as the Nursing Home Reform Act, instituted requirements for nursing homes with the purpose of strengthening and protecting patient rights. These requirements are as follows: "a facility must provide each patient with a level of care that enables him or her to attain or maintain the highest practicable physical, mental, and psychosocial wellbeing." OBRA 1987 required that all nursing home patients receive an initial evaluation with yearly follow-ups. Every patient is required to have a comprehensive care plan. Patients were ensured the right to medical care and the right to be informed about and refuse medical treatment. OBRA 1987 requires each state to establish, monitor, and enforce its own licensing requirements in addition to federal standards. Each state is also required to fund, staff, and maintain investigative and Ombudsman units.

OBRA 1990 (PSDA)

The Omnibus Budget Reconciliation Act of 1990 included the amendment called the **Patient Self Determination Act (PSDA)**. The PSDA required healthcare facilities to provide written information about advanced healthcare directives and the right to accept or reject medical or surgical treatments to all patients. Patients who make an advanced directive are leaving instructions about what medical interventions they authorize or refuse if they are incapacitated by illness or injury. They can also nominate another person to make these decisions for them in this situation. The PSDA also protected the right of patients to accept or refuse medical treatments. Healthcare facilities and hospitals are legally required to communicate these rights to all patients, to respect these rights, and to educate staff and personnel about these rights.

EMTALA

The **Emergency Medical Treatment and Active Labor Act (EMTALA)** is designed to prevent patient "dumping" from emergency departments (ED) and is an issue of concern for risk management that requires staff training for compliance:

- Transfers from the ED may be intrahospital or to another facility.
- Stabilization of the patient with emergency conditions or active labor must be done in the ED prior to transfer, and initial screening must be given prior to inquiring about insurance or ability to pay.
- Stabilization requires treatment for emergency conditions and reasonable belief that, although the emergency condition may not be completely resolved, the patient's condition will not deteriorate during transfer.
- Women in the ED in active labor should deliver both the child and placenta before transfer.
- The receiving department or facility should be capable of treating the patient and dealing with complications that might occur.
- Transfer to another facility is indicated if the patient requires specialized services not available intrahospital, such as to burn centers.

AHRQ

The **Agency for Healthcare Research and Quality (AHRQ)** is part of the U.S. Department of Health and Human Services. This agency is concerned about health care and primarily promotes scientific research into the safety, effectiveness, and quality of healthcare. It encourages evidence-based healthcare that produces the best possible outcome while containing healthcare costs. It makes contracts with institutions to review any published evidence on healthcare in order to produce reports used by other organizations to write guidelines. The agency operates the National Guideline Clearinghouse, which is available online. It is a repository of evidence-based guidelines that address various health conditions and diseases. These guidelines are written by many different health-related professional organizations and are used by primary healthcare providers, nurses, and healthcare facilities to guide patient treatment and care.

STANDARDS OF CARE

Standards of care provide a guideline that explains how a medication aide is expected to act in a given situation. The state government or the health care facility in which the medication aide is practicing typically sets these standards. It is the responsibility of the medication aide to be aware of the appropriate standards of care. If the medication aide were to fail to act appropriately in a given situation, they could be held responsible for any harm that might come to the patient as a result of them deviating from the expected way to practice.

Civil and Criminal Court Cases

There are two different types of court cases:

- **Civil court cases** take place between two people, when a wronged individual sues the person who did them wrong. If the accused is found guilty in a civil case, they are typically made to pay fines and restoration to the wronged party.
- In a **criminal court case**, the defendant is accused of committing crimes against society as a whole. If a person is found guilty in a criminal case, they are made to pay fines or serve time in jail.

Liability

Liability refers to the responsibility of a person to act within the confines of the law. In the eyes of the law, a person must take responsibility for their own actions. If a medication aide fails to perform a task to the best of their ability and harm comes to the patient, they can be considered liable. Similarly, if the medication aide performs a task that falls outside their scope of practice and harm comes to the patient, they are considered liable. In order to maintain safe practice, it is important for a medication aide to perform tasks exactly as they learned them, without taking shortcuts. The medication aide should also make an effort to keep their skills and knowledge up to date with current health care trends.

Tort

A tort is a wrong that is committed in a civil case. There are two types of torts: unintentional and intentional.

- In an **unintentional tort**, a person commits a wrong against another person without intending to cause harm. For example, if a medication aide forgets to put the side rails back up on the bed and the patient falls and is injured as a result, that could be considered an unintentional tort.
- An **intentional tort** occurs when a person has the intention of causing harm to another person. An example of an intentional tort is if the medication aide leaves the unit without telling anybody, and the patient becomes injured while they are not being monitored.

Assault

Assault refers to the threat or attempt to touch or inflict physical harm on another person. The threat could be verbal or physical, such as a threatening gesture or advancing toward a person in a threatening way. Caution must be taken while caring for a patient; if the patient refuses a treatment and the medication aide attempts to force the patient to receive the treatment, the aide may be liable for assault. It is important to remember that the patient does not have to be harmed in order for the medication aide to be found liable for assault. It is only necessary to prove that the patient felt threatened in a particular situation.

Battery

Battery refers to the act of touching a person without permission. It could refer to a violent act or an unintended act. A medication aide might also be accused of battery for performing a procedure on a patient without consent. In order to protect oneself from being accused of battery, a medication aide should take a moment to explain the procedure to the patient prior to beginning and obtain consent from the patient to perform the procedure. If the patient refuses the procedure, the medication aide should try to explain the reasons why the procedure is necessary but should not attempt to force the patient to have the procedure performed.

Negligence

Negligence is the failure to perform care in the manner in which that person was trained. A medication aide can be charged with negligence if they do not act in a way that is reasonable for a person with their level of training. For example, if the medication aide leaves a patient unattended in the shower and the patient falls and is injured, the medication aide could be found negligent. A medication aide can avoid being accused of negligence by performing procedures exactly as they learned how to do them, without taking shortcuts. If the medication aide is unsure how to perform a procedure, they should not hesitate to ask for assistance.

Review Video: Medical Negligence
Visit mometrix.com/academy and enter code: 928405

Malpractice

Malpractice is a **type of negligence** that is committed by a professional who needs to maintain a license in order to practice. In a case of malpractice, a professional fails to act according to standards of care within their profession, which results in harm to the patient. Malpractice is more severe than negligence; it takes into account the professional's higher level of training when considering the wrong that was committed by the health care professional. Medication aides cannot be sued for malpractice, as they are only required to maintain certification. However, they can still be sued for negligence.

Defamation

When a person makes statements about another person that causes damage to the individual's reputation, they can be accused of defamation.

- **Slander** refers to spoken defamation. For example, if a medication aide spreads rumors that a patient has HIV, that medication aide can be accused of slander. A medication aide can avoid being accused of slander by avoiding saying negative things about other people. By spreading rumors, the medication aide is acting unprofessionally and is at risk for being accused of defamation.
- **Libel** refers to a written statement that causes injury to another person's reputation. For example, if the medication aide writes an article that a doctor is practicing without appropriate licensure and that article is untrue, they can be accused of libel.

Invasion of Privacy

The patient has a right to keep details about himself or herself private. **Invasion of privacy** refers to failure to maintain the patient's right to privacy by relaying personal information without the patient's consent. The patient's privacy can be invaded if the medication aide shares details about the patient's health history with others or by inadvertently leaving sensitive documents where others can easily see them. A medication aide can avoid being accused of invasion of privacy by only discussing details of the case with those who are directly involved in the care of the patient. If a person who the patient has not identified as one who can receive their information wants details regarding the patient's treatment, the medication aide should refer them to the charge nurse.

Fraud

Committing **fraud** is deliberately misrepresenting oneself for personal gain. Fraud can be considered a violation of either civil or criminal law. A medication aide would commit fraud if they claimed to be a nurse or a doctor in the presence of a patient. It is also considered fraud to lie about one's qualifications or certifications on a resume in order to secure a job. A medication aide can avoid being accused of fraud by clearly identifying oneself when dealing with a patient. They can also avoid being accused of fraud by acting within their scope of practice.

Abandonment

Abandonment occurs when a medication aide leaves without notifying others or securing another person to provide care in their place. If harm befalls a patient while the medication aide is absent of their duties, the aide can be accused of abandonment. A medication aide can avoid being accused of abandonment by asking another medication aide to cover their patients and informing the charge nurse prior to leaving the unit. They should also make an effort to make sure all of their patients are safe and secure prior to giving report and leaving the unit.

False Imprisonment

False imprisonment refers to confining a person to an area against their will. It is typically used in reference to use of restraints. Restraints are an acceptable tool to be used as a last resort in order to protect both the patient and the safety of others. False imprisonment refers to the use of restraints without an order or in a situation in which it is inappropriate to restrain the patient. A patient could also be falsely imprisoned if they are confined to the health care facility when they wish to leave. If the patient expresses a desire to leave the hospital and is alert and able to make decisions, then the medication aide should avoid attempting to force the patient to stay. Instead, the aide should notify the charge nurse or the supervisor immediately.

Theft

Theft is the removal of another person's money or belongings without their knowledge. A medication aide is guilty of theft if they take a patient's belongings, even if the stolen item is not being used or is not of significant monetary value. Though the health care facility takes steps to avoid hiring people who might steal from patients, the medication aide should be vigilant as well. The medication aide should try to avoid theft by not leaving the patient's belongings in plain sight when they are not in use. If the aide sees someone stealing a patient's belongings or acting suspiciously, they should report the behavior to the charge nurse immediately.

Legal Ramifications of Abuse, Neglect, and Misappropriation of Property

A medication aide whom is guilty of abuse, neglect, and/or misappropriation of property may be liable to both criminal and civil penalties, depending on the type of act, the result, and the intention. Abuse of a patient (especially if it involved assault and battery or negligence and resulted in injury) and stealing from a patient are criminal offenses for which the medication aide may be arrested and charged. Non-criminal offenses, such as invasion of privacy, defamation of character, and libel, may result in a civil suit against not only the medication aide but also those responsible for delegating care, including supervising nurses and the organization. For that reason, if a medication aide commits or is suspected of non-criminal offenses, the medication aide is likely to lose employment, even if no civil complaint is filed. If found guilty of a non-criminal act, the medication aide has to pay a fine and may lose his or her employment and certification.

Grievance and Dispute Resolution

Grievance and dispute resolution is utilized when one or more parties believe that an agreement (work responsibilities, compensation) has been breached or treatment has been unfair or biased. Each organization should have a procedure in place for reporting grievances/disputes. Procedures usually begin with reporting the problem through the chain of command and/or to the human resources department. In some cases, the dispute may be resolved through supervisorial decision and direction, but with more complex issues, when agreement cannot be reached, or when the proposed agreement is unsatisfactory, the issue may be referred for a further process:

- **Mediation**: A facilitator helps the different parties to the grievance/dispute to discuss the issues and reach a satisfactory resolution. If unsuccessful, further action (arbitration, civil suit) may be needed.
- **Arbitration**: A neutral party listens to both parties to the grievance/dispute and makes a decision, which is usually binding.

Ethical Principles

Autonomy is the ethical principle that the individual has the right to make decisions about his or her own care. In the case of children or patients with dementia who cannot make autonomous decisions, parents or family members may serve as the legal decision maker. The medication aide must keep the patient and/or family fully informed so that they can exercise their autonomy in informed decision-making.

Justice is the ethical principle that relates to the distribution of the limited resources of healthcare benefits to the members of society. These resources must be distributed fairly. This issue may arise if there is only one bed left and two sick patients. Justice comes into play in deciding which patient should stay and which should be transported or otherwise cared for. The decision should be made according to what is best or most just for the patients and not colored by personal bias.

Beneficence is an ethical principle that involves performing actions that are for the purpose of benefitting another person. In the care of a patient, any procedure or treatment should be done with the ultimate goal of benefitting the patient, and any actions that are not beneficial should be reconsidered. As conditions change, procedures need to be continually reevaluated to determine if they are still of benefit.

Nonmaleficence is an ethical principle that means healthcare workers should provide care in a manner that does not cause direct intentional harm to the patient:

- The actual act must be good or morally neutral.
- The intent must be only for a good effect.
- A bad effect cannot serve as the means to get to a good effect.
- A good effect must have more benefit than a bad effect has harm.

Bioethics

Bioethics is a branch of ethics that involves making sure that the medical treatment given is the most morally correct choice given the different options that might be available and the differences inherent in the varied levels of treatment. In the health care unit, if the patients, family members, and the staff are in agreement when it comes to values and decision-making, then no ethical dilemma exists; however, when there is a difference in value beliefs between the patients/family members and the staff, there is a bioethical dilemma that must be resolved. Sometimes, discussion and explanation can resolve differences, but at times the institution's ethics committee must be brought in to resolve the conflict. The primary goal of bioethics is to determine the most morally correct action using the set of circumstances given.

Ethical Decision-Making Models

There are many ethical decision-making models. Some general guidelines to apply in using ethical decision-making models could be the following:

- Gather information about the identified problem
- State reasonable alternatives and solutions to the problem
- Utilize ethical resources (for example, clergy or ethics committees) to help determine the ethically important elements of each solution or alternative
- Suggest and attempt possible solutions
- Choose a solution to the problem

It is important to always consider the **ethical principles** of autonomy, beneficence, nonmaleficence, justice, and fidelity when attempting to facilitate ethical decision-making with family members, caregivers, and the healthcare team.

Professional Boundaries

Gifts

Over time, patients may develop a bond with medication aides they trust and may feel grateful to the them for the care provided and want to express thanks, but the medication aide must make sure to maintain professional boundaries. Patients often offer **gifts** to medication aides to show their appreciation, but some adults, especially those who are weak and ill or have cognitive impairment, may be taken advantage of easily. Patients may offer valuables and may sometimes be easily manipulated into giving large sums of money. Small tokens of appreciation that can be shared with other staff, such as a box of chocolates, are usually acceptable (depending upon the policy of the institution), but almost any other gifts (jewelry, money, clothes) should be declined: "I'm sorry, that's so kind of you, but medication aides are not allowed to accept gifts from patients." Declining may relieve the patient of the feeling of obligation.

Sexual Relations

When the boundary between the role of the professional medication aide and the vulnerability of the patient is breached, a boundary violation occurs. Because the medication aide is in the position of authority, the responsibility to maintain the boundary rests with the medication aide; however, the line separating them is a continuum and sometimes not easily defined. It is inappropriate for medication aides to engage in **sexual relations** with patients, and if the sexual behavior is coerced or the patient is cognitively impaired, it is **illegal**. However, more common violations with adults, particularly elderly patients, include exposing a patient unnecessarily, using sexually demeaning gestures or language (including off-color jokes), harassment, or inappropriate touching. Touching should be used with care, such as touching a hand or shoulder. Hugging may be misconstrued.

Attention

Health care is a giving profession, but the medication aide must temper giving with recognition of professional boundaries. Patients have many needs. As acts of kindness, medication aides (especially those involved in home care) often give certain patients extra attention and may offer to do **favors**, such as cooking or shopping. They may become overly invested in the patients' lives. While this may benefit a patient in the short term, it can establish a relationship of increasing **dependency** and **obligation** that does not resolve the long-term needs of the patient. Making referrals to the appropriate agencies or collaborating with family to find ways to provide services is more effective. Becoming overly invested may be evident by the medication aide showing favoritism or spending too much time with the patient while neglecting other duties. On the other end of the spectrum are medication aides who are disinterested and fail to provide adequate attention to the patient's detriment. Lack of adequate attention may lead to outright neglect.

Coercion

Power issues are inherent in matters associated with professional boundaries. Physical abuse is both unprofessional and illegal, but behavior can easily border on abusive without the patient being physically injured. Medication aides can easily **intimidate** older adults and sick patients into having procedures or treatments they do not want. Regardless of age, patients have the right to choose and the right to refuse treatment. Difficulties arise with cognitive impairment, and in that case, another responsible adult (often the patient's child or spouse) is designated to make decisions, but every effort should be made to gain patient cooperation. Forcing the patient to do something against his or her will borders on abuse and can sometimes degenerate into actual abuse if physical coercion is involved.

Personal Information

When pre-existing personal or business relationships exist, other medication aides should be assigned care of the patient whenever possible, but this may be difficult in small communities. However, the medication aide should strive to maintain a professional role separate from the personal role and respect professional boundaries. The medication aide must respect and maintain the confidentiality of the patient and family members, but the medication aide must also be very careful about **disclosing personal information** about him or herself because this establishes a social relationship that interferes with the professional role of the medication aide and the boundary between the patient and the medication aide. The medication aide and patient should never share secrets. When the medication aide divulges personal information, he or she may become vulnerable to the patient, a reversal of roles.

Resources and References

Patient Packet Inserts

Patient package inserts (PPIs), or medication guides, are informational leaflets designed to educate patients about a medication. PPIs have the following layout: table of contents, patient counseling information, highlights (boxed warnings, indications, usage, dosage, administration), recent changes to the leaflet, date of the initial drug approval, and toll-free phone number to report adverse drug reactions. These leaflets provide information about proper use of the medication, when the medication should not be used, and any serious adverse effects that may occur. PPIs must be approved by the FDA prior to use.

Certain medications require a PPI to be dispensed with it. These medications include oral contraceptives, IUDs, estrogen- or progesterone-containing products, and isoproterenol inhalations. Failure to provide a PPI for these medications is considered misbranding. For hospitalized patients, a PPI must be provided prior to the first administration, then every 30 days. For outpatients, a PPI must be provided for the first fill as well as each refill.

Medication Administration, Observation, and Reporting

Administering and Charting Medications

Units of Measurement

Common abbreviations indicating the different **units of measure**:

Abbreviation	Meaning
ss	One half, 1/2
L	Liter
mL	Milliliter
tsp	Teaspoon (5 mL)
tbsp	Tablespoon (15 mL)
Fl oz	Fluid ounce (30 mL)
gr	Grain
qs, qs ad	Dispense a sufficient quantity or add a sufficient quantity to make
Roman numerals	Number (e.g., number of tablets, capsules)
I	One
II	Two
III	Three
IV	Four
V	Five
aq	Water
ad	Up to
aa	Of each
gtt	Drop
G, g, gm	Gram
kg	Kilogram
mg	Milligram
mcg	Microgram
mEq	Milliequivalent
ds	Days' supply
lb	Pound
c	Cup

Common Medical Abbreviations Used in Prescriptions

Prescribers commonly used medical abbreviations when writing prescriptions, especially within the prescription instructions or directions (also known as the sig). You should be familiar with commonly used abbreviations, but if any part of the prescription is unclear, you should call the prescriber's office to clarify.

Abbreviation	Meaning
po	By mouth, per oral route (e.g., tablets, capsules)
tab	Tablet
cap	Capsule
SR, XR, XL	Extended-release or slow-release
liq	Liquid
syr	Syrup
sol	Solution
susp	Suspension
SL	Sublingually (e.g., sublingual tablet)
ou	Each eye
os	Left eye
od	Right eye
bid	Twice a day
tid	Three times a day
qid	Four times a day
am	Morning
pm	Evening
hs	At bedtime
q	Every
top	Topically (e.g., patch, cream, lotion, ointment)
crm	Cream
oint, ung	Ointment
Pr	Per rectum, rectally (e.g., suppository)
inh	Inhalation (e.g., inhaler)
per neb	By nebulizer
IV	Intravenously
SC, subc, subq	Subcutaneously
IM	Intramuscularly
au	Each ear
as	Left ear
ad	Right ear
UD	Use as directed
NR	No refills
DAW	Dispense as written (e.g., brand name requested)
w	With
w/o	Without
ac	Before food/meal
pc	After food/meal
stat	Immediately
prn	As needed

Medication Storage Requirements

Most medications can be stored at room temperature, which is defined as 20 °C to 25 °C or 59 °F to 77 °F. This includes most tablets, capsules, liquid solutions, creams, inhalers, and patches.

Some medications require refrigeration between 2 °C and 8 °C, or 36 °F and 46 °F. Medications that usually require refrigeration include injectables, vaccines, and antibiotic suspensions.

Controlled medications are usually kept in a locked cupboard, but not all states require them to be locked away.

Hazardous substances should be kept separately from regular pharmacy stock. Examples of hazardous substances include chemotherapy agents, including methotrexate. Pharmacy personnel who are handling hazardous substances should wear gloves. Some hazardous substances recommend that two layers of gloves (double gloving) should be worn. A separate counting tray should be used to count hazardous substances.

Hazardous wastes should also be stored separately from the rest of the pharmacy stock. Hazardous wastes include expired medications, recalled medications, damaged products, and incorrectly compounded products. These products should be put in designated bins and labeled as hazardous.

Refrigeration

Most injectable medications, biologics, blood factors, and vaccines require refrigeration. Oral antibiotic liquids that require reconstitution usually require refrigeration after mixing. There are also a few eye drops, inhalers, gels, and nasal sprays that must be stored in the refrigerator.

Brand Name	Generic Name
Acanya	Clindamycin/benzoyl peroxide
ActHIB	*Haemophilus influenzae* type B vaccine
Adacel	TDaP vaccine
Apidra	Insulin glulisine
Benzamycin gel (reconstituted)	Erythromycin/benzoyl peroxide
Byetta	Exenatide
CombiPatch	Estradiol/norethindrone
Enbrel	Etanercept
Engerix-B	Hepatitis B vaccine
Epogen	Epoetin alfa
Forteo	Teriparatide
Havrix	Hepatitis A vaccine
Humalog	Insulin lispro
Humira	Adalimumab
Humulin N	NPH insulin
Humulin R	Regular insulin
Lactinex	A blend of *Lactobacillus acidophilus* and *Lactobacillus helveticus* (*bulgaricus*)
Lantus	Insulin glargine
Levemir	Insulin detemir
Leukeran	Chlorambucil
Miacalcin nasal spray	Calcitonin
MMR II	Measles, mumps, and rubella vaccine

Brand Name	Generic Name
Neulasta	Pegfilgrastim
Neupogen	Filgrastim
Novolin N	NPH insulin
Novolin R	Regular insulin
Novolog	Insulin aspart
NovoSeven	Coagulation factor VII
NuvaRing	Etonogestrel/ethinyl estradiol
Perforomist	Formoterol
Phenergan suppositories	Promethazine
Pneumovax 23 Prevnar 13	Pneumococcal vaccine
Procrit	Epoetin alfa
Risperdal Consta	Risperidone
Sandostatin	Octreotide
Victoza	Liraglutide
Xalatan eye drops	Latanoprost

Storage Requirements for Injectable Medications

Some injectable medications should be stored at room temperature, whereas others must be stored in the refrigerator. It is important to read the storage information on the packaging or in the package insert if you are unsure of how to store a medication.

Most vaccines must be stored in a refrigerator, although there are a few that should be stored in a freezer or at room temperature. Insulin products should be stored in a refrigerator, although they can be stored at controlled room temperature for up to 28 days once dispensed. Most single-use injection solutions packaged in vials or IV bags can be kept at room temperature, although there are some exceptions. Most sterile compounded products must be stored in a refrigerator and have a short beyond-use date; however, there are a few products that should not be stored in the fridge, so refer to the preparation instructions or a pharmacist if you are not sure of how to store a medication.

Storage Requirements for Vaccinations

Most vaccinations must be stored in a refrigerator between 2°C and 8°C (36°F and 46°F). If the vaccine is stored outside of this temperature range or becomes frozen, it must be discarded. Some vaccines are formulated as powders for reconstitution. If a diluent is provided in the packaging, the diluent must also be stored in the refrigerator and cannot become frozen. Varivax and Zostavax must be stored in a freezer and maintained between –58°F and 5°F. They can be kept in a refrigerator for up to 72 hours prior to use. Note that one brand of the herpes zoster vaccine must be refrigerated, and the other brand must be frozen.

- **Vaccines that should be refrigerated:** influenza vaccine (Flulaval, Fluzone, Fluarix); TDaP vaccine (Adacel, Boostrix); hepatitis B vaccination (Engerix-B, Recombivax HB); hepatitis A vaccination (Havrix, Vaqta); *Haemophilus influenzae* type B (Pentacel, Vaxelis); meningococcal vaccinations (Menactra, Menveo, Menquadfi); MMR vaccination; human papillomavirus vaccination (Gardasil, Cervarix); pneumococcal vaccines (Pneumovax-23, Prevnar-13); and herpes zoster vaccine (Shingrix)
- **Vaccines that should be frozen:** varicella (chicken pox) vaccination (Varivax, Proquad); herpes zoster vaccines (Zostavax)

Storage Considerations for Light-Sensitive Medications

Some medications are sensitive to light and become unstable and adulterated if exposed to bright lights. Light-sensitive medications must be stored in amber or brown packaging to minimize their exposure to light, even if the drug is being transported within the pharmacy or hospital. There is a long list of medications that are sensitive to light, so if you are not sure whether a medication needs to be protected from light, refer to the manufacturer's information or the guidelines at your pharmacy. In time, you will become familiar with the medications that your pharmacy commonly dispenses.

Light-sensitive medications: aminophylline, amiodarone, amphotericin B, bupivacaine/epinephrine, cefepime, cefotaxime, cefazolin, chlorpheniramine, chlorpromazine, cisplatin, dacarbazine, diazepam, digoxin, diphenhydramine, dopamine, doxorubicin, doxycycline, epinephrine, fluorouracil, folic acid, furosemide, haloperidol, hydrocortisone, hydromorphone, iron (iron sucrose and ferrous gluconate), isoproterenol, methadone, morphine, nicardipine, nitroglycerine, nitroprusside, norepinephrine, phenylephrine, prochlorperazine, promethazine, propranolol, terbutaline, testosterone, thiamine, vincristine, vitamin B complex, vitamin K (menadiol and phytonadione), and vitamin B_{12} (cyanocobalamin)

Investigational Drugs

Storing, Ordering, Receiving, and Reporting When Lost or Stolen

Investigational or clinical trial drugs should be secured and **stored** in a separate room or separate storage area in the pharmacy. Only those pharmacy staff members that are delegated or authorized to work with investigational drugs should have access. Products should be stored under the storage conditions (e.g., temperature, humidity) specified by the manufacturer or study sponsor. Documentation of proper storage is important for validation of the trial.

Before investigational drugs can be ordered and received, the pharmacy must be approved by the study sponsor to participate in the trial. Once the study is ready to begin, the clinical protocol will specify how to **order and receive** the investigational product. When the products are shipped to the pharmacy, they should be clearly labeled as investigational drug products.

If an investigational drug product is **lost or stolen**, the sponsor of the trial should be notified immediately. For suspected thefts, the local police should also be notified. If the stolen medication is a controlled substance, the DEA should be notified using DEA Form 106.

Dispensing, Labeling, and Returning

When **dispensing** investigational drugs, handling requirements set out in the study protocol should be adhered to. Partial or empty vials of investigational drugs that are **returned** by patients/participants should be returned to the pharmacy's investigational drug team. Some study protocols require pharmacy staff to receive, count, and document drugs that are returned by patients. Patient returns, empty containers, and expired investigational drugs that are no longer dispensable must be stored in a separate, limited-access area until they can be destroyed or returned to the manufacturer/sponsor.

The immediate package or container for every investigational drug must contain the statement "Caution: New Drug — Limited by federal (or United States) law to investigational use." The pharmacy dispensing label for investigational drugs also requires additional information. The following information is required to be on the pharmacy label in addition to standard labeling requirements:

- Name of the investigational drug product (for blinded trials, the product name should read "[Drug product name] or placebo")
- Product strength or concentration (unless blinded)
- Quantity
- Lot number, container number, or kit number
- Expiration date, retest date, or period of use
- Manufacturer/sponsor name and address
- Clinical research protocol number

Packaging

Protecting from Light

Some products, such as nitroglycerin, furosemide, and doxycycline, are in dark-colored packaging because they are sensitive to light and are susceptible to instability and degradation if they are exposed to it. There are various packaging techniques that manufacturers use to prevent drugs from being exposed to light.

Most tablets today are packaged in white plastic bottles. White bottles contain the ingredient titanium dioxide that prevents light from entering the bottle; titanium dioxide is also an ingredient in sunscreens and cosmetics. Iron oxide is used to color medication bottles brown in order to prevent light from entering. Some products are packaged in brown plastic bottles or brown glass. The orange or amber vials that the pharmacy uses to dispense medications in also contain iron and are light-protective. Aluminum unit-dose blister packs can also be used for light protection. Secondary or outer packaging, such as cardboard boxes, also help protect products from light.

Glass Containers

Glass is used to package tablets, liquids, and solutions for injection (e.g., glass ampoules, glass vials). Glass is used less frequently than plastics due to cost, but it is still used to package medications that are incompatible with plastic. Glass is an excellent form of packaging because it is impervious (impenetrable) to water, oxygen, and carbon dioxide. Substances that react with and become unstable in the presence of water, oxygen, or carbon dioxide benefit from being packaged using glass. The weakest link for glass packing is the cap. Metal and plastic do not seal well against glass and may allow for the entry of contaminants. Rubber is often used in caps because it creates a more impenetrable seal and is tamper evident. However, penetration of the rubber seal for an injection solution (e.g., insulin vial) can cause rubber pieces to end up in the injection solution.

Safety and Rights of Medication Administration

HAZARDOUS SUBSTANCES

Hazardous substances are those that can cause potential harm to pharmacy personnel who are handling or dispensing them. Nearly all chemotherapy drugs used to treat cancer are hazardous substances. There are hundreds of hazardous chemotherapy agents, but a few of the more commonly dispensed substances are listed in the table below. Many immune modulators used to treat transplant rejection, inflammatory bowel diseases, and rheumatoid arthritis are also hazardous. Some antiviral drugs and hormone modulators are also potentially hazardous. These substances should be handled with extra caution, including wearing gloves during dispensing.

Brand Name	Generic Name
Anticancer Drugs	
Trexall, Otrexup	Methotrexate
Ellence	Epirubicin
Abraxane	Paclitaxel
Vincasar	Vincristine
Xeloda	Capecitabine
Afinitor, Zotress	Everolimus
Revlimid	Lenalidomide
Purixan	Mercaptopurine
Pomalyst	Pomalidomide
Temodar	Temozolomide
Thalomid	Thalidomide
Immune Modulators	
Azasan, Imuran	Azathioprine
Sandimmune, Neoral	Cyclosporine
Astagraf XL, Prograf	Tacrolimus
CellCept, Myfortic	Mycophenolate
Droxia, Hydrea	Hydroxyurea
Antivirals	
Valcyte	Valganciclovir
Rapivab	Peramivir
Veklury	Remdesivir
Retrovir	Zidovudine
Hormone Modulators	
Casodex	Bicalutamide
Propecia, Proscar	Finasteride
Retinoids	
Accutane	Isotretinoin
Retin-A	Tretinoin (topical)

The most up-to-date list of hazardous medications can be found on the CDC website.

EXPOSURES AND SPILLS

Immediately after **exposure to a hazardous substance**, a supervisor must be notified, and someone should be designated to call for medical help if required. The substance's Material Safety Data Sheet (MSDS) should be consulted on what to do in the event of an exposure.

- **Skin exposures** can cause burns, blisters, rashes, sores, or irritation. Remove clothing around the affected skin area, and wash the area with cool water for 15 minutes.
- **Eye exposures** require flushing the eyes for 15 minutes. Contact lenses should be removed prior to the eye wash. Instructions for eye wash stations may vary, so check with your manager on how to locate and use the eye wash station at your pharmacy.

In the event of a **hazardous substance spill**, every pharmacy should have a spill kit available. Notify your supervisor and coworkers of the spill, and evacuate the area if necessary. Check the MSDS for any special precautions or PPE required prior to cleaning up the spill. Use the spill kit to absorb the chemicals, and then place them in a chemical spill bag for disposal. Wash the area with water and detergent. For large spills, call a poison control center for assistance with cleaning up the spill.

STORAGE AND DISPOSAL

Pharmaceutical wastes include expired drugs, patient returned drugs, damaged drugs, partially used vials of single-use injection solutions, empty vials or containers of hazardous substances, syringes contaminated with hazardous substances, and any other items contaminated with hazardous substances or body fluids. Hazardous substances should be separated from other pharmacy stock and placed in leak-proof bags or bins labeled as hazardous waste. Sharps contaminated with a hazardous substance should be placed in a sharps bin labeled as hazardous.

Expired, damaged, or patient-returned medications can usually be sent to a reverse distributor for a credit. Items received from a wholesaler or distributor that are already damaged can usually be returned for a credit. Any other pharmaceutical hazardous wastes cannot be sent back to wholesalers or distributors for credit. Instead, they must be disposed of properly. A pharmaceutical waste management service, such as Stericycle, is usually contracted to periodically pick up waste from the pharmacy and dispose of it.

Bloodborne Pathogens

OSHA Standards

OSHA is the Occupational Safety and Health Administration, a government agency that helps protect employees and healthcare workers from exposure to potentially hazardous substances and chemicals. In 2000, OSHA developed the Needlestick Safety and Prevention Act to provide employers with standards for preventing the transmission of bloodborne pathogens. OSHA recommendations for reducing the risk of bloodborne pathogen transmission include the following:

- Require bloodborne pathogen training for all at-risk employees.
- Wear PPE whenever there is a reasonable risk of exposure.
- Wash hands prior to and after patient care, after removal of PPE, and after contact with blood or potentially infectious material.
- Use safer or needleless devices to reduce needlestick injuries or sharps exposures.
- Avoid splashing, spraying, or spattering body fluids.
- Use properly labeled biohazard containers or red bags labeled "Infectious Waste" for the transfer or disposal of contaminated materials.
- Use approved disinfectants on contaminated items and equipment before reuse.
- Offer hepatitis B vaccination to all employees that are at potential risk of exposure.
- Prohibit eating and drinking in work areas in which there is a risk of exposure.
- Ensure that a postexposure evaluation and a follow-up plan are in place to address exposures.

Needle Stick Injuries

A bloodborne pathogen exposure occurs when a healthcare worker or employee is exposed to human blood or any other potentially infectious material or body fluid. Body fluids other than blood that can carry infectious pathogens include cerebrospinal fluid, synovial joint fluid, pleural fluid, amniotic fluid, pericardial fluid, peritoneal fluid, semen, vaginal secretions, saliva, and fluids from tissues or body organs. All body fluids should be assumed to be infected even if the patient is not known to carry any infectious diseases. Standard precautions and exposure prevention procedures should be followed regardless of the patient being treated.

A needlestick injury results from piercing the skin or mucous membrane with a needle. If the needle was exposed to potentially infectious material prior to piercing the skin of the healthcare worker, then there is also a bloodborne pathogen exposure. Although needlestick injuries are a common type of bloodborne pathogen exposure, other common ways to be exposed to infectious material include contact with the eyes, nose, mouth, or broken/cut skin.

Protocol for Exposure to Blood

The OSHA standards and procedures for preventing bloodborne pathogen exposures should be followed by all healthcare workers. Despite our best efforts to prevent exposures, there will always be bloodborne pathogen and needlestick incidents. Therefore, we need to know how to react in the event of an exposure to blood or other potentially infectious material or body fluid. The following steps indicate the recommended procedure to follow immediately following a bloodborne pathogen exposure:

1. Wash or irrigate the site of exposure:
    a. For needlestick injuries, wash the puncture site with soap and water.
    b. For skin exposures, wash the exposure site with soap and water.
    c. For exposure into the nose or mouth, flush the area with water.
2. For eye exposures, irrigate the eyes with clean water, saline, or sterile irrigation fluid. If your department has an eye wash station, this is the best source for irrigation.
3. Report the exposure to your instructor, preceptor, or supervisor.
4. Seek medical evaluation as soon as possible. Postexposure prophylaxis treatments help prevent infection and are more effective if administered as soon as possible after exposure

Sharps Disposal

Sharp objects that require disposal, such as needles and syringes, must be place in a sharps bin. Sharps bins are usually plastic containers that have a one-way opening for the disposal of sharps that also prevent removal of objects from the container. After using a needle, lancet, syringe, or other sharp, place it in a sharps bin as soon as possible. Needles should NOT be recapped because the recapping process increases the risk of needlestick injury. Additionally, capped needles may be mistaken for new needles and may be used again. Do not attempt to remove the needles at the end of a syringe because this increases the risk of needlestick injury. Discard any used sharp along with whatever it is attached to without trying to remove it. Chemotherapy and other hazardous substances should be disposed of in a separate sharps bin labeled as hazardous. If a patient does not have a sharps container, they should dispose of their sharps in a hard, sealable container, such as a laundry detergent bottle.

HIGH-ALERT MEDICATIONS

High-alert medications are those that have the potential to cause significant harm if an error is made. Therefore, more caution and consideration must be taken when dispensing these medications.

High-Alert Medications		
IV adrenergic agonists (e.g., epinephrine)	Epidural administration of any medication	IV nitroprusside sodium
IV adrenergic antagonists (e.g., propranolol)	Oral hypoglycemic agents (e.g., glyburide, glimepiride, metformin)	Parenteral nutrition
Anesthetics (e.g., propofol)	IV inotropic agents (e.g., digoxin)	IV potassium chloride or potassium phosphate
IV antiarrhythmics (e.g., amiodarone)	Insulin	IV radiocontrast agents
Antithrombotic agents (e.g., warfarin, alteplase, apixaban)	Intrathecal administration of any medication	Sedation agents (e.g., chloral hydrate, midazolam, dexmedetomidine)
Chemotherapy agents (e.g., methotrexate)	Liposomal formulations (e.g., liposomal amphotericin B)	Sterile water for injection, inhalation, and irrigation in containers of ≥100 mL
Dextrose solutions ≥20% (hypertonic dextrose)	Narcotics/opioids (e.g., oxycodone, hydrocodone, hydromorphone)	IV sodium chloride >0.9% (hypertonic saline)
Dialysis solutions	Neuromuscular blocking agents (e.g., succinylcholine, rocuronium, vecuronium)	IV vasopressin

Controlled Substances

Classes

Schedule I — Drugs that have a high potential for abuse and no medical purpose. These cannot be obtained without a special license and are usually only used for research.

- Examples: heroin, illicit drugs

Schedule II — Drugs that have a high potential for abuse but have accepted medical uses.

- Examples: most opioids (oxycodone, morphine, hydrocodone), methadone, cocaine

Schedule III — Drugs that have less potential for abuse than schedule II drugs but can still cause low to moderate physical or psychological dependence. These drugs have accepted medical uses.

- Examples: anabolic steroids, ketamine

Schedule IV — Drugs that have less potential for abuse than schedule III drugs but can still lead to limited physical or psychological dependence. These drugs have accepted medical uses.

- Examples: benzodiazepines (alprazolam, clonazepam), sleeping tablets (zolpidem), propoxyphene

Schedule V — Drugs that have some potential for abuse but can still cause limited physical or psychological dependence. These drugs have accepted medical uses. In some states, certain schedule V medications can be sold OTC.

- Examples: diphenoxylate, pregabalin, promethazine with codeine cough syrup

Schedule II Controlled Substances

Schedule II controlled substances have a high potential for abuse and usually are kept locked up in the pharmacy safe. Schedule II substances must adhere to stricter prescription requirements. Only valid paper or electronic prescriptions are accepted, no refills are permitted, no prescription transfers are permitted, and prescriptions expire after 6 months. Substances that are classified as schedule II include opioid pain medications, CNS stimulants used to treat ADHD, and barbiturates used for sedation and to treat seizures. Codeine is only classified as a schedule II substance when it is not used in combination with another noncontrolled substance or if each dosage unit contains more than 90 mg of codeine. Diphenoxylate, a component of the laxative Lomotil, is a schedule II substance when not used in combination with another product.

Medications that are classified as schedule II controlled substances:

Brand Name	Generic Name
Codeine	Codeine
Lortab	Hydrocodone (with acetaminophen)
Dilaudid	Hydromorphone
MS Contin	Morphine
Oxycontin	Oxycodone
Actiq, Fentora, Subsys	Fentanyl
Methadone, Methadose	Methadone
Demerol	Meperidine
Adzenys, Dyanavel, Evekeo	Amphetamine
Adderall	Dextroamphetamine and amphetamine
Desoxyn	Methamphetamine
Ritalin, Concerta, Aptensio	Methylphenidate
Nembutal	Pentobarbital

Schedule III Controlled Substances

Schedule III controlled substances include the following:

- Some CNS stimulants used for weight loss are classified as schedule III substances, including benzphetamine and chlorphentermine.
- Synthetic cannabinoids (marijuana derivatives), such as dronabinol (Marinol) are also schedule III.
- Anabolic steroids are also schedule III substances, including testosterone (Depo-Testosterone) and dihydrotestosterone.
- Some barbiturates used to treat seizures that are normally classified as schedule II substances are classified as schedule III substances when formulated as a suppository or in combination with another noncontrolled substance. Pentobarbital and secobarbital suppositories are schedule III medications.
- Ketamine (Ketalar), which is used for pain and sedation, is a schedule III substance.
- Some opioid pain medications are also classified as schedule III substances, including buprenorphine with naloxone (Suboxone, Zubsolv). Codeine and dihydrocodeine are considered schedule III substances when the product contains ≤90 mg per dosage unit or ≤1.8 g per 100 mL of solution when used in combination with another noncontrolled substance. Morphine is a schedule III substance if it is used in combination with a noncontrolled substance and the product contains ≤50 mg per 100 mL or 100 g.

Schedule IV Controlled Substances

Most drugs in the schedule IV classification are benzodiazepines. Examples of benzodiazepines in this class include alprazolam (Xanax), chlordiazepoxide, clobazam, clonazepam (Klonopin), diazepam (Valium), flurazepam, loprazolam, lorazepam (Ativan), nitrazepam, oxazepam, temazepam, and triazolam. The Z-drugs used to treat insomnia are also schedule IV substances. Z-drugs include zaleplon, zolpidem (Ambien), zopiclone (Imovane), and eszopiclone (Lunesta).

The opioid pain medication tramadol (Qdolo) is also a schedule IV substance.

Some muscle relaxers are schedule IV controlled substances, including carisoprodol (Soma).

Many CNS stimulants used to aid in weight loss are classified as schedule IV controlled substances. This includes phentermine (Adipex-P) and diethylpropion. Modafinil (Provigil), a stimulant used to treat sleep disorders, is also a schedule IV substance.

The CNS depressant phenobarbital, which is used to treat seizure disorders, is also a schedule IV medication.

Schedule V Controlled Substances

Schedule V controlled substances are generally combination products that contain a schedule II, III, or IV controlled substance and at least one other noncontrolled substance.

Diphenoxylate, which is normally a schedule II controlled substance on its own, is classified as a schedule V substance when no more than 2.5 mg is combined with at least 25 mcg of atropine per dosage unit. Therefore, the medication Lomotil (2.5 mg diphenoxylate/0.025 mg atropine), used to treat diarrhea, is a schedule V substance.

The opiates codeine and dihydrocodeine may also be considered schedule V substances when combined in low concentrations with another noncontrolled ingredient. Products that contain ≤200 mg of codeine per 100 mL or 100 g of product are classified as schedule V substances. This includes promethazine with Codeine syrup, which contains 6.25 mg promethazine and 10 mg codeine per teaspoonful (5 mL) of syrup, and Coditussin AC, which contains 200 mg of guaifenesin and 10 mg of codeine per teaspoonful. Products that contain ≤100 mg of dihydrocodeine per 100 mL of 100 grams of product are also classified as schedule V substance. Many states allow some schedule V cough syrups to be sold OTC.

Disposal of Controlled Substances

A DEA Form 41 must be used to document the destruction of controlled substances. The form should include the name, address, phone number, and DEA number of the pharmacy/facility; name, strength, form, NDC number, and quantity of each controlled substance destroyed; date, location, and method of destruction; and signatures of two authorized witnesses. There are three main options for disposing of controlled substances.

- They can be transferred or returned to a reverse distributor who is authorized to possess controlled substances. The reverse distributor will issue a DEA Form 222 for the transfer/return of schedule II drugs.
- They may be destroyed in the presence of an authorized member of the DEA Drug Control Division or law enforcement. A DEA Form 41 detailing the controlled substances disposed of must be filled out and sent to the DEA.
- Hospitals or facilities that are licensed to administer medications may obtain a blanket authorization from the DEA to immediately destroy controlled substances on site in the presence of two authorized employees. A record of the destruction should be recorded using a DEA Form 41, and the form should be submitted to the DEA Drug Control Division within 10 days of the destruction.

Infection Control Standards

General Dispensing

- Pharmacy personnel should wash their hands before and after patient interactions (e.g., gel-in, gel-out).
- Equipment such as counting trays and spatulas should be cleaned and disinfected before and after use with 70% isopropyl alcohol.
- Certain medications should be prepared using designated and labeled counting trays and spatulas. This includes antibiotics and other agents that have allergy potential, warfarin, chemotherapy agents, and other hazardous medications.

Compounding

- **Nonsterile compounding** follows the standards set by *United States Pharmacopeia* 795 (USP 795).
- **Sterile compounding** follows the standards set by *United States Pharmacopeia* 797 (USP 797). Medications that are required to be compounded in a sterile environment include those administered through injection, IV infusion, intrathecal administration, or ocular administration.
- **Hazardous medications** should be compounded using biological safety cabinets or laminar flow hoods. Hazardous materials should not be stocked or worked with in an area with positive pressure relative to the surrounding areas.

Handwashing

You have been washing your hands since you were a toddler, so it may seem childish to be taught how to wash your hands. However, any new job in healthcare will require you to receive some sort of training on handwashing and hand hygiene. Below are the correct steps for washing your hands.

1. Stand far enough away from the sink so that your clothing does not touch the sink.
2. Wet your hands and forearms.
3. Apply soap.
4. Rub the soap into all areas of the hands, including under the nails, as well as the wrists and arms (up to the elbow). Do this for 15–30 seconds.
5. Rinse soapy areas of the hands, wrists, and arms thoroughly with water.
6. Keep the faucet running while you dry the hands, wrists, and arms with a paper towel.
7. Use the paper towel to turn off the faucet.

Routes of Administration and Influencing Factors

Medication Forms

Medications come in a variety of forms making them available and distributed throughout the body at different rates:

- **Tablets**: A compressed powder is administered orally (swallowed).
- **Sublingual or orally dissolving tablets**: A compressed powder tablet is placed under the tongue and left to dissolve (NOT swallowed).
- **Capsules:** A powder or liquid within a gelatin coating (capsules) is administered orally (swallowed).
- **Solutions**: Medication is dissolved in a water-based liquid and administered orally (swallowed).
- **Suspensions:** Medication is suspended in a liquid (NOT dissolved) and must be shaken before use to get an accurate dose. It is administered orally (swallowed).
- **Transdermal patches**: A patch is placed on the skin, and medication diffuses through the patch and the skin and into the bloodstream.
- **Suppositories**: Medication is incorporated into a waxy solid capsule that dissolves when exposed to body temperature. Can be inserted into the rectum, vagina, or urethra.
- **Ointments**: Oily semisolid preparation containing medication. They are applied topically.
- **Creams**: Water-based semisolid preparation containing medication. They are applied topically.
- **Inhalations:** Medication is either dissolved in a liquid and sprayed into the mouth (metered-dose inhalers), or the medication is compressed into powder particles and inhaled (dry powder inhalers [DPIs]).
- **Injections:** Medication is dissolved in a sterile (no bacteria), water-based liquid and can be injected into the body.

Infusion Pumps and Syringe Pumps

Infusion pumps are used to deliver large volumes of bagged fluids to a patient, including IV fluids, IV medications, and total parenteral nutrition. Although they are most commonly used in hospitals or care facilities, some patients use infusion pumps at home. These pumps may also be referred to as volumetric infusion pumps because they move a set volume of fluid along the tubing using mechanical methods (e.g., rotary or linear mechanisms).

Syringe drivers/pumps deliver small volumes of fluid to a patient directly from a compatible disposable syringe. Unlike infusion pumps that are driven by volume, syringe pumps are calibrated to move the syringe plunger a set distance over time. Syringe pumps are used in hospitals and medical facilities to administer certain medications, including patient-controlled analgesia. They are also very convenient for administration of medications to patients at home (e.g., insulin, chemotherapy) because there are small portable syringe pumps available.

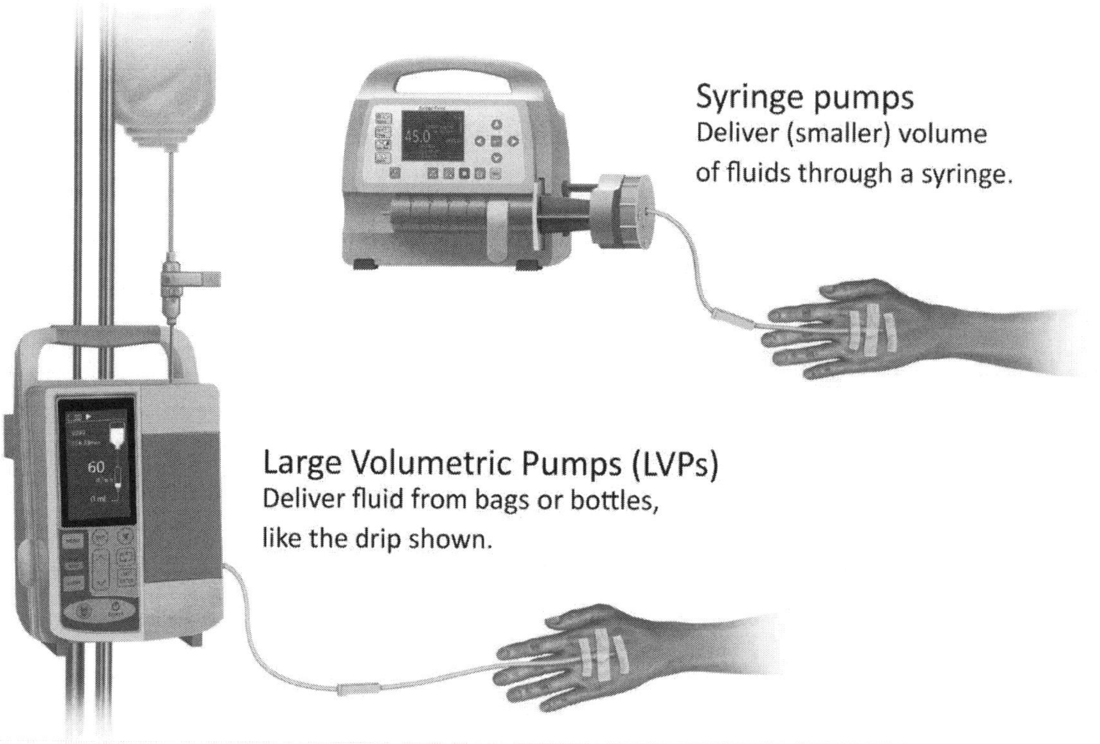

SPACERS

A spacer, also known as a holding chamber, is a device that makes using an inhaler easier and more effective. A mouthpiece or mask at one end of the device is attached to the patient, and the other end of the device is attached to the mouthpiece of the inhaler. Spacers are recommended for patients who have difficulty coordinating the action of pressing down on the inhaler and breathing in at the same time. Spacers are only used with MDIs because this type of inhaler requires the patient to press down on the metal canister to activate the release of a dose. DPIs are primed prior to use, then the dose can be inhaled without pressing a button. Most inhalers are used to treat asthma or COPD.

Spacers are commonly prescribed for children but are also used for elderly patients or those with arthritis who have difficulty pressing on the inhaler to activate it. Spacer devices can be purchased OTC without a prescription, but most patients obtain a prescription in order to bill the device to their insurance plan.

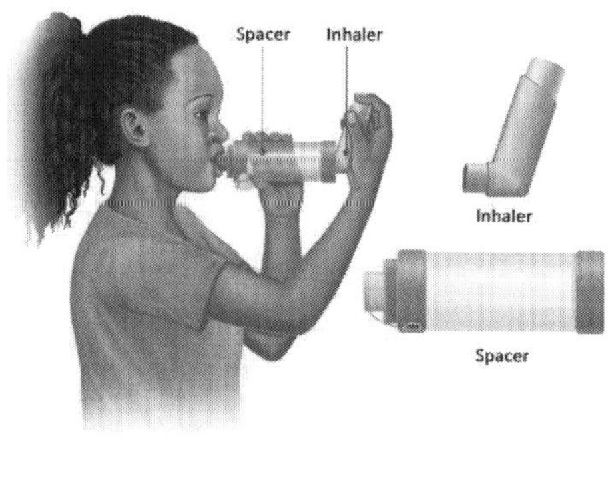

SYRINGES AND PEN NEEDLES

Syringes are used to administer injectable medications from a vial. With syringes, the patients or their caregiver must draw up the dose of medication from the vial using the syringe. The markings on the syringe are used to determine how much fluid or what amount of medication is in the syringe. Any insulin that is packaged in a multiuse vial requires syringes for administration. Examples include Lantus, Novolog, Humalog, Humulin R, and Novolin N. Many other medications require syringes to administer. In general, any injectable medication that is not packaged in an IV bag or pen device must be drawn up using syringes.

Pen needles are very short, thin needles that attach to injectable pen devices prior to administration. Pen needles are used for prefilled or refillable pen devices or cartridges. Examples of diabetic treatments that require pen needles for administration include Lantus SoloStar, Levemir FlexTouch, NovoLog FlexPen, Humalog KwikPen, Toujeo SoloStar, Byetta, and Victoza. Although pen devices are commonly used to administer insulin, there are some nondiabetic medications that use this technology as well, such as Forteo and Tymlos.

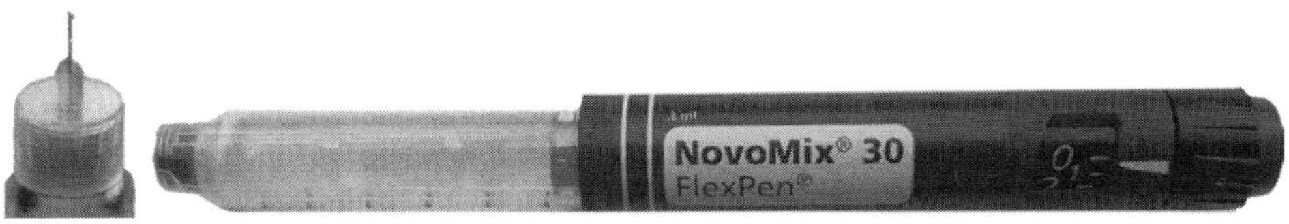

DIFFERENTIATING MEDICAL SYRINGES

Medical syringes are selected based on three different categories: volume, length, and gauge.

The **volume** of a syringe is simply the amount of volume that it holds. Syringes are available in many volumes, including 1 mL, 3 mL, 5 mL, 10 mL, 20 mL, and 50 mL. The abbreviation cc is often used instead of mL. The 1 mL syringes are the most common type dispensed in retail pharmacies because they are used to inject insulin. Each 1 mL insulin syringe holds 100 units of insulin and has markings that indicate the fill volume in units.

The **length** indicates the length of the needle. Subcutaneous medications, including insulin and some vaccinations, generally use a shorter syringe between 5/8 and 1/2 inch in length. Intramuscular injections, including many vaccines, require longer syringes between 1 inch and 1.5 inches.

The **gauge** refers to the diameter or thickness of the needle. Needles vary in size from 16- to 30-gauge. Needles with a larger gauge have a smaller diameter and are preferred in patients who are smaller or frail. Needles with smaller gauges are preferred for larger patient with more body fat. Certain types of injections may also require a specific gauge needle.

ORAL MEDICATIONS

Most medications are administered orally because it is convenient and relatively inexpensive. However, oral absorption of a drug can take a long time because it must pass through the digestive tract. Absorption can also be unpredictable and is dependent upon what is in the digestive tract (drug-food interactions). Some medications are absorbed better on an empty stomach, whereas others are absorbed better after a meal. One way to speed up oral absorption is to leave the tablet in the mouth instead of swallowing it so that it is absorbed directly into the veins in the mouth, bypassing the digestive tract. This is the idea behind sublingual and buccal tablets. Sublingual tablets dissolve on or under the tongue, whereas buccal tablets are placed on the inside of the cheek. Sublingual or buccal tablets may also be easier for patients with nausea or vomiting to tolerate.

- **Tablet examples** (most common): enalapril, Senna, amlodipine, atenolol, warfarin
- **Capsule examples:** doxycycline, Advil Liqui-Gels, omeprazole, ergocalciferol (vitamin D)
- **Sublingual examples:** Zofran ODT, Claritin RediTabs, Tylenol Meltaways, Maxalt-MLT, Prevacid SoluTab, Nitrostat
- **Buccal examples** (not as common): prochlorperazine buccal tablets, Nicorette lozenge

Parenteral Medications

Types of parenteral (injectable) medications include the following:

- **Subcutaneous (SC, SubQ)** medications are injected under the skin ("sub" means under, and "cutaneous" means skin). The skin near the injection site is pinched, and a needle is inserted into the fatty tissue beneath the skin. Most self-administered injectables, such as insulin, are administered subcutaneously.
- **Intramuscular (IM)** medications are injected into the muscle. The advantages of IM administration are that larger volumes of medication can be administered and longer acting formulations can be used. Most IM injections are administered into the deltoid muscle of the upper arm, but some are injected into the buttocks. Examples of IM medications include most vaccines, the Depo-Provera contraceptive, and most antipsychotic injections.
- **Intravenous (IV)** medications are injected directly into a vein. IV is the quickest way to get medication through your system, but administration requires medical training and is usually limited to hospital settings. Many oral medications are also available in IV form, such as nitroglycerin, verapamil, potassium, and sodium.
- **Intrathecal (IT)** means injecting a medication directly into the space around the spinal cord. This route of administration is rare and dangerous and is generally reserved for chemotherapy medications, such as methotrexate.

Otic and Optic Drops

Otic (ear) drops

- Examples: Ciprodex, ofloxacin, Cortisporin (polymyxin, neomycin, hydrocortisone)

Optic (eye) drops

- Examples: GoodSense Eye Drops, Restasis (single-use vials), latanoprost, sodium cromoglycate, Optilast

Otic and optic drops are solutions manufactured in small-volume package sizes, such as 1, 5, 8, 10, or 15 mL dropper bottles. Drops are usually in multidose bottles that expire 28 days after opening, but some manufacturers offer single-use packaging. Some ophthalmic drugs are formulated as gels or ointments instead of liquids so they last longer. They do not need to be applied as often, but they can cause temporary blurred vision in the patient. Both otic and optic dosage forms are considered topical because they are applied directly to their site of action and do NOT have significant systemic (widespread) effects.

Optic drops must be sterilized during manufacturing because the eye is an environment that is free of bacteria. Otic drops are manufactured in a clean environment, but they do not necessarily need to be sterile. For this reason, it is permissible to use an optic drop in the ear, but it is NOT permissible to use an otic drop in the eye.

Administering Optic Drops

Eye drops are administered into the eye to treat eye conditions or infections. The eye is sterile (no bacteria are present), and it must remain that way in order to prevent infection. Therefore, eye drops should be administered carefully to prevent contamination or infection.

- Step 1: Wash your hands before applying eye drops or eye ointments.
- Step 2: Tilt your head backwards while sitting, standing, or lying down.
- Step 3: Place your index finger on the soft spot of skin just under the lower eyelid, and gently pull the eyelid downward to form a pocket.
- Step 4: While looking up, squeeze one drop into the pocket formed in the lower eyelid. Ensure that you do not allow the eyedropper to touch the eye or face.

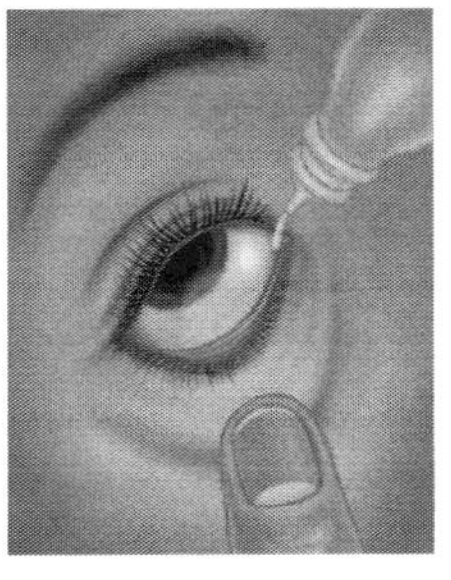

- Step 5: Close your eye for approximately 3 minutes. Do not blink or rub/wipe your eyes.

If multiple eye drops need to be applied, wait 5 minutes between applications. If using an eye ointment, apply this last and use it at bedtime because ointments can cause blurred vision.

Inhaled Medications

Inhaled medications are designed to work specifically in the lungs rather than systemically (throughout the whole body). However, small amounts of inhaled medications can be absorbed into the body and can cause side effects.

- **Metered-dose inhalers (MDIs)** contain a drug solution within a canister. When the patient presses down on the canister, a propellant (e.g., hydrofluoroalkane [HFA]) helps spray a set amount of drug solution into the patient's mouth to be inhaled. Examples of MDIs include Proair HFA, Ventolin HFA, Proventil HFA, Flovent HFA, Atrovent HFA, Advair HFA, and QVAR RediHaler.
- **Dry powder inhalers (DPIs)** contain a drug within small granules of powder. Before inhaling, the patient must prep the device. Then, the patient must inhale deeply to draw the powder into their lungs. Examples of DPIs include Advair Diskus, Spiriva HandiHaler, and Symbicort Turbuhaler.

- **Nebulizer solutions** are small vials/ampoules of drug solution that are designed to be inserted into a nebulizer machine. Nebulizers aerosolize the solution into small particles that can be inhaled into the lungs more quickly and efficiently than with inhalers. Examples include albuterol sulfate nebulization solution 2.5 mg/3 mL, sodium chloride inhalation solution, and tobramycin inhalation solution.

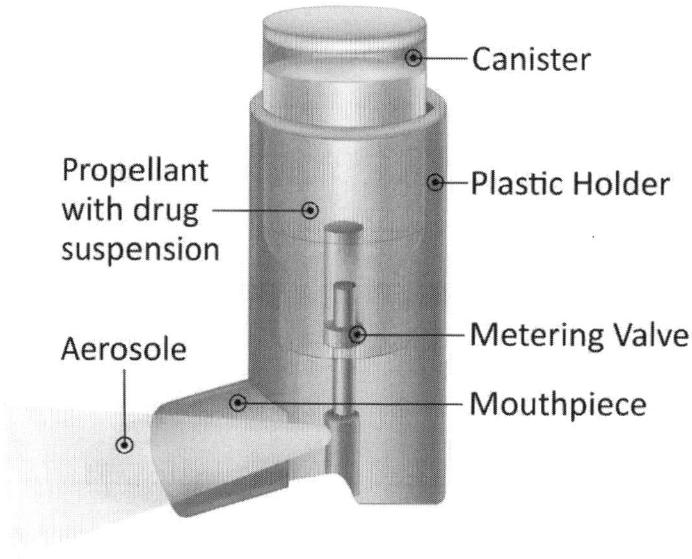

Metered-dose inhaler (MDI)

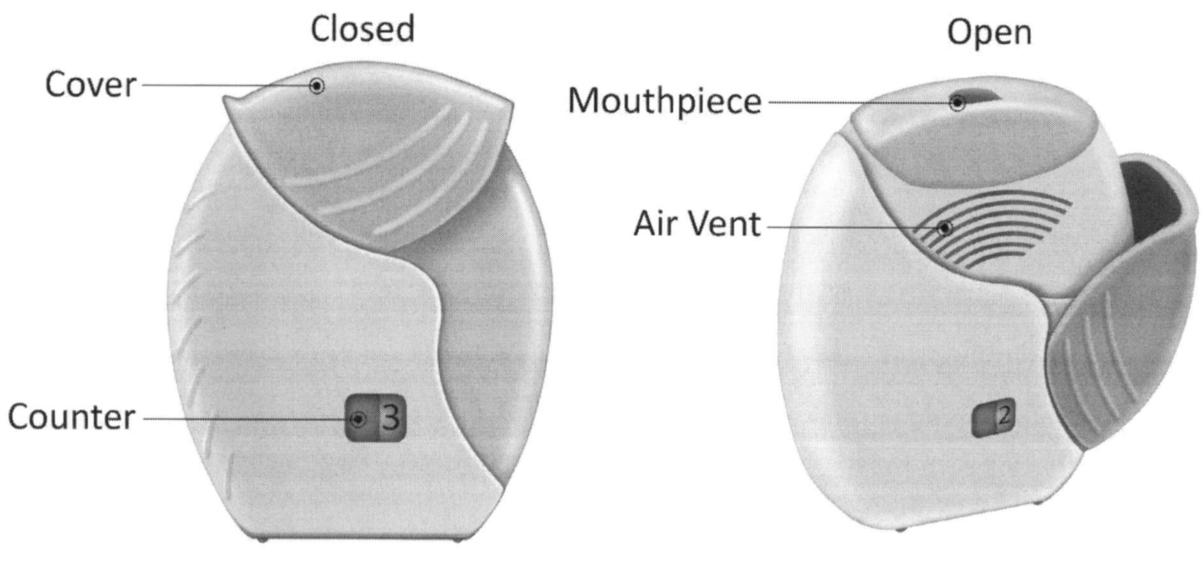

Dry powder inhaler (DPI)

Factors Influencing the Effects of Medications on the Patient

Patients respond differently to drugs depending upon their age, race, genetics, height, weight, gender, and diet. Most drugs have different recommended doses for pediatric patients because children metabolize medications at a different rate. Many medications have a greater or longer lasting effect in elderly patients because those patients break down drugs more slowly. Some medications require dosage adjustment in the elderly. Height and weight may also influence drug effects. Some drugs are dosed based on weight or body surface area. Gender, race, and genetics can also play roles in drug dosing. Patients of a certain race or gender and those with certain genetic conditions may require dosage adjustments for certain medications. Diet can also affect the metabolism of certain medications. For example, patients who take warfarin should be cautious of their vitamin K intake because it can affect the actions of warfarin. Some other medications (e.g., tetracyclines) can be affected by ions, such as calcium, and should not be taken with milk.

Classifications/Categories of Medications

Cardiovascular Drugs

Cardiovascular medications are among the most commonly prescribed drugs. They are used to treat hypertension (high blood pressure), hyperlipidemia (high cholesterol), blood clots, angina (chest pain), and heart arrhythmias.

Generic Name	Brand Name
Antihypertensives	
Lisinopril	Zestril
Lisinopril/hydrochlorothiazide	Zestoretic
Metoprolol	Lopressor
Amlodipine	Norvasc
Furosemide	Lasix
Atenolol	Tenormin
Carvedilol	Coreg
Losartan	Cozaar
Losartan/hydrochlorothiazide	Hyzaar
Tamsulosin	Flomax
Propranolol	Inderal
Spironolactone	Aldactone
Triamterene/hydrochlorothiazide	Maxzide
Valsartan	Diovan
Valsartan/hydrochlorothiazide	Diovan HCT
Enalapril	Vasotec
Amlodipine/benazepril	Lotrel
Benazepril	Lotensin
Clonidine	Catapres
Hydralazine	Apresoline
Ramipril	Altace
Nifedipine	Procardia XL
Olmesartan	Benicar
Nebivolol	Bystolic
Doxazosin	Cardura
Irbesartan	Avapro
Terazosin	APO-Terazosin
Chlorthalidone	Thalitone
Guanfacine	Intuniv
Antihyperlipidemics	
Atorvastatin	Lipitor
Simvastatin	Zocor
Rosuvastatin	Crestor
Lovastatin	Altoprev
Fenofibrate	Tricor
Ezetimibe	Zetia
Gemfibrozil	Lopid
Omega-3 acid	Lovaza

Generic Name	Brand Name
Blood Thinners (Antiplatelets and Anticoagulants)	
Aspirin	Bayer
Clopidogrel	Plavix
Warfarin	Coumadin
Rivaroxaban	Xarelto
Apixaban	Eliquis
Enoxaparin	Lovenox
Angina Drugs (Nitrates and Calcium Channel Blockers)	
Nitroglycerin	Nitrostat
Isosorbide mononitrate	Imdur
Diltiazem	Cardizem
Verapamil	Calan SR
Antiarrhythmics	
Amiodarone	Nexterone

Antihypertensive Drugs

Hypertension means high blood pressure, so antihypertensive medications help lower blood pressure. High blood pressure is one of the most common conditions treated with medication. There are many classes of cardiovascular drugs that are prescribed in the treatment of high blood pressure. The most common classes of medications are beta-blockers (they end in the suffix "-olol"), calcium channel blockers (most end in "-pine"), angiotensin-converting enzyme (ACE) inhibitors (end with the suffix "-pril"), alpha-blockers (end in "-zosin"), and diuretics (there are various naming systems, but some end in "-thiazide").

Beta-blockers and alpha-blockers block the fight-or-flight response in our bodies that triggers increased heart rate, increased force of contraction of the heart, and increased blood pressure. By blocking this response, beta blockers lower heart rate and blood pressure to treat hypertension.

Calcium channel blockers prevent calcium from entering the cells of the heart and blood vessel walls. Because calcium is needed for muscle contraction, calcium channel blockers reduce the force of contraction of the heart and the muscles surrounding blood vessels, resulting in lower blood pressure.

ACE inhibitors block angiotensin-converting enzyme, which is responsible for producing a substance called angiotensin II. Angiotensin II narrows blood vessels and helps the body retain water, which leads to a rise in blood pressure.

Diuretics decrease the volume of blood by promoting water loss in the urine. This volume loss results in lower blood pressure.

Review Video: Antihypertensives: ACE inhibitors and ARBs
Visit mometrix.com/academy and enter code: **525864**

Review Video: Antiadrenergics: Alpha and Beta-Blockers
Visit mometrix.com/academy and enter code: **947779**

Commonly dispensed antihypertensive drugs:

Classification	Generic Name	Brand Name
Beta-blocker	Atenolol	Tenormin
Beta-blocker	Metoprolol	Lopressor, Toprol
Beta-blocker	Nadolol	Corgard
Beta-blocker	Propranolol	Inderal
Calcium channel blocker	Amlodipine	Norvasc
Calcium channel blocker	Diltiazem	Cardizem, Cartia, Tiazac
Calcium channel blocker	Nifedipine	Procardia
Calcium channel blocker	Verapamil	Calan
ACE inhibitor	Benazepril	Lotensin
ACE inhibitor	Captopril	APO-Captopril
ACE inhibitor	Enalapril	Vasotec
ACE inhibitor	Lisinopril	Zestril
ACE inhibitor	Ramipril	Altace
Alpha-blocker	Prazosin	Minipress
Alpha-blocker	Doxazosin	Cardura
Diuretic	Hydrochlorothiazide	APO-Hydro
Diuretic	Furosemide	Lasix
Diuretic	Spironolactone	Aldactone

Heart Failure Drugs

Heart failure occurs when a patient's heart is not functioning efficiently, often as a result of a heart attack or cardiovascular disease. These patients get chest pain (angina) when they exert themselves and overwork their heart. They will be prescribed an antianginal agent, also referred to as nitrates, to use to prevent or treat angina pains. Heart failure patients are usually prescribed antihypertensive medications and diuretics as well to lower blood pressure and reduce the rate and force of the contraction of the heart. Some patients may have an irregularity in their heartbeat, which is treated with antiarrhythmic medications.

Vasodilators and **antianginal agents** cause vasodilation (widening) of blood vessels, which lowers blood pressure. **Antihypertensive medications** and **diuretics** also reduce blood pressure. Lower blood pressures reduce the strain on an overworked heart to reduce angina pains.

Antiarrhythmic drugs help restore a normal heart rhythm and improve the efficiency of the heart.

Drug Classification	Generic Name	Brand Name
Vasodilator	Hydralazine	Apresoline
Antianginal	Nitroglycerin	Nitrostat, Nitrolingual, Rectiv
Antianginal	Isosorbide mononitrate	(None currently on the market)
Antiarrhythmic	Amiodarone	Nexterone
Antiarrhythmic	Digoxin	Lanoxin

ANTIARRHYTHMIC DRUGS

An arrhythmia is an irregularity in the rate or rhythm at which the heart beats. The most common types of arrhythmias are ventricular tachycardia and atrial fibrillation.

Some classes of medications that are used to treat hypertension are also used to treat arrhythmias, including beta-blockers (end in "-olol") and calcium channel blockers. These medications slow the heart rate and are used to treat tachycardias. Tachycardia is a type of heart arrhythmia in which the heart beats too fast. Several other classes of antiarrhythmic drugs also exist. The common antiarrhythmic drugs are used to treat tachycardias and/or atrial fibrillation. You may notice that many of the brand names for antiarrhythmic drugs contain the root words "pace" or "rhythm," which is helpful for indicating that they are used to control the pace or rhythm of the heart.

Generic Name	Brand Name
Metoprolol	Lopressor, Toprol
Atenolol	Tenormin
Sotalol	Betapace
Verapamil	Calan SR, Verelan
Amiodarone	Pacerone, Nexterone
Propafenone	Rythmol
Disopyramide	Norpace
Flecainide	Tambocor
Digoxin	Lanoxin

ANTIHYPERLIPIDEMIC DRUGS

Hypercholesterolemia is defined as high cholesterol levels. Cholesterol is a lipid molecule that is transported in the blood and is linked to cardiovascular disease. Most antihyperlipidemic medications inhibit the enzyme HMG-CoA reductase, which is involved in the production of cholesterol in the body. HMG-CoA reductase inhibitors are commonly referred to as **statins** because they end in the suffix "-statin." Some antihyperlipidemic medications, such as ezetimibe, work by inhibiting the absorption of cholesterol in the gastrointestinal tract. Cholestyramine and colestipol act by binding to and removing bile salts in the gastrointestinal tract. Because cholesterol is used by the body to make bile salts, removing bile salts helps use up excess cholesterol to make more bile salts. Cholesterol or bile salt binding antihyperlipidemic medications are usually well tolerated, but some patients experience abdominal cramping, constipation, nausea, or vomiting.

Generic Name	Brand Name
Ezetimibe	Zetia
Pravastatin	(None currently on the market)
Simvastatin	Zocor
Atorvastatin	Lipitor
Rosuvastatin	Crestor
Cholestyramine	Questran
Colestipol	Colestid

SIDE EFFECTS OF ANTIHYPERLIPIDEMIC AND ANTIHYPERTENSIVE DRUGS

The most common class of antihyperlipidemic medications is the HMG CoA reductase inhibitors, commonly referred to as **statins**. Common side effects of statins include headache, nausea, abdominal pain, drowsiness, dizziness, and muscle aches. Many patients experience minor muscle aches with statin use, but some patients may experience more serious muscle side effects called myopathy or rhabdomyolysis. Patients should be referred to their doctor if they experience any muscle pains while taking a statin. Some other antihyperlipidemic medications act in the digestive tract, including bile acid binders (e.g., cholestyramine and colestipol). These medications are usually well tolerated, but some patients experience abdominal cramping, constipation, nausea, or vomiting.

Antihypertensives have the following known side effects:

- **Beta-blockers and alpha-blockers** commonly cause fatigue (tiredness), cold hands, upset stomach, constipation, dizziness, shortness of breath, low blood pressure (hypotension), low heart rate (bradycardia), and fainting.
- **Calcium channel blockers** can cause adverse effects such as dizziness, swelling, blurred vision, fatigue, and weight gain.
- **ACE inhibitors** are known for causing an unproductive dry cough, high potassium levels (hyperkalemia), nausea, and loss of appetite.
- **Diuretics** can lead to adverse effects such as dry mouth, weakness, loss of appetite, muscle twitching, upset stomach, and electrolyte imbalances.

RESPIRATORY DRUGS

Respiratory medications include tablets, capsules, inhalers, and nebulizer solutions. Commonly treated respiratory conditions include asthma, emphysema, chronic obstructive pulmonary disease (COPD), bronchitis, flu, cold, and allergies.

- **Antihistamines** reduce inflammation by inhibiting histamine, a chemical messenger in the body that promotes inflammation. Antihistamines are used to treat allergies such as hay fever, flu symptoms, and cold symptoms.
- **Decongestants** constrict the blood vessels in the nose to reduce mucus buildup and congestion. Decongestants are used to treat head and sinus congestions associated with colds and flus.
- **Antitussives** prevent coughing and are used to treat cold and flu symptoms. The mechanism of action varies depending upon the specific medication. Some medications soothe the lining of the throat, whereas others act on cough reflex centers in the brain.
- **Expectorants** help thin the mucus that builds up during a cold or respiratory illness. They help patients with productive coughs bring up excess mucus and relieve chest congestion.
- **Bronchodilators** dilate or open the airways to make it easier for patients to breathe. They are used to treat respiratory diseases, such as asthma and chronic obstructive pulmonary disease (COPD), but they can also be used short term during a respiratory illness to help relieve shortness of breath.
- **Corticosteroids** are anti-inflammatory medications that are used to treat a wide range of diseases, including respiratory illnesses.

Commonly Used Respiratory Drug Generic and Brand Names

Medications that can be purchased over the counter (OTC) without a prescription are italicized in the table below. Pseudoephedrine is a special case because, although it can be purchased without a prescription, it is kept behind the pharmacy counter and the customer must show identification and sign for it in order to purchase it.

Drug Classification	Generic Name	Brand Name
Antihistamine	Loratadine	*Claritin, Alavert*
Antihistamine	Cetirizine	*Zyrtec*
Antihistamine	Fexofenadine	*Allegra*
Antihistamine	Chlorpheniramine	*Chlor-Trimeton*
Antihistamine	Diphenhydramine	*Benadryl*
Antihistamine	Promethazine	Phenergan
Decongestant	Pseudoephedrine	Sudafed (available without prescription)
Decongestant	Phenylephrine	*Sudafed-PE*
Antitussive	Dextromethorphan	*Delsym*
Antitussive	Codeine (used in combination cough syrups)	Phenergan with codeine
Expectorant	Guaifenesin	*Robitussin (most formulations), Mucinex*
Bronchodilator	Albuterol	Ventolin, Airomir
Bronchodilator	Levalbuterol	Xopenex
Bronchodilator	Ipratropium	Atrovent
Bronchodilator	Formoterol	Perforomist
Bronchodilator	Salmeterol	Serevent
Corticosteroid	Budesonide	*Pulmicort* (only nasal version is OTC)
Corticosteroid	Beclomethasone	Qvar
Corticosteroid	Mometasone	Asmanex
Corticosteroid	Fluticasone	Generic version only
Corticosteroid	Triamcinolone	Hexatrione, Kenalog
Antiasthmatic drug (leukotriene receptor antagonist)	Montelukast	Singulair

DRUGS FOR RESPIRATORY INFECTIONS

The top drugs used to treat infections and respiratory disorders:

Generic Name	Brand Name
Antibiotics	
Amoxicillin	APO-Amoxi, Novamoxin
Azithromycin	Zithromax
Sulfamethoxazole/trimethoprim	Bactrim
Amoxicillin/clavulanate potassium	Augmentin
Bacitracin/neomycin/polymyxin B cream	Neosporin
Ciprofloxacin	Cipro
Cephalexin	(None currently on the market)
Doxycycline	Doryx
Clindamycin	Cleocin
Levofloxacin	Levaquin
Metronidazole	Flagyl
Nitrofurantoin	Macrobid
Antivirals	
Acyclovir	(None currently on the market)
Valacyclovir	Valtrex
Antifungals	
Fluconazole	Diflucan
Bronchodilators	
Albuterol inhaler	Ventolin, ProAir, Proventil
Tiotropium inhaler	Spiriva
Albuterol/ipratropium nebulized, inhaled	Combivent
Fluticasone/salmeterol inhaler	Advair
Budesonide/formoterol inhaler	Symbicort
Oral Antiasthma Drugs	
Montelukast	Singulair
Antihistamines	
Loratadine	Claritin
Cetirizine	Zyrtec
Hydroxyzine	Vistaril
Promethazine	Phenergan
Meclizine	Bonine
Antitussives	
Benzonatate	(None currently on the market)

Anti-infectives include antibiotics, antivirals, and antifungals. Bronchodilators are used to treat asthma and COPD. Antihistamines can be used to relieve the respiratory symptoms of respiratory illnesses and seasonal allergies, such as runny nose, congestion, watery eyes, and nasal congestion. Some antihistamines, such as meclizine, can also be used to relieve nausea and vomiting. Antitussives are used to relieve cough.

ANALGESICS

Analgesics are medications that are used to reduce pain. They can be given in the form of a tablet/capsule, oral liquid, or parenteral injection. Most nonsteroidal anti-inflammatory drugs (NSAIDs) as well as aspirin and acetaminophen are available over the counter (OTC). Opioids are stronger, have more side effects, and have a higher potential for abuse, so they are prescription only. Most opioids are classified as controlled substances.

Commonly used **analgesics**:

Drug Classification	Generic Name	Brand Name	Legal Classification
Salicylate	Aspirin	Bayer	OTC
NSAID	Ibuprofen	Motrin, Advil	OTC
NSAID	Naproxen	Aleve	OTC
NSAID	Celecoxib	Celebrex	℞ only, noncontrolled
Non-aspirin, non-NSAID	Acetaminophen	Tylenol	OTC
Opiate	Tramadol	Ultram	Sch IV
Opiate	Acetaminophen with codeine Promethazine with codeine	Tylenol with Codeine (None currently on the market)	Sch II if >90 mg per dosage unit Sch III if <90 mg per dosage unit Sch V if ≤200 mg per 100 mL or 100 g
Opiate	Hydrocodone	Hysingla, Zoyhydro	Sch II
Opiate	Hydromorphone	Dilaudid	Sch II
Opiate	Morphine	MS Contin, Duramorph, Infumorph, Mitigo	Sch II
Opiate	Oxycodone	Oxycontin, Oxaydo, Roxicodone, Roxybond	Sch II
Opiate	Meperidine	Demerol	Sch II

ANTIMICROBIALS

ANTIBIOTIC DRUGS

Antibiotics are used to treat bacterial or microbial infections. Broad-spectrum antibiotics are less specific and kill a wide range of bacteria, but they have more side effects. Narrow-spectrum antibiotics are more specific and are used to treat infections when the bacterial cause is known.

Commonly prescribed **antibiotics**:

Class	Drug Examples	Class Details
Penicillins	Amoxicillin, penicillin, ampicillin	Broad-spectrum antibiotics used to treat respiratory infections.
Cephalosporins	Cefaclor (Cefaclor), cefixime (Suprax)	Broad-spectrum antibiotics.
Tetracyclines	Tetracycline, doxycycline (Vibramycin, Monodoxyne), minocycline (Minocin, Solodyn)	Broad-spectrum, but many bacteria are resistant. Used to treat acne.
Macrolides	Erythromycin (Erythrocin), clarithromycin (Biaxin)	Similar spectrum to penicillins, so they are used as an alternative in penicillin allergy. Used to treat respiratory infections, acne, and chlamydia.
Quinolones	Ciprofloxacin (Cipro), levofloxacin (Levaquin)	Narrower spectrum, commonly used to treat pneumonia.
Sulfonamides (sulfa drugs)	Sulfamethoxazole-trimethoprim (Bactrim)	Used to treat urinary tract infections.
Glycopeptides	Vancomycin	Narrow spectrum, used to treat MRSA (IV only). Oral vancomycin is used to treat colitis and *Clostridioides difficile*.

Antiviral Drugs

Antiviral medications are used to treat viral infections. Viruses are different in structure and behavior than bacteria and require different types of medications to eradicate them. In general, drug names that end in "-vir" are antiviral drugs. Some viral infections are short term (e.g., influenza), whereas others are chronic and require life-long treatment (e.g., human immunodeficiency virus [HIV]). In addition to therapeutic medications, there are several vaccinations that are used to prevent viral infections before the patient becomes infected (e.g., flu vaccine, hepatitis B vaccine).

Commonly prescribed **antiviral medications**:

Generic Name	Brand Name	Indication
Acyclovir	(None currently on the market)	Herpes infections
Valacyclovir	Valtrex	Herpes infections
Oseltamivir	Tamiflu	Influenza viruses
Zanamivir	Relenza	Influenza viruses
Emtricitabine and tenofovir disoproxil fumarate	Truvada	HIV prevention in at-risk patients
Dolutegravir, abacavir, and lamivudine	Triumeq	HIV
Dolutegravir	Tivicay	HIV
Tenofovir alafenamide and emtricitabine	Descovy	HIV
Elvitegravir, cobicistat, emtricitabine, and tenofovir alafenamide	Genvoya	HIV
Darunavir and ritonavir	Prezista	HIV
Ledipasvir and sofosbuvir	Harvoni	Hepatitis C
Sofosbuvir and velpatasvir	Epclusa	Hepatitis C

Antifungal Drugs

Fungi differ from bacteria and viruses in their structure and behavior, so a different set of medications are required to treat a fungal infection. Antifungal medications can easily be identified because they either end in the suffix "-conazole" or "-fungin." However, there are always exceptions to the rule and there are a few antifungal medications that do not follow this naming rule. Common types of fungal infections include oral thrush, vaginal candidiasis (yeast infection), athlete's foot, jock itch, and fungal skin infections. Most of these conditions are minor and can be treated with OTC medications. The OTC medications are italicized in the table below. Occasionally, fungal infections can get into the body and cause more serious widespread infections, meningitis, or pneumonia.

Generic Name	Brand Name
Caspofungin	Cancidas
Micafungin	Mycamine
Clotrimazole	*Gyne-Lotrimin* (cream is OTC; tablets are ℞-only)
Fluconazole	Diflucan
Itraconazole	Sporanox
Miconazole	*Cavilon, Desenex*
Terbinafine	*Lamisil* (cream is OTC; tablets are ℞-only)
Amphotericin B	(None currently on the market)
Nystatin	Nyamyc, Nystop
Griseofulvin	(None currently on the market)

Cancer Drugs

Drugs used to treat cancer are also called antineoplastic agents or anticancer agents.

- **Antimetabolites** inhibit cancer cell growth by interfering with their metabolism (cellular processes).
- Examples: methotrexate (Rasuvo, Otrexup, Trexall), fluorouracil, mercaptopurine (Purixan), capecitabine (Xeloda), azathioprine (Imuran)
- **Alkylating agents and antitumor antibiotics** interfere with and cause damage to DNA. This prevents cancer cells from replicating or growing.
- Examples: cyclophosphamide (Procytox), temozolomide (Temodar), carmustine, daunorubicin, bleomycin
- **Hormonal anticancer therapies** are used to treat cancers that require certain hormones to grow (e.g., breast cancer, prostate cancer). By blocking the necessary hormone, these therapies inhibit the growth of cancer cells. These therapies are more selective and have fewer classic antineoplastic agent side effects.
- Examples: tamoxifen (Soltamox), letrozole (Femara), anastrozole (Arimidex), bicalutamide (Casodex), leuprolide (Lupron, Eligard)
- **Radioactive isotopes** act in a similar way to radiation therapy. The radiation enters cancer cells and causes damage, preventing the cells from growing and dividing. Example: cesium-137

Endocrine Drugs

Endocrine system disorder drugs include antihyperglycemic treatments for diabetes, contraceptives, hormone replacement therapies, hormonal cancer treatments, treatments for thyroid disorders, and corticosteroid hormones that are used to treat a wide range of inflammatory conditions. The brand names and generic names of the top medications used to treat **endocrine system disorders**:

Generic Name	Brand Name
Antihyperglycemics	
Metformin	Glucophage
Glipizide	Glucotrol
Glimepiride	Amaryl
Sitagliptin	Januvia
Sitagliptin/metformin	Janumet
Glyburide	Glynase
Pioglitazone	Actos
Canagliflozin	Invokana
Insulin lispro	Humalog
Insulin glargine	Lantus
Insulin detemir	Levemir
Insulin aspart	Novolog
Insulin regular	Humulin
Liraglutide	Victoza

Generic Name	Brand Name
Corticosteroid Hormones (Anti-inflammatory, Bronchodilators)	
Fluticasone inhaler	Flovent
Budesonide inhaler	Pulmicort
Fluticasone/salmeterol inhaler	Advair
Budesonide/formoterol inhaler	Symbicort
Methylprednisolone	Solu-Medrol, Medrol
Prednisone	Prednisone Intensol, Rayos
Prednisolone	Millpred
Hydrocortisone	Cortef
Clobetasol propionate cream	Clobex
Triamcinolone cream	Kenalog
Mometasone nasal spray	Propel
Contraceptives (Birth Control)	
Ethinyl estradiol/norethindrone	Estrostep. Loestrin
Ethinyl estradiol/levonorgestrel	Altavera, Levonest
Ethinyl estradiol/drospirenone	Ocella, Yasmin
Ethinyl estradiol/norgestimate	Mili, Monolinyah
Ethinyl estradiol/desogestrel	Apri
Ethinyl estradiol/etonogestrel vaginal ring	NuvaRing
Postmenopausal Hormone Replacement Therapy	
Estradiol vaginal ring	Estring
Conjugated estrogens	Premarin
Hormonal Anticancer Drugs	
Anastrozole	Arimidex
Male Hormone Replacement Therapy	
Testosterone	Andriol, Androgel
Antiandrogens (to Treat Prostate Enlargement and Pattern Baldness)	
Finasteride	Proscar
Thyroid Hormone Replacements	
Levothyroxine	Synthroid, Levoxyl

Drugs for Thyroid-Related Disorders

Hypothyroidism is defined as thyroid hormone levels that are too low, and **hyperthyroidism** is defined as thyroid hormone levels that are too high. Recall that the prefix "hypo-" means less than normal or low and "hyper-" means greater than normal or high. The thyroid gland sits low in the front of the neck and is responsible for secreting thyroid hormone. This gland is part of the body's endocrine system, which is responsible for secreting hormones that regulate body processes. Hypothyroidism is more common than hyperthyroidism in the United States and is easily treatable with hormone replacement therapy. Symptoms of hypothyroidism include fatigue, weakness, joint pain, sensitivity to cold, weight gain, hair thinning, depression, impaired memory, slow heart rate, and irregular menstrual periods. Symptoms of hyperthyroidism are essentially the opposite: restlessness, tremors, intolerance to heat, weight loss, increased appetite, sweating, anxiety, rapid heart rate, and agitation.

Indication	Generic Name	Brand Name
Hypothyroidism	Levothyroxine	Synthroid, Levoxyl
Hypothyroidism	Liothyronine	Cytomel
Hyperthyroidism	Propylthiouracil	Halycil

DIABETES MELLITUS DRUGS

Diabetes mellitus is a chronic disease in which patients have too much glucose in their blood. It is related to dysfunction of insulin, a hormone that shuttles glucose from the blood into the tissues. In diabetics, either too little insulin is being produced or the tissues are not sensitive or responsive enough to insulin. Because insulin is not shuttling glucose from the blood into the tissues, glucose builds up in the blood.

- **Type 1 diabetes** is a genetic disorder that is diagnosed at a young age. Immune cells in the body attack and destroy the beta cells in the pancreas that produce insulin. Therefore, type 1 diabetics must replace the missing insulin using insulin injections.
- **Type 2 diabetes** is characterized by decreased sensitivity to insulin. Although there may also be reduced insulin production, the tissues are not responding to the insulin that is present. Type 2 diabetes is usually diagnosed later in life. Although there are genetic risk factors, lifestyle factors such as obesity increase the risk of getting the disease. Type 2 diabetes can be treated by diet and lifestyle modifications, oral or injectable antihyperglycemic medications, and insulin.

Review Video: Diet, Exercise, and Medications for Diabetes
Visit mometrix.com/academy and enter code: 774388

Review Video: Diabetes Mellitus
Visit mometrix.com/academy and enter code: 501396

Review Video: Diabetes Mellitus: Complications
Visit mometrix.com/academy and enter code: 996788

ORAL ANTIHYPERGLYCEMIC DRUGS

Diabetes is caused by either a lack of insulin or reduced sensitivity to insulin. Insulin is a hormone that shuttles glucose from the blood into the tissues. The mechanism of action for common oral antihyperglycemic drugs are as follows:

- **Biguanides** decrease glucose production in the liver, decrease absorption of glucose in the intestines, and improve glucose uptake into tissues.
- **Alpha-glucosidase inhibitors** delay the digestion of carbohydrates in the intestines, thereby slowing the release of glucose into the blood.
- **Sulfonylureas** stimulate the release of insulin from the pancreas.
- **Thiazolidinediones** decrease glucose production in the liver and enhance the sensitivity of tissues to insulin, allowing them to take up more glucose from the blood.
- **DPP-4 inhibitors** promote insulin production by increasing the levels of a hormone called glucagon-like peptide-1 (GLP-1).
- **SGLT-2 inhibitors** inhibit a sodium-glucose transporter in the kidney, which promotes the excretion of glucose in the urine.

Commonly used **oral antihyperglycemic drugs** include the following:

Drug Class	Generic Name	Brand Name
Biguanide	Metformin	Glucophage
Alpha-glucosidase inhibitor	Acarbose	(None currently on the market)
Sulfonylurea	Glipizide	Glucotrol
Sulfonylurea	Glyburide	Glynase
Sulfonylurea	Glimepiride	Amaryl
Thiazolidinedione	Pioglitazone	Actos
Thiazolidinedione	Rosiglitazone	(None currently on the market)
DPP inhibitor	Saxagliptin	Onglyza
DPP-4 inhibitor	Sitagliptin	Januvia
DPP-4 inhibitor	Linagliptin	Tradjenta
SGLT-2 inhibitor	Canagliflozin	Invokana
SGLT-2 inhibitor	Dapagliflozin	Farxiga
SGLT-2 inhibitor	Empagliflozin	Jardiance

Injectable Antihyperglycemic Medications

Insulin injections replace insulin that is missing or lacking in the body. They are usually used to treat type 1 diabetes, but they may also be used in type 2 diabetes. Common side effects of using insulin are hypoglycemia, weight gain, and injection site reactions.

Incretin mimetics are a newer class of injectable antihyperglycemic drugs. They increase the activity of the hormone GLP-1, which increases insulin production, decreases glucagon (stored glucose) release, slows glucose digestion, and reduces appetite. Because they do not replace insulin, they are only used in type 2 diabetes. Incretin mimetics are becoming increasing popular because they have a low risk of causing hypoglycemia and they help patients lose weight.

Amylin mimetics decrease the production of glucagon (stored glucose), slow gastric emptying (this slows glucose digestion), enhances satiety (the feeling of fullness after a meal), and cause weight loss. They are not very popular because they can cause severe hypoglycemia. However, they can be used in combination with insulin in type 1 or type 2 diabetics who have failed other regimens.

Drug Class	Generic Name	Brand Name
Incretin mimetic	Liraglutide	Victoza
Incretin mimetic	Exenatide	Byetta, Bydureon BCise
Amylin mimetic	Pramlintide	SymlinPen

Commonly Used Insulin Regimens

Basal bolus regimen (first-line, preferred regimen)

The basal bolus regimen involves injecting a long-acting insulin once or twice daily in addition to injecting a dose of rapid-acting insulin before every meal.

Insulin Type/Generic Name	Brand Name	Duration of Action
Rapid-Acting Insulins		
Insulin glulisine	Apidra	1–3 hours
Insulin aspart	NovoLog	3–5 hours
Insulin lispro	Humalog, Admelog	3–4 hours
Long-Acting Insulins		
Insulin glargine	Lantus	24 hours
Insulin detemir	Levemir	18–24 hours

Twice-Daily Mixed Insulin Regimen

The mixed insulin regimen involves the patient injecting a mixture of intermediate- and short-acting insulin twice daily. This regimen does not provide as steady of an insulin level compared to the basal bolus regimen, and it increases the patient's risk for a hypoglycemic event.

Insulin Type/Generic Name	Brand Name	Duration of Action
Short-Acting Insulins		
Insulin regular	Novolin R, Humulin R	4–6 hours
Intermediate-Acting Insulins		
Insulin NPH	Novolin N, Humulin N	10–18 hours
Premixed Formulations		
70% Insulin NPH + 30% insulin regular	Novolin 70/30 Humulin 70/30	
50% Insulin NPH + 30% insulin regular	Humulin 50/50	

Hypoglycemia Medications

Diabetes mellitus is defined by hyperglycemia (high blood glucose). Treatments for diabetes aim to lower blood glucose. Therefore, many antihyperglycemic medications can cause hypoglycemia (low blood glucose). Some classes of antihyperglycemic medications have a higher risk of causing hypoglycemia (e.g., sulfonylureas, insulin, amylin mimetics) than others.

Hypoglycemia is a potentially serious side effect of antihyperglycemic medications. If too high of a dose is administered or if a patient does not eat enough carbohydrates, the patient's blood glucose levels can become too low. Symptoms of hypoglycemia include tremors, dizziness, sweating, hunger, irritability, slurred speech, anxiety, and headache.

If hypoglycemia is suspected, the patient should be given a sugary snack or drink, glucose tablets, or a glucagon injection (if the patient is unconscious) as soon as possible. If left untreated, hypoglycemia can cause the patient to pass out, have a seizure, or even die.

Glucose tablets	Glucolift, Dex4, Relion
Glucose oral gel	Dex4, Glutose, Transcend
Glucagon injection	GlucaGen

Hormonal Replacement Therapy

After menopause, women experience a decline in estrogen levels. This causes menopausal symptoms such as hot flashes, vaginal dryness, and osteoporosis. Some women are placed on **estrogen hormone replacement therapy** to combat menopausal symptoms and reduce the risk of osteoporosis. However, estrogen replacement can cause adverse effects such as breast tenderness, acne, blood clots, and increased risk of breast cancer.

Men may require **testosterone hormone replacement therapy**. Symptoms of testosterone deficiency include decreased sexual desire and decreased energy. Testosterone replacement therapy may be prescribed to combat these symptoms. Side effects of testosterone replacement therapy include raised cholesterol levels, fluid retention, and liver failure. Testosterone also helps the body build muscle, so it is often abused by body builders. Therefore, testosterone products are schedule III controlled substances.

The generic and brand names for commonly prescribed hormone replacement therapies:

Generic Name	Brand Name
Testosterone	Androgel
Estradiol vaginal cream	Estrace
Estradiol pessary	Vagifem
Estradiol vaginal ring	Estring, Femring
Estradiol tablets	Estrace, Femtrace
Estradiol patch	Vivelle-Dot, Climara
Conjugated estrogens tablets and cream	Premarin
Estradiol/levonorgestrel patch	Climara Pro
Estradiol/norethindrone patch	CombiPatch
Estradiol/norethindrone tablets	Activella
Conjugated estrogen/medroxyprogesterone tablets	Prempro

Combined Oral Contraceptives

Combined oral contraceptives (COCs) contain an estrogen and a progesterone. COCs are available as daily tablets, once-weekly patches, and once-monthly vaginal rings. There are hundreds of oral COCs available on the market that contain different strengths and different forms of hormones in order to help women regulate their menstrual cycle.

Common adverse effects of COCs include breast tenderness, nausea, vomiting, headache, high blood pressure, weight gain, and breakthrough vaginal bleeding. The estrogens in COCs increase the risk of developing breast cancer and blood clots. The different combined oral contraceptive (COC) products:

Dosage Form	Generic Name	Brand Names
Oral tablet	Ethinyl estradiol/norethindrone	Loestrin, Necon, Nortrel, Ortho Novum
Oral tablet	Ethinyl estradiol/levonorgestrel	Aviane, Levora, Trivora, Seasonique, Jolessa
Oral tablet	Ethinyl estradiol/drospirenone	Yasmin, Ocella, Yaz
Oral tablet	Ethinyl estradiol/norgestrel	Cryselle, Elinest, Low Ogestrel
Oral tablet	Ethinyl estradiol/desogestrel	Apri, Cyred, Mircette, Pimtrea
Oral tablet	Ethinyl estradiol/norgestimate	Estarylla, Mili, TriLinya
Patch	Ethinyl estradiol/norelgestromin	Xulane, Zafemy
Vaginal ring	Ethinyl estradiol/etonogestrel	NuvaRing

Progesterone-Only Contraceptives

Progesterone-only contraceptives (POCs) are safer than birth controls that contain estrogen because there is a lower risk of blood clot and breast cancer development. Additionally, POCs are safe to use in women who are breastfeeding, whereas estrogen-containing products are not. Common side effects of POCs include weight gain, irregular menstrual periods, acne, breast tenderness, fatigue, and depression.

Oral tablets should be taken daily at the same time each day for 21 days, followed by a 7-day tablet-free period during menstruation. With POCs, it is important that patients are compliant because missing a dose by 3 hours or more constitutes a missed dose. If a dose is missed, another form of contraceptive must be used for at least 2 days.

For patients who do not want to take a tablet every day, there are several more convenient formulations available. Long-acting **medroxyprogesterone injections** only need to be administered every 3 months. **Subdermal implants** are placed under the skin for up to 3 years, and **intrauterine devices** are effective for up to 5 years.

Dosage Form	Generic Name	Brand Name
Oral tablet	Norethindrone	Aygestin, Camila
Long-acting injection	Medroxyprogesterone	Depo-Provera
Implant/Subdermal injection	Etonogestrel	Nexplanon
Intrauterine device (IUD)	Levonorgestrel	Mirena

Dermatologic Medications

Acne

Acne occurs when oil glands in the skin become blocked, infected, and inflamed. Acne is common in teenagers because puberty causes overproduction of skin oils. Acne treatments include antibiotics to treat the infection, exfoliants that remove excess dead skin and oils to prevent blockage of glands, and retinoids that decrease oil production.

Some topical treatments are available as OTC medications. The oral retinoid isotretinoin is reserved for severe cases of acne that have not responded to topical therapies or oral antibiotics. Isotretinoin can cause serious birth defects if taken during pregnancy, so it is part of an iPledge risk evaluation and mitigation strategy (REMS) program that places restrictions on its use.

Commonly prescribed acne medications are below. Those available OTC are italicized.

Drug Classification	Generic Name	Brand Name
Topical antibiotic	Clindamycin	Cleocin T
Topical antibiotic	Erythromycin	Erygel
Topical antibiotic	*Benzoyl peroxide*	*PanOxyl*
Topical antibiotic	Dapsone	Aczone
Topical antibiotic/exfoliant	Azelaic acid	Finacea
Topical exfoliant	*Salicylic acid*	*Stridex, Noxzema, Neutrogena, Clearasil*
Oral antibiotic	Tetracycline	(None currently on the market)
Oral antibiotic	Erythromycin	Erythrocin, E.E.S.
Oral antibiotic	Doxycycline	Vibramycin
Oral antibiotic	Minocycline	Minocin
Topical retinoid	Tretinoin	Retin-A
Topical retinoid	Adapalene	Differin
Topical retinoid	Tazarotene	Tazorac
Oral retinoid	Isotretinoin	Accutane, Amnesteem, Claravis

Gastrointestinal Drugs

Heartburn and GERD Drugs

Heartburn is a burning sensation in the chest caused by acid from the stomach entering the esophagus. Gastroesophageal reflux disease (GERD) is the medical term for heartburn. Gastric acid in the stomach moves upward into the esophagus, causing discomfort and a burning sensation. Treatments for heartburn, or GERD, include medications that reduce the amount of acid in the stomach. Antacids act quickly by combining with existing stomach acid and neutralizing it. Acid reducers, such as proton pump inhibitors (PPIs) or histamine-$_2$ antagonists (H_2 blockers) prevent the production of stomach acid. Therefore, they take longer to start working than antacids. Many of these medications are available as OTC formulas (they are italicized in the table).

Drug Classification	Generic Name	Brand Name
Antacid	*Calcium carbonate*	*Tums, Rolaids*
Antacid	*Magnesium hydroxide*	*Milk of Magnesia, Maalox*
PPI	*Lansoprazole*	*Prevacid*
PPI	Dexlansoprazole	Dexilant
PPI	*Omeprazole*	*Prilosec*
PPI	*Esomeprazole*	*Nexium*
PPI	Rabeprazole	Aciphex
PPI	Pantoprazole	Protonix
H_2 blocker	*Famotidine*	*Pepcid*

LAXATIVES FOR CONSTIPATION

Constipation is defined as hard stools or difficulty with bowel movements. Common causes include dehydration (reduced fluid intake), lack of fiber in the diet, lack of exercise, and medications. Opioid pain medications are a common cause of constipation.

Drug Classification	Generic Name	Brand Name
Bulk-forming laxative	Psyllium	Metamucil
Bulk-forming laxative	Methylcellulose	Citrucel
Stool softener	Docusate	Colace
Osmotic laxative	Magnesium salts (magnesium hydroxide, magnesium citrate, magnesium sulfate), Epsom salts	Milk of Magnesia
Osmotic laxative	Sodium phosphate	Fleet Enema
Osmotic laxative	Polyethylene glycol	MiraLAX
Stimulant laxative	Senna	Senokot, Ex-Lax
Stimulant laxative	Bisacodyl	Dulcolax
Stimulant laxative	Glycerin	Avedana Glycerin, Fleet Liquid Glycerin Supp

MECHANISMS OF ACTION FOR VARIOUS LAXATIVES

The mechanisms of action for various laxatives are as follows:

- **Bulk-forming laxatives** absorb water into the stool to increase its bulkiness so that it moves along the colon easier. They usually start working within 2–3 days.
- **Stool softeners** are emollients (oils) that soften and lubricate the stool, making it easier to pass. Their onset of action is 2–3 days.
- **Osmotic laxatives** pull water into the colon to hydrate the stool. They start working in 1–3 days.
- **Stimulant laxatives** stimulate bowel movements by causing local irritation to the lining of the bowel. Stimulants work more quickly than other laxatives. Glycerin works within 30 minutes, whereas senna and bisacodyl work within 6–12 hours.

DIARRHEA MEDICATIONS

Diarrhea is defined as loose, runny, or frequent bowel movements. Diarrhea can be caused by overeating in general and by certain foods, illnesses, and medications. Foods that commonly cause diarrhea include spicy foods and meals high in carbohydrates. Cold and flu viruses can cause diarrhea as well as bacterial infections, such as food poisoning and traveler's diarrhea. Medications that commonly cause diarrhea include antibiotics, magnesium-containing antacids, and antineoplastic agents (chemotherapy). Patients with diarrhea can lose a lot of water in their stool, so it is important to drink water or electrolyte drinks to stay hydrated.

There are two OTC medications available to treat diarrhea. **Loperamide (Imodium)** is an opioid agonist that slows the movement of food along the digestive tract. **Bismuth subsalicylate (Pepto-Bismol)** works as an antacid as well as reduces the frequency of bowel movements.

The prescription only medication **diphenoxylate 2.5 mg/atropine 0.025 mg (Lomotil)** can be prescribed to treat cases of diarrhea that are not resolved by OTC Imodium. The diphenoxylate ingredient in Lomotil is an opioid agonist that helps slow down the digestive system. Because it contains an opioid ingredient, Lomotil is a schedule V controlled substance.

Medications for Nausea and Vomiting

Nausea and vomiting can be caused by gastrointestinal issues, such as infection or obstruction. Certain medical disorders can also cause nausea and vomiting including headaches or migraines, pregnancy, recent surgery, motion sickness, ear infections, vertigo (dizziness), and drug or alcohol withdrawal. Many medications include nausea and vomiting as a common side effect: antibiotics, antivirals, cancer treatments (chemotherapy), opioid pain medications, NSAIDs (e.g., naproxen, ibuprofen), antidepressants, digoxin, theophylline, iron supplements. Patients who have been vomiting should try to remain hydrated by drinking water or electrolyte drinks. Untreated vomiting can lead to dehydration, electrolyte imbalances, and postsurgical complications in patients who have recently had surgery.

Medications that are used to treat nausea and vomiting are called antiemetics. Some antiemetics are available as OTC medicines (they are italicized in the table), whereas others require a prescription.

Generic Name	Brand Name
Ondansetron	Zofran
Granisetron	Sancuso, Sustol
Promethazine	Phenergan
Prochlorperazine	Compro
Aprepitant	Emend
Dexamethasone	Dexabliss, DoubleDex
Dimenhydrinate	*Driminate*
Diphenhydramine	*Benadryl*
Meclizine	*Bonine, Travel-Ease*

Urinary Medications

Classes medications that target the urinary system include:

- **Alpha-blockers**, such as tamsulosin and finasteride, improve urine flow in patients with benign prostatic hyperplasia or prostate enlargement. They relax the muscles of the prostate and bladder to alleviate the symptoms of urinary retention associated with prostate cancer. Common side effects include headache, hypotension, and erectile dysfunction.
- **Alpha-reductase inhibitors** block the conversion of testosterone into a molecule that contributes to prostate enlargement. These are used to treat urinary retention caused by prostate issues in patients where alpha-blockers have failed.
- **Anticholinergic drugs**, such as solifenacin and tolterodine, relax the bladder to treat symptoms of overactive bladder and urinary urgency.
- **Phosphodiesterase (PDE) inhibitors** (end in "-afil") are used to treat erectile dysfunction by increasing blood flow to the penis. Common side effects include headache and nausea. PDE inhibitors should not be used in combination with nitrate drugs that are used to treat chest pain.

The different classes of medications used to treat urinary system disorders, including prostate enlargement, overactive bladder, and erectile dysfunction:

Drug Classification	Generic Name	Brand Name
Alpha-blocker	Tamsulosin	Flomax
Alpha-blocker	Doxazosin	Cardura
Alpha-blocker	Terazosin	APO-Terazosin
Alpha-blocker	Alfuzosin	Uroxatral
Alpha-reductase inhibitor	Dutasteride	Avodart
Alpha-reductase inhibitor	Finasteride	Proscar
Anticholinergic	Solifenacin	Vesicare
Anticholinergic	Tolterodine	Detrol
Anticholinergic	Oxybutynin	Ditropan
PDE inhibitor	Sildenafil	Viagra
PDE inhibitor	Tadalafil	Cialis

DIURETICS

Diuretics are medications that promote the excretion of water from the body in the urine. They are used to treat high blood pressure (hypertension) and edema (swelling). There are three main classes of diuretics: thiazide diuretics, loop diuretics, and potassium-sparing diuretics.

- **Thiazide diuretics** promote the excretion of sodium and water by the kidney, allowing more water to leave the body in the urine. Thiazide diuretics are not very potent, but they can be combined with other diuretics for an additive effect. The most commonly prescribed thiazide diuretic is hydrochlorothiazide.
- **Loop diuretics** also promote the excretion of sodium and water in the urine, but they act on a different part of the kidney than thiazide diuretics. Loop diuretics act quickly and are far more potent than thiazide diuretics. Commonly prescribed loop diuretics include furosemide (Lasix) and bumetanide (Bumex).
- Because diuretics promote the excretion of water and electrolytes from the body, one of their main side effects is hypokalemia (low potassium). **Potassium-sparing diuretics** do not cause hypokalemia like other diuretics do, so they are often used in combination with another class of diuretic to help prevent low potassium levels. Potassium-sparing diuretics include amiloride, triamterene (Dyrenium), and spironolactone (Aldactone).

Review Video: Diuretics
Visit mometrix.com/academy and enter code: 373276

ADDITIONAL DRUGS FOR GASTROINTESTINAL AND URINARY CONDITIONS

The most common vitamins/supplements and drugs used to treat gastrointestinal and urinary conditions:

Generic Name	Brand Name
Ulcerative Colitis Drugs	
Mesalamine	Pentasa
Urinary Incontinence Drugs	
Oxybutynin	Ditropan
Solifenacin	Vesicare
Irritable Bowel Syndrome Drugs	
Dicyclomine	Bentyl

Urinary incontinence drugs relax the bladder muscles and treat urinary urgency. Drugs used to treat irritable bowel syndrome help reduce stomach cramping by relaxing the muscles in the intestines.

Hematologic Drugs

Anemia Drugs

Anemia occurs when there are not enough healthy red blood cells to carry oxygen around the body. Symptoms include fatigue (tiredness), shortness of breath, headache, rapid heart rate, pale skin, dizziness, difficulty concentrating, and leg cramps. Potential dietary causes include inadequate intake of iron, folic acid, or vitamin B_{12}. In addition, some medications interfere with iron absorption, including tetracyclines, antacids, and acid reducers. Reduced absorption also occurs in patients with alcoholism, Crohn's disease, ulcerative colitis, or a history of gastric bypass or bowel resection. Disease states such as cancer, rheumatoid arthritis, and kidney disease also increase anemia risk. Infants, elderly, pregnant, lactating, and menstruating patients are at higher risk. Blood loss from trauma, surgery, gastrointestinal ulcers, or heavy menstruation can also lead to anemia.

Treatment of anemia depends upon the cause but may include iron, folic acid, or vitamin B_{12} supplements. Patients with kidney disease may require injections of erythropoietin, a hormone produced in the kidney that stimulates red blood cell production. Italicized drugs are available over the counter.

Generic Name	Brand Name
Ferrous sulfate	*Fer-in-Sol, Ferosol*
Ferrous gluconate	*Ferate*
Ferrous fumarate	*Ferretts, Fumerin*
Folic acid	*FA-8*
Vitamin B_{12} (cyanocobalamin)	Dodex
Polysaccharide iron complex (IV only)	*Myferon, Ferrex*
Epoetin alfa (IV only)	Procrit, Epogen
Darbepoetin alfa	Aranesp

Blood Thinners

Thrombolytics dissolve blood clots that have already formed, whereas antiplatelets and anticoagulants are blood thinners that prevent blood clot formation. Antiplatelets prevent the platelets in the blood from sticking together and forming a clot. Anticoagulants prevent the formation of fibrin, a protein that holds blood clots together.

Thrombolytics, also called clot busters, are used in emergency situations to break up clots associated with a stroke, pulmonary embolism, or heart attack.

Antiplatelets and anticoagulants are given to at-risk patients to prevent clot formation. Patients who are hospitalized or immobile after surgery are usually prescribed an anticoagulant to prevent clots from forming in their legs. Patients who have heart arrhythmias, such as atrial fibrillation, are also at higher risk of clot formation and may be prescribed an anticoagulant. Other risk factors that may justify the use of a blood thinner include cardiovascular disease or history of stroke, heart attack, or pulmonary embolism.

Commonly prescribed **blood thinners** include the following:

Drug Classification	Generic Name	Brand Name
Anticoagulant	Warfarin	Coumadin
Anticoagulant	Heparin	(None currently on the market)
Anticoagulant	Enoxaparin	Lovenox
Anticoagulant	Rivaroxaban	Xarelto
Anticoagulant	Apixaban	Eliquis
Anticoagulant	Dabigatran	Pradaxa
Antiplatelet	Aspirin	Bayer
Antiplatelet	Clopidogrel	Plavix
Antiplatelet	Prasugrel	Effient
Antiplatelet	Ticagrelor	Brilinta
Antiplatelet	Dipyridamole	Persantine
Thrombolytic	Alteplase	Activase, Cathflo

Review Video: Heparin – An Injectable Anti-Coagulant
Visit mometrix.com/academy and enter code: 127426

Review Video: Warfarin - Uses and Side Effects
Visit mometrix.com/academy and enter code: 844117

Review Video: Antiplatelets and Thrombolytics
Visit mometrix.com/academy and enter code: 711284

Musculoskeletal Drugs

Rheumatoid Arthritis Drugs

Rheumatoid arthritis is an autoimmune disease that causes the body's own immune system to attack the joints. It affects about 1% of the population and is far more common in women than men. There is a strong genetic component to the disease, but it is also known to have environmental triggers, such as infection. Disease progression varies greatly among individuals, but symptoms usually begin in the patient's late 20s or early 30s. Diagnosis is based on the patient's symptoms as well as a lab test for rheumatoid factor.

Symptoms of rheumatoid arthritis include fatigue, joint pain, joint swelling, and morning stiffness. Although these symptoms seem very nonspecific, the chronic morning joint stiffness is a key symptom in diagnosis. Rheumatoid arthritis is a progressive disease, and without effective treatment, permanent joint damage can occur. The joints that are usually affected include the fingers, wrists, ankles, elbows, shoulders, hips, knees, and jaw.

Disease-modifying antirheumatic drugs (DMARDs) halt disease progression and prevent joint damage. The downsides are that they become less effective over time and they are associated with significant side effects, such as increased infection risk, liver damage, and infertility.

Biologic drugs are newer, more expensive treatments that target specific molecules to prevent disease progression. Most biologics are subcutaneous injections that can be administered at home by patients after an initial training session. However, some biologics (e.g., Remicade) can only be administered intravenously at an infusion center. Like DMARDs, many biologics are associated with an increased risk of infection.

Nonsteroidal anti-inflammatory drugs (NSAIDs) are used to control joint pain and inflammation. Most rheumatoid arthritis patients take an NSAID long term and should be aware that long-term NSAID use can cause stomach ulcers. Taking NSAIDs with food or in combination with an acid reducer can help prevent this.

Medications for rheumatoid arthritis:

Drug Classification	Generic Name	Brand Name
Biologic	Adalimumab	Humira
Biologic	Etanercept	Enbrel
Biologic	Infliximab	Remicade
Biologic	Abatacept	Orencia
Biologic	Tocilizumab	Actemra
DMARD	Leflunomide	Arava
DMARD	Methotrexate	Otrexup, Rasuvo, Trexall
DMARD	Hydroxychloroquine	Plaquenil
DMARD	Sulfasalazine	Azulfidine
DMARD	Azathioprine	Imuran
DMARD	Tofacitinib	Xeljanz
NSAID	Diclofenac	Cambia, Lofena, Zipsor
NSAID	Ibuprofen	Motrin
NSAID	Naproxen	Naprosyn, Aleve
NSAID	Meloxicam	Anjeso
NSAID	Celecoxib	Celebrex

Osteoporosis Drugs

Osteoporosis is defined as low bone mineral density that results in deterioration of bone tissue, bone fragility, and increased risk of bone fracture. Symptoms include bone pain, bone fractures, and loss of height. Risk factors for osteoporosis include being elderly, cigarette smoking, ethnicity (Caucasians and Asians are at higher risk), alcoholism, sex (females are at higher risk), family history, low calcium and/or vitamin D intake, and sedentary lifestyle. Certain medical conditions can also reduce bone density and lead to osteoporosis: acquired immunodeficiency syndrome, anorexia, hyperthyroidism, hyperparathyroidism, inflammatory bowel disease, type 1 diabetes mellitus, rheumatoid arthritis, chronic kidney disease, and COPD. In addition, some classes of medications can increase the risk of developing osteoporosis: anticonvulsants, glucocorticoids (steroids), long-term heparin therapy, high doses of thyroid hormone, hormonal antineoplastic agents, antivirals, antidepressants, and acid reducers.

Review Video: Osteoporosis
Visit mometrix.com/academy and enter code: 421205

Medications commonly used to treat **osteoporosis**:

Drug Classification	Generic Name	Brand Name
Bisphosphonate	Ibandronate	(None currently on the market)
Bisphosphonate	Risedronate	Actonel
Bisphosphonate	Alendronate	Fosamax
Calcium supplement	Calcium citrate	Citracal
Calcium supplement	Calcium carbonate	Tums
Estrogen receptor modulator	Raloxifene	Evista

Gout Drugs

Gout is a disease caused by the buildup of uric acid in the joints. This leads to joint pain, inflammation, and swelling. Patients may also experience fever, chills, and general body aches. Gout occurs in about 1% of the population and is far more common in men. Gout usually attacks one joint at a time, and symptoms last for 1–2 weeks if left untreated. Commonly affected joints include the ankle, heel, knee, wrist, fingers, and elbow.

Uric acid is a product of the metabolism of ribose, a sugar that is found in RNA. Patients with gout should avoid foods that are high in ribose, including red meats, seafood, sugary drinks, processed foods, and alcohol.

Drug treatment of gout includes anti-inflammatory drugs to reduce joint pain and swelling, uricosuric agents that promote the excretion of excess uric acid in the urine, and xanthine oxidase inhibitors that stop the production of uric acid.

Drug Classification	Generic Name	Brand Name
Uricosuric drug	Probenecid	(None currently on the market)
Xanthine oxidase inhibitor	Allopurinol	Zyloprim, Aloprim
Xanthine oxidase inhibitor	Febuxostat	Uloric
Anti-inflammatory	Colchicine	Colcrys
Anti-inflammatory (NSAID)	Indomethacin	Indocin

Muscle Relaxants

Muscle relaxants, also known as spasmolytics, are used to treat muscle spasms, muscle cramps, and muscle pains. They do this by reducing muscle tone and relaxing the muscles. Muscle relaxers may be used to treat a variety of muscle conditions, including lower back pain, neck pain, fibromyalgia, multiple sclerosis, cerebral palsy, and amyotrophic lateral sclerosis. Most muscle relaxers are centrally acting, so they lead to significant drowsiness. Some benzodiazepines that are used to treat anxiety can also be used as muscle relaxers, such as diazepam. Muscle relaxers are generally only used in the short term because they can lead to dependence or addiction. For this reason, some of the muscle relaxants are schedule IV controlled medications, including diazepam and carisoprodol.

Generic Name	Brand Name
Carisoprodol	Soma
Cyclobenzaprine	Amrix, Fexmid
Metaxalone	(None currently on the market)
Methocarbamol	Robaxin
Tizanidine	Zanaflex
Baclofen	Lioresal
Dantrolene	Dantrium
Diazepam	Valium

Neurological Drugs

The top medications used to treat neurological disorders:

Generic Name	Brand Name
Antidepressants	
Sertraline	Zoloft
Fluoxetine	Prozac
Citalopram	Celexa
Trazodone	APO-Trazadone, TEVA-Trazodone
Bupropion	Wellbutrin
Escitalopram	Lexapro
Duloxetine	Cymbalta
Venlafaxine	Effexor
Paroxetine	Paxil
Amitriptyline	Elavil
Mirtazapine	Remeron
Antipsychotics	
Quetiapine	Seroquel
Divalproex	Depakote
Risperidone	Risperdal
Aripiprazole	Abilify
Lithium	Lithobid
ADHD Treatments	
Dextroamphetamine and amphetamine	Adderall
Methylphenidate	Ritalin
Lisdexamfetamine	Vyvanse
Atomoxetine	Strattera
Stimulants Used for Weight Loss	
Phentermine	Lomaira, Adipex-P
Muscle Relaxers	
Cyclobenzaprine	Amrix, Fexmid
Tizanidine	Zanaflex
Baclofen	Lioresal
Carisoprodol	Soma
Methocarbamol	Robaxin
Antiparkinsonian drugs	
Ropinirole	Requip
Pramipexole	Mirapex ER
Antiepileptics	
Gabapentin	Neurontin
Lamotrigine	Lamictal
Topiramate	Topamax
Pregabalin	Lyrica
Levetiracetam	Keppra
Phenytoin	Dilantin
Oxcarbazepine	Trileptal
Divalproex	Depakote

Generic Name	Brand Name
Sedatives/Antianxiety Drugs	
Alprazolam	Xanax
Clonazepam	Klonopin
Zolpidem	Ambien
Lorazepam	Ativan
Diazepam	Valium
Buspirone	Buspar
Temazepam	Restoril
Alzheimer's Drugs	
Memantine	Namenda
Donepezil	Aricept
Analgesics	
Acetaminophen	Tylenol
Acetaminophen/hydrocodone	Lortab
Tramadol	Conzip, Qdolo
Ibuprofen	Motrin, Advil
Meloxicam	Anjeso
Oxycodone	Oxycontin
Naproxen	Aleve
Hydrocodone	Hysingla ER
Diclofenac	Cambia
Celecoxib	Celebrex
Morphine	Duramorph, Infumorph
Lidocaine	Xylocaine
Migraine Treatments	
Sumatriptan	Imitrex

Analgesics are pain relievers. These include Tylenol, NSAIDs, and opioids. Many antiepileptic drugs can also be used as analgesics to relieve nerve pain.

Parkinson's Disease Drugs

Parkinson's disease (PD) is a chronic, progressive neuromuscular disorder in which the brain has difficulty communicating with the muscles. In PD, there is a progressive degeneration of cells in the brain that produce dopamine, a neurotransmitter that is involved in muscle movements. Therefore, drug treatments aim to replace or enhance the activity of dopamine.

The cause of PD is not fully known, although it is known to have genetic links as well as environmental risk factors, such as infection, trauma, and medication use. Antipsychotic medications usually act on dopamine and aim to block the effects of dopamine. Therefore, antipsychotic medications cause Parkinson-like side effects, which are usually reversible with discontinued use.

Symptoms of PD include tremors, muscle rigidity (stiffness), akinesia (an inability to initiate movement), bradykinesia (slowed movements), postural instability, abnormal gait (walk), difficulty standing, drooling, decreased blinking, dysphagia (difficulty swallowing), dysphasia (difficulty speaking), constipation, and urinary incontinence.

One of the causes of PD is a reduction in the levels of dopamine in the brain. Dopamine is a neurotransmitter that is involved in muscle movement. Most drug treatments for PD aim to replace or enhance the effects of dopamine. Mechanisms of actions are as follows:

- **Dopaminergic drugs** mimic dopamine in the body by binding to and stimulating dopamine receptors.
- **MAO-B inhibitors** block an enzyme called monoamine oxidase type B that breaks down dopamine in the body. Preventing the breakdown of dopamine leads to an increase in dopamine levels.
- **Anticholinergic drugs** block the effects of acetylcholine, another neurotransmitter that is involved in muscle movements.

Drug Classification	Generic Name	Brand Name
Dopaminergic	Carbidopa-levodopa	Sinemet
Dopaminergic	Bromocriptine	Parlodel
Dopaminergic	Pramipexole	Mirapex ER
Dopaminergic	Rotigotine	Neupro (patch available)
MAO-B inhibitor	Selegiline	Eldepryl, Zelapar
MAO-B inhibitor	Rasagiline	Azilect
MAO-B inhibitor	Amantadine	Gocovri, Osmolex
Anticholinergic	Benztropine	Cogentin

Alzheimer's Disease Drugs

Cholinesterase inhibitors are the recommended first line treatment of mild Alzheimer's disease (AD). One of the key neurological changes in AD is significantly reduced levels of the neurotransmitter acetylcholine. Cholinesterase inhibitors increase acetylcholine levels by blocking the enzyme acetylcholinesterase, which is responsible for breaking down acetylcholine. These drugs are usually started at a low dose and gradually titrated up to minimize side effects.

***N*-Methyl-D-aspartate (NMDA) receptor antagonists (blockers)** are used to treat moderate to severe cases of AD. *N*-Methyl-D-aspartate (NMDA) receptors release glutamate and are overactive in AD. The buildup of glutamate is one of the causes of neurological dysfunction and cell death in AD. NMDA receptor antagonists block the actions of NMDA receptors and reduce glutamate levels.

Drug Classification	Generic Name	Brand Name
Cholinesterase inhibitor	Donepezil	Aricept
Cholinesterase inhibitor	Rivastigmine	Exelon (patch is available)
Cholinesterase inhibitor	Galantamine	Razadyne
NMDA receptor antagonist	Memantine	Namenda

Migraine Drugs

Patients who experience recurring migraines may be prescribed a preventative therapy to reduce the frequency of attacks and improve their responsiveness to on-demand treatments. Although the exact cause of migraine disorders is not known, there are genetic risk factors as well as known environmental triggers. Environmental triggers vary among individuals, but they often include weather or air pressure changes, bright lights, chemical fumes, hormonal changes during the menstrual cycle, and certain foods (e.g., red wine, beer, cheeses, etc.). Trigger avoidance is an important part of migraine prevention.

Medications that are normally used to treat hypertension or heart failure, such as beta-blockers and calcium channel blockers, have proven to be effective in preventing migraines. Drugs that act on the central nervous system (CNS), including antidepressants and anticonvulsant drugs, also play a role in migraine prevention.

Prevention

Medications that are commonly prescribed to prevent migraines:

Drug Classification	Generic Name	Brand Name
Beta-blocker	Propranolol	Inderal
Beta-blocker	Metoprolol	Toprol, Lopressor
Beta-blocker	Atenolol	Tenormin
Antidepressant	Amitriptyline	Elavil
Antidepressant	Fluoxetine	Prozac
Calcium channel blocker	Diltiazem	Cartia, Cardizem
Calcium channel blocker	Verapamil	Calan SR
Anticonvulsant	Valproate	Depakene
Anticonvulsant	Gabapentin	Neurontin
Anticonvulsant	Topiramate	Topamax

Relief

Migraines are a severe form of headache associated with pain in the front and sides of the head (usually only one side of the head is affected), nausea, vomiting, and sensitivity to light and sound. Some patients also experience aural, visual, or sensory symptoms. There may also be prodromal symptoms that occur before the migraine begins, such as mood changes, fatigue, or neck pain.

- **Nonsteroidal anti-inflammatory drugs (NSAIDs)** help reduce some of the pain associated with headaches, although their ability to relieve migraine symptoms is limited.
- **Selective serotonin receptor agonists (triptans)** are taken on an as-needed basis at the first sign of a migraine. They start acting relatively quickly, within 10–60 minutes depending upon the drug. The potential adverse effects are relatively minor: dizziness, flushing, neck pain or stiffness, and fatigue. Triptans are available in a variety of dosage forms in order to get past the nausea and vomiting that many patients experience during a migraine, including orally disintegrating tablets, nasal sprays, transdermal patches, and infusions.

Therapeutic Classification	Generic Name	Brand Name
Triptan	Sumatriptan	Imitrex
Triptan	Eletriptan	Relpax
Triptan	Rizatriptan	Maxalt
Triptan	Zolmitriptan	Zomig
Triptan	Naratriptan	(None currently on the market)
NSAID	Ibuprofen	Motrin, Advil
NSAID	Naproxen	Naprosyn, Aleve

Epilepsy Drugs

Drugs used to treat epilepsy are referred to as antiepileptics or anticonvulsants. Epilepsy is notoriously difficult to treat, and not all patients respond to drug treatments. Antiepileptic medications are a diverse group of medications with many different mechanisms of action. Benzodiazepines (normally used to treat anxiety) may also be used to treat some seizure types. Each type of seizure disorder has a preferred drug regimen that involves the specific antiepileptic drugs that work best for that condition. Most patients will start out on the recommended first-line monotherapy (one-drug treatment), and a second adjunctive therapy will be added if the patient is not responding.

Medications commonly used to treat seizure disorders (epilepsy):

Generic Name	Brand Name
Phenytoin	Dilantin, Phenytek
Carbamazepine	Tegretol
Oxcarbazepine	Trileptal
Tiagabine	Gabitril
Ethosuximide	Zarontin
Phenobarbital	Sezaby
Primidone	Mysoline
Perampanel	Fycompa
Felbamate	Felbatol
Valproic acid/ Divalproex sodium	Depakote
Clobazam	Onfi
Eslicarbazepine	Aptiom
Ezogabine	(None currently on the market)
Vigabatrin	Sabril
Zonisamide	Zonegran
Lacosamide	Vimpat
Lamotrigine	Lamictal
Topiramate	Topamax
Levetiracetam	Keppra
Gabapentin	Neurontin
Pregabalin	Lyrica

Ophthalmic Drugs

Glaucoma Drugs

Glaucoma is an eye condition characterized by increased pressure in the eye. Glaucoma is treated using eye drops that act locally and have minimal adverse effects.

Initial treatment is with either a **prostaglandin** drug (they end in "-prost") or a **beta-blocker** (they end in "-olol"). Prostaglandins stimulate drainage of fluid from the eye, and beta-blockers prevent the production of fluid. Prostaglandins are more popular because they are administered once daily at bedtime, whereas most beta-blockers are administered twice daily. Treatment is started with a single drug; additional drugs are added if required.

Second-line add-on treatments include **carbonic anhydrase inhibitors** (they end in "-zolamide") and **alpha-agonists** (they end in "-onidine"), which decrease the production of fluid in the eye. Most of these eye drops must be applied three times a day.

Review Video: Glaucoma and Cataracts
Visit mometrix.com/academy and enter code: 279024

Drug Classification	Generic Name	Brand Name
Beta-blocker	Betaxolol	Betoptic
Beta-blocker	Timolol	Timoptic
Beta-blocker	Levobunolol	(None currently on the market)
Prostaglandin	Bimatoprost	Lumigan
Prostaglandin	Latanoprost	Xalatan
Prostaglandin	Travoprost	Travatan
Carbonic anhydrase inhibitor	Dorzolamide	(None currently on the market)
Carbonic anhydrase inhibitor	Brinzolamide	Azopt
Alpha-agonist	Brimonidine	Alphagan

Eye Infections, Inflammation, and Dry Eye

Antibiotic eye drops are used to treat bacterial **eye infections**, such as conjunctivitis. Ciprofloxacin and gentamicin are available in eye drop form and are commonly prescribed to treat conjunctivitis.

Patients who experience **seasonal allergies** often use an antihistamine eye drop such as olopatadine to treat their symptoms.

Some anti-inflammatory medications are available in eye drop form to treat **eye inflammation**. Inflammation can occur in the eye due to infection or recent eye surgery. Corticosteroids, such as budesonide and prednisolone, and NSAIDs, such as flurbiprofen and ketorolac, are available in eye drop form for treating inflammation.

Dry eye is another condition for which patients seek treatment using eye drops. Most of these treatments contain harmless lubricants or saline, and most are available as OTC medications.

Drug Classification	Generic Name	Brand Name
Antibiotic	Ciprofloxacin	Ciloxan
Antibiotic	Gentamicin	Gentak
Antihistamine	Olopatadine	Pataday
Antihistamine	Azelastine	(None currently on the market)
Anti-inflammatory	Prednisolone	Pred Forte
Anti-inflammatory	Flurbiprofen	(None currently on the market)
Anti-inflammatory	Ketorolac	Acular
Eye lubricant	Propylene glycol	Systane

Otic Drugs

Antibiotic ear drops are used to treat bacterial **ear infections**, such as swimmer's ear or otitis media. Common antibiotics used in the ear include ciprofloxacin, neomycin, and polymyxin b. If necessary, ophthalmic drops can also be administered into the ear.

Anti-inflammatory corticosteroid drugs are also available in otic form to treat **ear inflammation**. Because ear inflammation is usually associated with an infection, anti-inflammatory drugs are usually an ingredient in combination ear drops that also contain an antibiotic. Common drugs used to treat ear inflammation include dexamethasone and hydrocortisone.

Earwax buildup is another common condition for which patients seek treatment using ear drops. Most of these treatments contain a weak acid (e.g., acetic acid) or an oily substance that helps soften earwax and make it easier to remove. Many earwax softening treatments are available as OTC formulas.

Drug Classification	Generic Name	Brand Name
Antibiotic/anti-inflammatory	Ciprofloxacin, dexamethasone	Ciprodex
Antibiotic/anti-inflammatory	Neomycin, polymyxin b, hydrocortisone	(None currently on the market)
Ear wax softener	Acetic acid (vinegar)	Acetasol HC
Ear wax softener	Carbamide peroxide	Clinere

Psychological Drugs

ADHD Drugs

Attention-deficit/hyperactivity disorder (ADHD) is defined by a persistent pattern of inattention, hyperactivity, and/or impulsiveness that interferes with daily activities.

Stimulants are the first-line treatment for ADHD. Stimulants increase levels of dopamine in the brain, which is a neurotransmitter that is associated with attention, motivation, and pleasure. All of the stimulants used to treat ADHD are schedule II controlled substances with a high potential for abuse. Therefore, prescriptions cannot be received by telephone or fax and refills are not allowed. Stimulants can also be used to treat narcolepsy (daytime drowsiness) and are used by military pilots to maintain wakefulness.

Nonstimulants are used as a second-line treatment if stimulants have failed. These medications are prescription only but are not controlled substances.

Therapeutic Category	Generic Name	Brand Name
Stimulant	Methylphenidate	Ritalin, Methylin, Metadate, Concerta, Daytrana
Stimulant	Dexmethylphenidate	Focalin
Stimulant	Dextroamphetamine	Dexedrine
Stimulant	Lisdexamfetamine	Vyvanse
Stimulant	Dextroamphetamine-amphetamine	Adderall
Nonstimulant	Atomoxetine	Strattera
Nonstimulant	Guanfacine	Intuniv

Bipolar Disorder Drugs

Bipolar disorder is a mood disorder characterized by alternating highs (mania) and lows (depression). Many **mood stabilizer drugs** were originally developed to treat epilepsy but were found to be effective in treating bipolar disorder as well. Most mood stabilizers have a narrow therapeutic index (a narrow safe dosage range), so extra monitoring and blood tests are often involved. Many of the drugs in this class also have the potential to cause serious side effects, such as increased risk of infection, electrolyte imbalances, birth defects, liver damage, and kidney damage. Mood stabilizers also interact with many other medications, so refer any computer alerts to a pharmacist.

Antipsychotic drugs have a long list of commonly experienced side effects. These include drowsiness, weight gain, orthostatic hypotension (dizziness upon standing), dry mouth, constipation, and urinary retention. Because they block dopamine, they also cause Parkinson-like side effects including involuntary muscle spasms (dystonia), restlessness, bradykinesia (slow movements), and tremors.

Examples of different classes of drugs used to treat **bipolar disorder**:

Drug Classification	Generic Name	Brand Name
Antipsychotic	Aripiprazole	Abilify
Antipsychotic	Risperidone	Risperdal
Antipsychotic	Quetiapine	Seroquel
Antipsychotic	Olanzapine	Zyprexa
Mood stabilizer	Lithium	Lithobid
Mood stabilizer	Lamotrigine	Lamictal
Mood stabilizer	Valproate	Epilim, Depakote
Mood stabilizer	Carbamazepine	Tegretol

Schizophrenia Drugs

Schizophrenia is a psychological disorder associated with delusions, hallucinations, disorganized speech, personality and mood disorders, and behavioral symptoms. Overactivity of dopamine plays a major role in the disorder, so most **antipsychotic drug treatments** target and block dopamine. Because Parkinson's disease is characterized by a lack of dopamine, antipsychotic medications can cause Parkinson-like side effects, such as tremors, involuntary muscle spasms (dystonia), restlessness, and bradykinesia (slow movements). Older, conventional antipsychotics tend to have more Parkinson-like side effects. Newer, atypical antipsychotics have fewer Parkinson-like side effects and usually cause more significant weight gain, elevations in cholesterol levels, and hyperglycemia. Clozapine requires extra lab tests and monitoring as part of a REMS program because it causes a rare but serious side effect that reduces the body's ability to fight infection.

The generic and brand names of commonly prescribed antipsychotic drugs:

Generic Name	Brand Name
Aripiprazole	Abilify
Risperidone	Risperdal
Ziprasidone	Geodon
Quetiapine	Seroquel
Olanzapine	Zyprexa
Haloperidol	Haldol
Clozapine	Clozaril
Fluphenazine	(None currently on the market)
Lurasidone	Latuda
Asenapine	Saphris

Review Video: Antipsychotic Drugs
Visit mometrix.com/academy and enter code: 369601

Depression Drugs

Depression is characterized by low mood, fatigue, body aches, sleep disturbances, appetite changes, anxiety, and suicidal thoughts. Treatment usually involves a selective serotonin reuptake inhibitor

(SSRI), serotonin-norepinephrine reuptake inhibitor (SNRI), or TCA, although antipsychotics and other classes of antidepressants can be used in resistant depression.

- **Tricyclic antidepressants (TCAs)** increase the concentration of serotonin and norepinephrine in the brain. They cause significant sedation, increased heart rate, hypotension, increased risk of arrhythmia, weight gain, sexual dysfunction, dry mouth, and urinary retention.
- **Selective serotonin reuptake inhibitors (SSRIs)** increase the concentration of serotonin in the brain. They are the most popular class of antidepressant because they are safer than other medications. Adverse effects are limited to headache, fatigue, insomnia, nausea, and sexual dysfunction.
- **Serotonin-norepinephrine reuptake inhibitors (SNRIs)** increase the concentration of serotonin and norepinephrine in the brain. Possible adverse effects are similar to those of SSRIs.

The generic and brand names of commonly prescribed antidepressants:

Drug Classification	Generic Name	Brand Name
TCA	Amitriptyline	Elavil
TCA	Nortriptyline	Pamelor
TCA	Doxepin	Silenor
TCA	Clomipramine	Anafranil
SSRI	Citalopram	Celexa
SSRI	Escitalopram	Lexapro
SSRI	Fluoxetine	Prozac
SSRI	Paroxetine	Paxil
SSRI	Sertraline	Zoloft
SNRI	Venlafaxine	Effexor
SNRI	Desvenlafaxine	Pristiq
SNRI	Duloxetine	Cymbalta

Review Video: Major Depression
Visit mometrix.com/academy and enter code: 632694

Review Video: Effects of Prozac as an Antidepressant
Visit mometrix.com/academy and enter code: 620613

Benzodiazepines and Hypnotics

Benzodiazepines are a class of medication that enhances the action of gamma-aminobutyric acid, a neurotransmitter that relaxes the neurons. Benzodiazepines are used to treat a variety of conditions including anxiety, epilepsy, alcohol withdrawal, insomnia, obsessive-compulsive disorder, and post-traumatic stress. Due to their relaxing and euphoric effects, benzodiazepines have a high potential for abuse and are classified as schedule IV controlled substances. Long-term use is not recommended because tolerance develops quickly. Patients are encouraged to use these medications on an as-needed basis. Other adverse effects include significant sedation, dizziness, confusion, and blurred vision. Elderly patients should be particularly cautious because these adverse effects increase the risk of falls. Patients should also be advised not to take benzodiazepines with alcohol or opiate pain medications.

The **hypnotic Z-drugs** are benzodiazepine-like medications used to treat insomnia. They have similar side effects and are also schedule IV controlled substances. They include zolpidem, zopiclone, eszopiclone, and zaleplon.

The generic and brand names for commonly prescribed **benzodiazepines and hypnotics**:

Generic Name	Brand Name	Indications (Uses)
Alprazolam	Xanax	Anxiety, insomnia
Chlordiazepoxide	Librium	Alcohol withdrawal
Clonazepam	Klonopin	Anxiety
Diazepam	Valium	Anxiety
Lorazepam	Ativan	Anxiety
Temazepam	Restoril	Anxiety, insomnia
Triazolam	Halcion	Insomnia
Zolpidem	Ambien	Insomnia
Zaleplon	(None currently on the market)	Insomnia
Eszopiclone	Lunesta	Insomnia

CHILDHOOD VACCINATIONS

Childhood vaccination recommendations per CDC guidelines are as follows:

- The annual **influenza vaccine** (Afluria, Flulaval, Fluzone, Fluarix) is recommended for all children over 6 months old.
- The **DTaP vaccine** (Daptacel, Infanrix, Kinrix, Pediarix, Pentacel, Quadracel, Vaxelis) protects against diphtheria, tetanus, and pertussis (whooping cough). Infants receive initial doses starting at 6 weeks, or children 7 years and older receive the **Tdap vaccine** (Adacel or Boostrix) as a catch up vaccine. Children age 11 also receive the Tdap vaccine routinely.
- **Hepatitis B vaccination** (Engerix-B, Recombivax HB) and **hepatitis A vaccination** (Havrix, Vaqta) are recommended for infants or toddlers.
- **Haemophilus influenzae type B** (ActHIB) is recommended as part of routine childhood vaccinations.
- **Meningococcal vaccinations** defend against certain types of bacterial meningitis. The two different forms available in the US have different age recommendations (MenACWY for children 11–16 and MenB for children 16–18).
- **Measles, mumps, and rubella (MMR) vaccination** is recommended as part of routine childhood vaccinations, with one dose at 12–15 months and the second at 4–6 years.
- **Varicella (chicken pox) vaccination** (Varivax) is now routine for all children aged 12–15 months, and a booster is given at 4–6 years of age. This can also be given in conjunction with the measles, mumps, and rubella vaccination (MMRV).
- **Human papillomavirus vaccination** (Gardasil) helps protect against a common sexually transmitted disease that causes cervical cancer. Vaccination is recommended for males and females from ages 9–12.

ADULT VACCINATIONS

Adult vaccination recommendations per CDC guidelines are as follows:

- The annual **influenza vaccine** (Afluria, Flulaval, Fluzone, Fluarix) is recommended for all adults, especially those with a medical condition that puts them at increased risk for flu complications.

- **TDaP vaccine** protects against tetanus, diphtheria, and pertussis (whooping cough). Although initially administered during childhood, adults should receive a booster shot every 10 years as well as during pregnancy.
- **Hepatitis B vaccination** (Engerix-B, Recombivax HB) is recommended for all adults ages 19–59 and **hepatitis A vaccination** (Havrix, Vaqta) is only recommended to patients who are at high risk.
- **Meningococcal vaccination** (Menactra, Menveo, Trumenba, Bexsero) should be given to patients at high risk for exposure, including military service members, college students, travelers, and patients with a compromised immune system.
- **Pneumococcal vaccines** protect against various strains of Streptococcus pneumoniae bacteria. Patients over the age of 65 should receive both pneumococcal vaccines, Pneumovax-23 and Prevnar-13, spaced 1 year apart.
- **Herpes zoster vaccines** (Shingrix) protect against shingles, a painful condition in which the virus attacks the nerves. It usually occurs in elderly patients or those who are immunocompromised. Shingles is caused by the same varicella virus that causes chicken pox, but it presents with different symptoms once it is reactivated. Vaccination is recommended in adults over the age of 50 and patients with reduced immunity.

Live vs. Inactivated Vaccines

Vaccinations work by taking advantage of our body's acquired immune system. After exposure to a pathogen (a harmful virus or bacteria), our body remembers that specific pathogen and produces specific cells that fight off the infection quickly if we encounter that same pathogen again. A vaccination is the first exposure that signals the body to produce immune cells against the pathogen and prevents us from getting ill from that pathogen in the future. Common side effects of vaccines include redness, swelling, and pain at the injection site. Patients may also experience fever and soreness at the site of injection.

- **Live vaccines** contain the actual pathogen, but it has been attenuated or made to be less harmful. Most patients do not get ill from live vaccines, but patients who have a compromised immune system might. Therefore, live vaccines should not be administered to certain groups of patients: pregnant women, patients receiving chemotherapy, patients who have had an organ transplant in the past, patients taking medications that lower their immune response, and HIV patients. Vaccinations that are live include Varivax, Zostavax, MMR, the yellow fever vaccine, and the typhoid vaccine.
- **Inactivated vaccines** contain parts of a pathogen, which are not disease-causing. Immunocompromised patients can receive inactivated vaccines.

Dietary Supplements

Nonprescription, or over-the-counter (OTC), medications are drugs that are preapproved by the Food and Drug Administration (FDA) for sale to patients without a prescription. The product packaging must contain complete product information and a drug facts panel that includes directions for use, warnings, active and inactive ingredients, and a telephone number to call with questions. OTC drugs must go through the same drug approval process as prescription drugs and must be proven to be safe and effective.

Dietary supplements, such as vitamins, minerals, and medical foods, are still regulated by the FDA, but regulations are not as strict as they are for drugs. The FDA ensures that dietary supplements are manufactured using good manufacturing practices, but no proof of safety or efficacy is required. The packaging must state the name and quantity of each ingredient, but no other information is required. Dietary supplements cannot advertise that the product can cure, diagnose, or prevent any disease. However, dietary supplements can claim that they improve general structures or functions in the body. If a dietary supplement wants to claim that it can be used to treat or prevent a disease or condition, this claim must first be preapproved by the FDA.

HERBAL SUPPLEMENTS

An herbal supplement is a product derived from a plant that is used to treat an illness, condition, or disorder. Herbal supplements can be purchased as OTC formulas. Although they are regulated by the FDA, they are not monitored as closely as drugs.

Supplement	Indication
Aloe vera	Used topically for burns, cuts, scrapes, and psoriasis; taken orally for constipation and other gastrointestinal disorders
Coenzyme Q10	Hypertension, heart failure, and to reduce the muscle aches associated with statins
Echinacea	Respiratory infections
Evening primrose oil	Eczema/dermatitis
Fish oil	Hypercholesterolemia, hypertension, coronary artery disease, prevention of cardiovascular disease, and rheumatoid arthritis
Garlic	Hypercholesterolemia and prevention of cardiovascular disease
Ginger	Nausea, vomiting
Ginkgo biloba	Enhancement of memory/cognition, dementia, anxiety disorders, and schizophrenia
Ginseng	Improvement of immune function and mental performance
Glucosamine and chondroitin	Osteoarthritis
Green tea	Performance enhancement, prevention of cardiovascular disease, and prevention of cancer
Melatonin	Sleep disorders
Probiotics	Antibiotic-induced diarrhea, gastrointestinal disorders, and dermatitis
St. John's wort (Hypericum perforatum)	Depression, anxiety

VITAMINS

A vitamin is an organic molecule that is required for the normal growth and function of the human body.

Vitamin	Indication(s)
Vitamin D (ergocalciferol, calcitriol, alfacalcidol)	Dietary deficiency, hypoparathyroidism, renal failure, prevention of osteoporosis, and topical treatment of psoriasis
Vitamin K (menadiol, phytomenadione)	Treatment of neonatal vitamin K deficiency, overtreatment with warfarin, dietary malabsorption, drug-induced malabsorption (e.g., cholestyramine), and hepatic cirrhosis induced clotting disorders
Vitamin B_{12} (hydroxocobalamin, cyanocobalamin)	Treatment and prevention of deficiency, especially following gastric bypass surgery

Folic acid (vitamin B_9)	Prevention and treatment of folate deficiency, prevention of neural tube defects during pregnancy, and reduction of bone marrow toxicity in patients taking methotrexate

Minerals

Minerals, such as iron and magnesium, are inorganic substances that are essential for normal body functions.

Mineral	Indication(s)
Calcium	Low calcium levels, high potassium levels (renal impairment), osteoporosis
Magnesium	Low magnesium levels, cardiac arrhythmias, severe asthma
Potassium	Low potassium levels (e.g., due to diuretic or corticosteroid use)
Iron	Treatment and prevention of deficiency, anemia

Drugs Intended for Short- vs. Long-Term Use

The duration of treatment is the amount of time that the patient is expected to take a medication in order to treat their condition. Some medications are intended for short-term use, whereas others are intended to be taken for the long term.

Medications that are intended for short-term use are generally used to treat an acute (sudden or temporary) illness. Examples of acute indications include infections, electrolyte imbalances, perioperative treatment (around the time of surgery), bone fracture, trauma, headaches/migraines, gastrointestinal disturbances (nausea, vomiting, and diarrhea), and treatment of poisoning. For acute conditions, medication treatments will be stopped once symptoms have improved.

Medications that are intended for long-term use are generally used to treat a chronic (persistent, recurrent) illness. Examples of chronic illnesses that require long-term drug therapy include hypertension, diabetes, rheumatoid arthritis, hypothyroidism, epilepsy, asthma, hypercholesterolemia, psychosis, inflammatory bowel disease, PD, and glaucoma. Medication for chronic conditions will be prescribed for a long period of time, if not indefinitely.

Causes and Reporting of Medication Errors

Common Causes of Medication Errors

A medication error is any preventable medication event that has the potential to lead to medication misuse or patient harm. A near-miss is a medication error that is caught before the medication leaves the pharmacy. Medication error is a broad term that includes a variety of medication events including prescribing errors, computer entry errors, dispensing errors, labeling errors, and administration errors.

We are all human, and we all make mistakes. Making ourselves aware of the common causes of errors can help us reduce the number of errors that we make. Common causes of medication errors include look-alike medication names, sound-alike medication names, the use of error-prone abbreviations, alert fatigue, human error, distractions (noise, music, conversations), multitasking, and failure to use available barcode scanning technologies. Alert fatigue occurs when the computer system constantly prompts you with too many alerts, so you become less responsive to the alerts and miss an important one. Although multitasking may be helpful in some job roles, it is best to avoid working on multiple patient prescriptions at one time to avoid errors or mix-ups.

Preventing Common Medication Error

Methods in place for preventing common medication errors include the following:

- Verify patient identity using at least two patient identifiers (name, date of birth, address, etc.) during each encounter (drop-off and pick-up).
- Maintain up-to-date records of patient allergies, medications, and disease states (e.g., pregnancy) in the patient's medication profile.
- If any part of a prescription is unclear, alert the pharmacist and contact the prescriber's office to clarify.
- Verify the prescription information with the patient to ensure that what is prescribed is what is expected or intended.
- Only work on one patient's prescription at a time. Although pharmacies can get busy, it is quicker and safer to finish one patient's prescription before moving on to another.
- Use baskets to keep patient's prescription separate from each other.
- Keep pharmacy shelves neat and tidy, and separate LASA medications from each other.
- Check that the drug NDC number dispensed matches the NDC number on the label (use barcode technology if available).
- Avoid using error-prone abbreviations.
- Use tall-man lettering to help differentiate between look-alike and sound-alike medications. For example, NIFEdipine versus niCARdipine.

Look-Alike/Sound-Alike Medications

Look-alike/sound-alike (LASA) medications are drugs with names that are either spelled similarly or sound similar when pronounced. Medications with similar names are prone to confusion and mix-up and can lead to medication errors.

Amlodipine	Amiloride
Alprazolam	Lorazepam
Bupropion	Buspirone
Ceftazidime	Ceftriaxone
Cefazolin	Cefoxitin
Celebrex	Celexa
Chlorpromazine	Chlordiazepoxide
Cisplatin	Carboplatin
Clobazam	Clonazepam
Clonidine	Klonopin, Clonazepam
Cyclosporine	Cycloserine
Dactinomycin	Daptomycin
Dobutamine	Dopamine
Docetaxel	Paclitaxel
Doxorubicin	Daunorubicin
Duloxetine	Fluoxetine
Epinephrine	Ephedrine
Flonase	Flovent
Fluoxetine	Fluvoxamine
Fluphenazine	Fluvoxamine
Glipizide	Glyburide
Guaifenesin	Guanfacine
Hydralazine	Hydroxyzine
Hydrocodone	Oxycodone
Hydromorphone	Oxymorphone

Humulin	Humalog
Infliximab	Rituximab
Isotretinoin	Tretinoin
Lamictal	Lamisil
Medroxyprogesterone	Methylprednisolone
Mifepristone	Misoprostol
Methimazole	Metolazone
Nifedipine	Nicardipine
Novolin	Novolog
Oxcarbazepine	Carbamazepine
Oxycodone	Oxymorphone
Paroxetine	Fluoxetine
Penicillin	Penicillamine
Phenobarbital	Pentobarbital
Prednisone	Prednisolone
Quinidine	Quinine
Rifaximin	Rifampin
Risperidone	Ropinirole
Sitagliptin	Saxagliptin
Sulfasalazine	Sulfadiazine
Tizanidine	Tiagabine
Tramadol	Trazodone
Valacyclovir	Valganciclovir
Vincristine	Vinblastine
Zyprexa	Zyrtec

Prescription Errors

A prescription error is a mix-up or mistake that occurs any time during the prescribing, dispensing, or administration process and has the potential to cause patient harm. Near-misses are prescription errors that are caught before the medication reaches the patient. Prescription errors encompass a variety of different medication events:

- Dispensing the wrong drug, the wrong strength of drug, or the wrong formulation of drug (e.g., tablets instead of liquid)
- Dispensing a drug to the incorrect patient (patient name mix-ups)
- Dispensing the incorrect quantity of medication
- Refilling a prescription too early (which can lead to medication abuse or overdose)
- Incorrect labeling, directions, or infusion rate information
- Compounding a medication incorrectly (e.g., adding too much or too little water)
- Preparing an IV admixture in an incompatible solution or in an incompatible bag
- Dispensing a drug to a patient with a known allergy or contraindication
- Dispensing a drug that interacts with another medication that the patient is taking
- Failure to provide adequate counseling or information to the patient
- Shipping a medication order to the incorrect address

Error-Prone Abbreviations

Examples of error-prone abbreviations:

Abbreviation NOT to Use	Use Instead	Potential Error
U (for unit)	Unit	Mistaken for mL, cc., 0, or 4
IU (for international unit)	International unit	Mistaken for IV or 10
Q.D., QD, q.d., or qd	Daily	Mistaken for every other day, drops
Q.O.D., QOD, q.o.d., qod	Every other day	Mistaken for daily, four times a day
Chemical abbreviations (e.g., $MgSO_4$, NaCl, KCl)	Write out the full chemical/drug name	Easily confused for another drug
Drug name abbreviations (e.g., MS, HCTZ, NS)	Write out the full name of the medication (e.g., morphine sulfate, hydrochlorothiazide, normal saline)	Easily mistaken for another medication
Trailing zero (e.g., 1.0 mg)	For whole numbers, do not put a decimal and a zero after the number	The decimal point may be missed, and an extra zero can be added to the dose. The patient could receive 10× the intended dose (e.g., 10 mg instead of 1 mg).
Lack of a leading zero (e.g., .5 mg)	For numbers less than 1, place a 0 in front of the decimal point (e.g., 0.5 mg)	The decimal point may be missed, and the number can be mistaken for a whole number. The patient may receive 10× the intended dose (e.g., 5 mg instead of 0.5 mg).

Reducing Medication Errors Using Technology

Pharmacy technology has come a long way in the past decade. Pharmacy computer systems have made significant advancements, and dispensing robots are now commonplace in large pharmacies. A popular English proverb tells us that to err is human. Therefore, we should use technology to try to reduce the number of errors that we make.

- Take notice of computerized alerts or warnings, and relay this information to a pharmacist prior to dispensing.
- Use barcode scanning technology every time you dispense a medication to ensure that the NDC number that is dispensed matches the NDC number on the label or in the computer system.
- If your pharmacy computer system allows you to prefill prescription information from an electronic prescription, use this feature to prevent manual typing errors.
- If available, use dispensing robots to dispense, count, and label prescriptions.
- Use a patient's electronic profile to document and identify allergy information, current medication information, and other medication information.
- Use the linking of Pyxis machines with pharmacy computer systems to monitor medication inventory and administration records to identify potential errors.

Barcode and Data Entry Technologies

Each product has a unique scannable bar code that is linked to its National Drug Code (NDC) number. During the dispensing process, the bar code of each stock bottle is scanned to ensure that it matches the NDC number dispensed. Drug bar codes are also scanned when they are loaded into automated dispensing robots or cabinets (e.g., Pyxis machines). This helps ensure that the correct medication is loaded into the correct container, drawer, or pocket. When medications are loaded into or dispensed from an automated dispensing system, inventory levels are also updated. This helps ensure that the correct on-hand inventory for each medication is maintained in the computer system.

Data entry technologies are also used by pharmacies for quality assurance. Many pharmacy computer systems allow new prescriptions to be scanned into the system, and most of the prescription details are prefilled. In most hospitals, prescribers order medications using the same software that the pharmacy uses to dispense medications. Therefore, medication aides can pull prescription details from the computer system without manually entering the information. This reduces the risk of human error. Additionally, the computer system will usually automatically select preferred formulary products that are in stock at the pharmacy.

Use of Barcode Scanning

Barcode scanning is used in the dispensing process to verify that the correct medication was dispensed. In retail or outpatient settings, the bar code of each stock bottle is scanned during the dispensing process to ensure that the NDC number matches the NDC number dispensed on the label or in the computer system. In hospital pharmacies, barcode scanning is also used when delivering medication to automated dispensing cabinets (e.g., Pyxis machines). When the medication aide restocks the machine, they first scan the medication. This triggers the machine to open the pocket or drawer assigned to that medication. This reduces the likelihood of stocking the drug in the wrong location. It also reduces the likelihood that nurses or providers will dispense and administer the wrong medication. Additionally, nurses use barcode scanning technology to ensure that they are administering the right drug to the right patient. First, they scan the drug, and then they scan the patient identifier code on the patient's wristband before drug administration.

Documenting and Reporting Medication Errors

All pharmacies should keep a medication error logbook in the pharmacy at all times, and all pharmacy staff members should know where it is located and how to document medication errors. Any time a dispensing error occurs, regardless of whether it reaches the patient or the pharmacist, the error should be recorded in the medication error log. Each pharmacy will have a policy that states who is responsible for reviewing medication errors and how often the error log should be reviewed. The types of information usually recorded in the error log includes the date the error occurred, the names of the medication(s) involved, the stage at which the error occurred, the stage at which the error was discovered, and the staff members that were involved. It is important to record as many details of the event as possible because this information will help during the review process. The idea of the logbook is not to place blame on specific employees, but to try to establish trends and come up with ideas for how to prevent the reoccurrence of common errors.

Analyzing Medication Errors

Root cause analysis is a problem-solving method used by pharmacies to determine the causes of medication errors and suggest methods for error prevention. Root cause analysis is triggered by a sentinel event, a medication error, or an undesirable event. Event analysis is not a simple 5-minute meeting. Analysis can take days to weeks to complete. Every pharmacy should have a multidisciplinary team in place that is trained on how to analyze sentinel events using root cause analysis.

The first step in root cause analysis is to collect data about the event and what happened. Data collection involves interviewing staff members, reviewing dispensing records, etc. Data collection can be time-consuming, but it is important to collect as much data as possible. Next, the team can brainstorm potential causes of the event. Then, a corrective action plan and report can be developed by the team. At a specified time period, the team should follow up with the action plan to ensure that it is effective and does not need to be revised.

Symptoms and Side Effects

Common Side Effects of Medications

Antineoplastic Agents

Most antineoplastic agents have the same classic chemotherapy side effects. These include hair loss, increased risk of infection (immunosuppression), low red blood cell count (anemia), bruising or bleeding easily, skin rashes (especially at the site of injection), fatigue, nausea, vomiting, diarrhea, constipation, gastrointestinal ulcers, mouth sores, and weight loss. Most of these side effects are due to the fact that antineoplastic agents are so good at killing cells that they kill normal body cells in addition to cancer cells. Some of the newer cancer medications are better at targeting cancer cells and have fewer side effects.

Hormonal anticancer therapies are among the targeted antineoplastic agents. Because they target cancer cells and avoid killing healthy body cells, hormonal therapies have fewer of the classic chemotherapy side effects. However, they do cause hormone-related side effects in the patient. For instance, tamoxifen causes menopause-like symptoms in women because it blocks estrogen. These symptoms include hot flashes, mood swings, depression, headache, hair thinning, loss of libido (sex drive), and fatigue. Bicalutamide also causes menopause-like side effects when taken by men because it blocks androgens (male sex hormones). Side effects include hot flashes, breast tenderness, weight changes, headaches, and difficulty sleeping.

Oral Antihyperglycemic Drugs

Oral antihyperglycemic drugs have various side effects:

- **Metformin** is a first-line drug for treating type 2 diabetes mellitus because it has fewer side effects than many of the other antihyperglycemic drugs. It commonly causes nausea and stomach pains, but it does not cause hypoglycemia (too-low blood sugar) or weight gain like many other agents.
- **Sulfonylureas** are very effective at lowering blood glucose and are commonly used as an addition to metformin. However, they are associated with an increased risk of hypoglycemia and weight gain.
- **Thiazolidinediones** are no longer commonly used because there were found to be associated with an increased risk of cardiovascular disease and heart failure. They also cause weight gain and edema (swelling).
- **Acarbose** is rarely used because it often causes abdominal discomfort.
- **DPP-4 inhibitors** are well tolerated by patients and have few side effects. They do not cause weight gain or hypoglycemia like many of the other antidiabetic medications, but they are newer and more expensive.
- **SGLT-2 inhibitors** are becoming popular because instead of causing weight gain, they can help diabetic patients lose weight. This is beneficial to diabetics because they are already susceptible to weight gain. Unfortunately, they do increase the risk of genital and urinary tract infections.

Parkinson's and Alzheimer's Disease Drugs

Side effects of Parkinson's disease (PD) drugs include:

- **Dopaminergic drugs** commonly cause nausea, vomiting, agitation, confusion, depression, psychosis, dyskinesias (involuntary muscle movements), compulsive disorders (e.g., gambling), and orthostatic hypotension (dizziness upon standing).
- **MAO-B inhibitors** also cause a number of adverse effects that are similar to those of dopaminergic drugs. The common side effects for MAO-B inhibitors include nausea, vomiting, agitation, confusion, dizziness, dyskinesias, insomnia, lack of appetite, depression, anxiety, and psychosis.
- **Anticholinergic drugs** used for PD cause adverse effects similar to those of other anticholinergics that are used to treat urinary retention. Anticholinergic side effects include dry mouth, blurred vision, constipation, urinary retention, confusion, agitation, and psychosis.

Side effects of Alzheimer's disease (AD) drugs include:

- **Cholinesterase inhibitors** have an opposite effect to that of anticholinergic drugs. They increase acetylcholine levels by blocking the enzyme acetylcholinesterase, which is responsible for breaking down acetylcholine. Common side effects of cholinesterase inhibitors include nausea, vomiting, upset stomach, and weight loss. Starting at a low dose and gradually titrating the dose up to the intended maintenance dose helps minimize gastrointestinal adverse side effects.
- **NMDA receptor antagonists (blockers)** are used to treat moderate to severe cases of AD. NMDA blockers commonly cause dizziness, headache, drowsiness, high blood pressure, and restlessness.

Stimulants

Attention-deficit/hyperactivity disorder (ADHD) is treated using stimulants, such as amphetamines, that excite the brain and help with focus, concentration, and motivation. Common side effects of stimulants include restlessness, nervousness, insomnia, mood swings, headache, raised blood pressure, loss of appetite, stomachaches, headaches, and weight loss. The stimulants used to treat ADHD are schedule II controlled substances and are prone to abuse. Some noncontrolled nonstimulant medications, such as Strattera, are now used to treat more resistant forms of ADHD. The adverse effects of these nonstimulants include dry mouth, nausea, upset stomach, weight loss, and insomnia.

The side effects of appetite loss and weight loss have made stimulants a target for weight loss treatments. Phentermine is a schedule IV drug prescribed to assist in weight loss in patients who have not responded to diet and exercise alone. In addition to its ability to improve attention and wakefulness, caffeine is also available as an OTC medication in tablet form as a weight loss supplement. The OTC nasal decongestant pseudoephedrine also has stimulant effects and similar side effects to ADHD stimulants. They should be avoided in patients with hypertension because of their effects on blood pressure.

Osteoporosis

There are two main types of medications used to prevent or treat osteoporosis: calcium with vitamin D supplements and bisphosphonates.

- Adverse effects associated with calcium and vitamin D supplements are uncommon. In rare cases, they can cause hypercalcemia (high blood calcium levels). Signs of hypercalcemia include nausea, vomiting, and thirst. High doses of vitamin D are contraindicated in pregnancy.
- Bisphosphonates used to treat osteoporosis include alendronate (Fosamax), risedronate (Actonel), and zoledronate (Reclast). The main side effects of bisphosphonates include hypocalcemia (low blood calcium levels) and gastrointestinal ulceration. These medications irritate the esophagus, so they should be taken with a full glass of water, and the patient should not lie down for at least 30 minutes after taking the medication in order to avoid irritation to the esophagus. Bisphosphonates are contraindicated in patients with gastrointestinal ulcers, patients with moderate to severe renal impairment, and pregnant women.

Adverse Effects

An adverse effect is an unintended or undesired effect of a drug. A side effect is an unintended secondary effect of a medication. An adverse effect is different from a side effect because side effects may be desired or wanted, whereas an adverse effect is undesired or harmful. Adverse effects may be local (e.g., rash) or systemic (e.g., raised blood pressure). Local effects remain in one area of the body, whereas systemic effects are spread throughout the body. Adverse effects can range from mild (e.g., nausea) to severe (e.g., kidney failure).

Types of adverse effects: allergies, gastrointestinal effects (e.g., nausea, vomiting, diarrhea, abdominal pain), central nervous system (CNS) effects (drug dependence, tolerance, drowsiness), hematological effects (blood clotting, bleeding), nephrotoxicity (kidney[renal] impairment), hepatotoxicity (liver impairment), ototoxicity (causes damage to the ear), immunosuppression (reduces the ability to fight infection), carcinogenicity (ability to cause cancer), and teratogenicity (the ability to harm the fetus or cause birth defects in pregnant women).

Review Video: Mnemonics for Drug Side Effects
Visit mometrix.com/academy and enter code: 452450

MEDICAL TERMS DESCRIBING ADVERSE EFFECTS

Key terms describing adverse effects of medications include the following:

- **Hypoglycemia**: Low blood glucose (hint: "hypo" means less than normal). This is a common adverse effect of antidiabetic medications.
- **Hyperkalemia**: High blood potassium levels (hint: "hyper" means above, and the chemical abbreviation for potassium is "K").
- **Hypokalemia**: Low blood potassium levels. This is a common adverse effect of diuretics or water tablets.
- **Orthostatic hypotension**: Low blood pressure upon standing, which often leads to dizziness and blurred vision.
- **Fatigue**: Tiredness, drowsiness, or sleepiness.
- **Malaise**: A general feeling of discomfort or illness.
- **Dyspepsia**: Heartburn, indigestion, bloating, or abdominal pain (hint: "dys" means painful, and "pepsia" means digestion).
- **Pruritus**: Itching.
- **Diaphoresis**: Sweating.
- **Alopecia**: Hair loss.
- **Myalgia**: Muscle pain (hint: "my" refers to muscles, and "algia" means pain).
- **Edema**: Swelling
- **Xerostomia**: Dry mouth (hint: "xero" means dry, and "stomy" refers to an opening such as the mouth).
- **Anuria**: Lack of urination (hint: "an" means without, and "urea" means urination). Oliguria may also be used to refer to reduced urination.

SEIZURES

Epilepsy is a disorder in which a patient has seizures. Epilepsy is complex to diagnose because not every patient that has a seizure is diagnosed with a seizure disorder. Some patients have recurrent seizures, whereas others have had one seizure caused by an acute illness or a drug therapy.

Some forms of epilepsy have genetic links and run in families. Other seizure disorders may be linked to another medical issue, such as a birth defect, head injury, tumor, stroke, electrolyte imbalance (e.g., low sodium), hypoglycemia (low glucose), fever, or infection.

Certain medications can also increase a patient's risk of having a seizure. Recreational substances, including alcohol and cocaine, can cause seizures. Prescription medications can also increase seizure risk: narcotic pain medications (e.g., tramadol, meperidine), methylphenidate (used to treat ADHD), anesthesia drugs, metoclopramide, some antidepressants, and some antibiotics. Paradoxically, anticonvulsants that are used to treat epilepsy are also known to cause seizures. This adverse effect is of most concern when anticonvulsants are being used to treat a different disorder, such as migraines or bipolar disorder.

Antibiotics

Antibiotics are used to treat bacterial or microbial infections. All antibiotics have the potential to cause nausea, vomiting, diarrhea, stomach upset, and abdominal pain. Antibiotics can also kill the normal flora (good bacteria) in the body and lead to secondary infections, such as thrush or intestinal infection (colitis, *Clostridioides difficile*). This is more common with broad-spectrum (less specific) antibiotics and longer courses of treatment. Patients can take a probiotic to help prevent this side effect.

Review Video: Antibiotics: An Overview
Visit mometrix.com/academy and enter code: 165628

The potential adverse effects associated with antibiotics:

Antibiotic Classification	Drug Examples	Potential Side Effects
Penicillins	Amoxicillin, penicillin	Allergy in 1–10% of patients. Anaphylaxis (a rare but serious form of allergy). Skin rash (a common, less severe form of allergy).
Cephalosporins	Cefaclor, cefixime	Allergy: About 10% of patients with a penicillin allergy are also allergic to cephalosporins.
Tetracyclines	Tetracycline, doxycycline, minocycline	Sensitivity to sunlight. Tooth staining, so avoid in children.
Macrolides	Erythromycin, clarithromycin	Arrhythmias. Ototoxicity (ear problems) with high doses.
Quinolones	Ciprofloxacin, levofloxacin	Arrhythmias. Muscle tendon rupture. Increased seizure risk.
Sulfonamides (sulfa drugs)	Sulfamethoxazole-trimethoprim (Bactrim)	Allergy — anaphylaxis or skin rash.

Opioids

Opioids are central nervous system (CNS) depressants used to treat pain. One of the main adverse effects is a high risk of dependence and addiction, and there are many widely seen advertisements warning of the potentially addictive properties of opioids. Prescription opioids are one of the main culprits of the current opioid epidemic alongside other illegal opioids, including heroin and cocaine. Patients receiving a prescription for an opioid should be warned about this potential adverse effect and encouraged to only use these medications on an as-needed basis. Some state laws require additional warning stickers for opioid bottles or restrict the quantity of opioids that can be dispensed at a time.

Opioids can also cause nausea and vomiting in many patients. They also commonly cause constipation. Opioids slow down the movement of the digestive tract and can lead to reduced bowel movements.

In addition to slowing the digestive system, opioids also slow down respiration or breathing. This adverse effect is exploited by using opioids to suppress coughing, such as with Phenergan with Codeine cough syrup. However, high doses of more potent opioids, such as oxycodone or morphine, can reduce the respiration rate to dangerous levels.

Inhaled Medications

Inhaled dosage forms include MDIs, DPIs, and nebulizer solutions. Nebulization delivers higher doses of medication to the body compared to inhalers, so it is associated with a higher risk of side effects. Inhaled medications used to treat asthma and COPD include bronchodilators, such as beta agonists and muscarinic antagonists, and anti-inflammatory corticosteroids.

- **Beta agonists** can cause tachycardia (a fast heart rate), cardiac arrhythmias, and tremors. They are also known to cause hypokalemia (low potassium levels). Examples of inhaled beta agonists include albuterol, levalbuterol, terbutaline, salmeterol, and formoterol.
- **Muscarinic antagonists** are selective and act locally, so they rarely cause significant adverse effects. However, they can potentially cause dry mouth, blurred vision, difficulty urinating, and glaucoma. The patient's eyes should be protected when administering nebulizers. Examples of inhaled muscarinic antagonists include ipratropium and tiotropium.
- **Inhaled corticosteroids** provide localized actions, so they do not cause as many adverse effects as oral steroids. However, they still have the potential to cause fluid retention, weight gain, hyperglycemia (high blood glucose), and hypokalemia (low potassium). Because corticosteroids reduce the body's immune response, patients frequently get a localized infection called thrush, a fungal infection in the mouth or throat.

Allergic Reactions

An allergy occurs when the body's own immune system reacts to the presence of a foreign substance (e.g., a drug) and causes an adverse effect. Allergic reactions can range in severity from a mild rash to anaphylactic shock. Anaphylactic shock is a life-threatening reaction that results from dangerously low blood pressure and shortness of breath. Anaphylaxis should be treated immediately with epinephrine (e.g., EpiPen).

It is important to get a thorough allergy history before dispensing for a patient. However, patients who have not yet been exposed to a medication will not know if they are allergic to it, so they should be cautioned on the warning signs. A rash is a sign of minor allergy and usually goes away on its own after the medication course is complete. Signs of a more severe allergy include swelling of the face, tongue, or throat and difficulty breathing. These symptoms require immediate medical attention and discontinuation of the medication. Fortunately, rashes are far more common than anaphylactic allergies. Many patients also report an allergy to a drug because they experienced a side effect, so be sure to document the details of the allergy in the patient profile if known.

Types of Drugs That Commonly Cause Allergic Reactions

A patient can be allergic to any medication, but medication allergies are more common in some drug classes than in others. Antibiotics are a common culprit, particularly older classes of antibiotics including penicillins, cephalosporins, and sulfa drugs (e.g., Bactrim). Up to 10% of the population reports being allergic to penicillin, but most patients only experience a minor rash. Only about 1% of the population experiences a true anaphylactic allergy to penicillin. Cephalosporin antibiotics are structurally related to penicillins, so some patients who are allergic to penicillin are also allergic to cephalosporins. The chance of cross-reactivity is thought to be about 10%.

Antifungals and antiviral drugs are also among the commonly reported allergies. Chemotherapy drugs, NSAIDs, insulin, antiepileptic drugs, and biologic injections are also common culprits of drug allergies. An allergy is far more likely with injectable medications compared to the oral route. Certain injectable medications require test doses and allergy monitoring as part of their infusion protocol.

Reporting Adverse Reactions to the FDA

The FDA's MedWatch program can be used to report adverse effects associated with any human drug (whether OTC or prescription-only), biologic (blood component, tissue-based products), medical device, vaccine, dietary supplement, infant formula, cosmetic, food, or beverage. MedWatch can even be used to report medication errors. Pharmacists, pharmacy technicians, and medication aides in practice rarely submit information on adverse drug reactions to the FDA because it is voluntary and time-consuming. However, the FDA encourages use of the MedWatch reporting system, even if you are not certain of all the details of the event.

Adverse event reporting through MedWatch is particularly encouraged for serious adverse reactions that involve hospitalization, involve a life-threatening reaction, result in disability or permanent damage, or result in death. The FDA also encourages the reporting of quality or safety concerns with a product, such as suspected contamination, suspected counterfeit products, defective products, inadequate packaging or labeling, or stability issues.

Resources for Reporting

All drugs have the potential to cause adverse effects or reactions. For older medications that have been on the market for a while, the frequency and nature of commonly experienced adverse events are well known. However, less is known about the adverse effects associated with newer medications or rare adverse reactions. Therefore, it is important to report adverse drug events to MedWatch, the FDA's online voluntary reporting system for adverse drug reactions. Anyone can report an adverse drug event to MedWatch, including doctors, pharmacy technicians, pharmacists, medication aides, patients, or caregivers. Reports can be made online, by phone, by mail, or by fax. The FDA's Adverse Event Reporting System database contains information about all the adverse events reported to the FDA through the MedWatch program. This database is especially useful in reporting severe reactions, rare reactions, or events related to drugs that have recently entered the market. The Vaccine Adverse Event Reporting System is an FDA program specifically designed to monitor adverse reactions associated with vaccinations.

Medication Concepts and Measurements

Medication Concepts

Brand Name vs. Generic Name

The brand name for a drug is its advertised name assigned by the original inventor. The generic name is its chemical, scientific, or nonproprietary name. The generic name is always listed on the label of the container, but a brand name is not required for generic versions. For example, when you go to the store to purchase household cleaner, you will have the choice of purchasing Clorox (brand name) or the store brand of bleach cleaner (generic name).

The same system applies to pharmacy. If you browse the OTC section of your local pharmacy for the nasal spray Flonase (brand name), you will also have the option to purchase a generic version labeled fluticasone. Both product labels are required to contain the generic name of fluticasone.

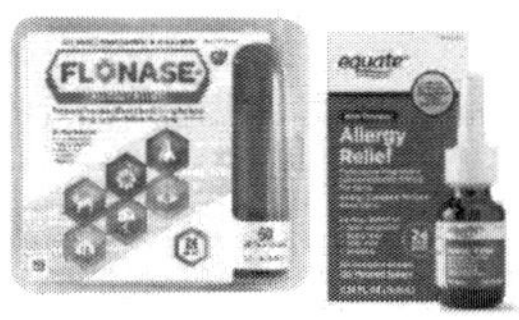

Inventors/manufacturers of a new drug will file for a patent, which gives them exclusive rights to produce that drug for the next 20 years. During this period, the drug will only be available as a brand-name product. Once the patent expires, other companies will be allowed to produce generic versions of the drug once they obtain Food and Drug Administration (FDA) approval and prove that the ingredients and formulation are equivalent to the branded product.

Medical Root Words

A root word is part of a word that tells us the primary meaning of the word. In medical terminology, the root of the word is usually in Latin. Knowing the meanings of the Latin root words helps us understand what the word means even if we have never seen it before.

Common medical root words:

Root Word	Meaning
Acous, audi	Hearing
Adip	Fat
Alges	Pain
Andr	Male
Aneur	Widening
Angi	Vessel
Aort	Aorta
Arthr	Joint
Cardi	Heart
Carp	Wrist
Cere	Cerebrum (part of brain)
Crani	Skull
Cutane, derm	Skin

Root Word	Meaning
Dactyl	Finger, toe
Encephal	Brain
Esthes	Sensation
Gastr	Stomach
Gynec	Women
Hem, hemat	Blood
Hepat	Liver
Hyster	Uterus
Ichthy	Dry, scaly
Kerat	Hard
Lapar	Abdomen
Lord	Curve
Mamm, mast	Breast
My	Muscle

Root Word	Meaning
Myel	Spinal cord
Necr	Death
Nephr	Kidney
Neur	Nerve
Ocul, ophthalm, optic	Eye
Pector	Chest
Ped, pod	Foot
Phalang	Bones of the fingers and toes
Phas	Speech
Pneum	Lung, air
Psycho	Mind

Root Word	Meaning
Pulmon	Lung
Onych	Nail
Oste	Bone
Prurit, psor	Itching
Rhin	Nose
Scoli	Bent
Somat	Body
Sten	Narrow
Stern	Sternum, breastbone
Tars	Ankle
Thromb	Clot
Ven	Vein

Medical Suffixes

Many medical words are Latin in origin, so knowing parts of the Latin words can help us define medical terms. A suffix is the ending of a word. Knowing the suffix of a word can help us understand what the word means, even if we haven't seen that word before.

Common medical suffixes:

Suffix	Meaning
-ac, -al, -ar, -ary	Pertaining to
-algia, -dynia	Pain
-asthenia	Weakness
-cele	Hernia, bulging
-cyesis	Pregnancy
-ectasis	Dilation
-ectomy	Surgical removal
-edema	Swelling
-emesis	Vomiting
-emia	Blood condition
-esthenia	Lack of sensation
-genic	Producing, forming
-gram	Record
-iatry	Treatment
-icle	Small
-itis	Inflammation
-lepsy	Seizure
-lith	Stone
-lysis	Breaking down
-malacia	Softening

Suffix	Meaning
-megaly	Enlargement
-oma	Tumor
-opia, -opsia	Vision
-orexia	Appetite
-paresis	Partial paralysis
-pathy	Disease
-pepsia	Digestion
-phagia	Swallowing
-phasia	Speech
-philic	Attraction
-plegia	Paralysis, stroke
-pnea	Breathing
-rrhage	To burst
-rrhea	Discharge
-sclerosis	To harden
-spasm	Involuntary contraction
-stasis	Stop, control
-stomy	Artificial opening
-trophy	Growth, nourishment
-uria	Urination

Review Video: Drug Suffixes
Visit mometrix.com/academy and enter code: 882876

Medical Prefixes

A prefix is the beginning of a word.

Prefix	Meaning
A-, An-	Without
Ambi-	Both
Ante-	Before
Anti-	Against
Auto-	Self
Bi-	Two, both
Brady-	Slow
Circum-	Around
Cirrh-	Yellow
Con-	With
Contra-	Against
Dia-	Completely
Dipl-	Double
Dis-	Separate, apart
Dys-	Painful, difficult
Ec-	Away, out of
Ecto-	Outside
En-	In
Endo-	Within
Epi-	Above
Eso-	Inward
Eu-	Normal, good
Exo-	Outside
Hemi-	Half
Heter-	Different
Hyper-	Above, over
Hypo-	Below, under
Im-	Not, without
Immune-	Immunity

Prefix	Meaning
Infra-	Below, under
Inter-	Between
Intra-	Within
Iso-	Equal
Leuk-	White
Lip-	Fat
Macro-	Large
Mal-	Poor
Medi-, meso-, mid-	Middle
Meta-	Beyond, after
Micro-	Small
Mono-	One
Multi-	Many
Neo-	New
Pachy-	Heavy, thick
Pan-	All
Para-	Near, abnormal
Peri-	Around
Poly-	Many
Post-, retro-	After
Pre-, pro-	Before
Pseudo-	FALSE
Super-, supra-	Above
Sym-, syn-	With
Tachy-	Fast
Trans-	Across
Tri-	Three
Uni-	One
Xero-	Dry

Common Medical Abbreviations

Common medical abbreviations:

ACE	Angiotensin-converting enzyme
ADH	Antidiuretic hormone
ADR	Adverse drug reaction
AF, AFib	Atrial fibrillation (a type of heart arrhythmia)
BMI	Body mass index
BP	Blood pressure
BPH	Benign prostatic hyperplasia
CNS	Central nervous system
CVS	Cardiovascular system
DEA	Drug Enforcement Administration
DMARD	Disease-modifying antirheumatic drug
DVT	Deep vein thrombosis
ECG/EKG	Electrocardiogram
ED	Erectile dysfunction
FDA	Food and Drug Administration
GFR	Glomerular filtration rate (measure of kidney function)
HBP	High blood pressure
HIV	Human immunodeficiency virus
HRT	Hormone replacement therapy
HSV	Herpes simplex virus
HTN	Hypertension
Ig	Immunoglobulin
INR	International normalized ratio (a test used to dose warfarin)
IR	Immediate release
LMWH	Low-molecular-weight heparin
MDI	Metered-dose inhaler
MI	Myocardial infarction (heart attack)
MR	Modified release (formulation)
MRI	Magnetic resonance imaging
MRSA	Methicillin-resistant Staphylococcus aureus
N/V/D	Nausea, vomiting, and diarrhea
NSAID	Nonsteroidal anti-inflammatory drug
NSTEMI	Non-ST elevation myocardial infarction (ST refers to the ST segment)
OTC	Over-the-counter
PCA	Patient-controlled analgesia
PE	Pulmonary embolism
PPI	Proton pump inhibitor (acid suppressor)
PRN	As needed
SR	Sustained release (long acting)
SSRI	Selective serotonin reuptake inhibitor (antidepressant)
STEMI	ST elevation myocardial infarction
TB	Tuberculosis
TCA	Tricyclic antidepressant
TIA	Transient ischemic attack (ministroke)
VTE	Venous thromboembolism
XR	Extended release (long acting)

Medical Conditions

Definitions of common medical conditions include:

- **Myocardial infarction**: Heart attack (hint: "myo" means muscle, "cardi" means heart, and "infarction" means tissue death). When a blood clot obstructs blood flow to the heart, the heart muscles cannot get enough oxygen and the tissue eventually dies.
- **Pulmonary embolism**: Blood clot in the lung (hint: "pulm" means lung, and an embolism is a blood clot).
- **Benign prostatic hyperplasia**: Enlarged prostate (hint: "hyper" means greater than normal).
- **Thrombus**: A blood clot that develops in a blood vessel (hint: "thromb" means clot).
- **Embolism**: A thrombus that breaks off and gets stuck in another blood vessel.
- **Hypertension**: High blood pressure (hint: "hyper" means greater than normal).
- **Hypotension**: Low blood pressure (hint: "hypo" means less than normal).
- **Hyperglycemia**: High blood glucose (hint: "glyc" means sugar or glucose, and "emia" refers to a condition of the blood). This is the main clinical feature of diabetes mellitus.
- **Neuropathy**: A disease of the nerves, usually resulting in nerve pain or unusual sensations (hint: "neur" refers to nerves, and "pathy" means disease).

Therapeutic Contraindications

A therapeutic contraindication is a specific situation or condition in which a drug should not be administered because it may increase the risk of causing harm to the patient. A contraindication is usually a disease state, patient group, or medical diagnosis. For example, if a drug is contraindicated in hypertension, that means that patients with hypertension (high blood pressure) should not use that drug.

Many drugs are contraindicated in pregnancy, including tetracyclines, vancomycin, ACE inhibitors, NSAIDs, and lithium. Another common contraindication is advanced age (elderly patients). Extra caution should be taken when antidepressants, antihistamines, antipsychotics, and sedatives are used in elderly patients because they are at increased risk of experiencing side effects. Other examples of common contraindications to drug treatments include alcohol use, liver (hepatic) impairment, kidney(renal) impairment, hypertension, asthma, cardiac arrhythmias, epilepsy, PD, childhood, electrolyte imbalances, immune disorders, and active infection.

Drug Interactions

Common drug interactions include:

Interaction	Description	Example
Drug-disease	A drug interacts with or interferes with an existing medical condition.	Pseudoephedrine increases blood pressure and is not recommended in patients who have high blood pressure (aka hypertension).
Drug-drug	The effects of one drug are changed when taken in combination with another drug.	Enalapril and amlodipine are both antihypertensive medications. When taken together, the patient's blood pressure will be lower than if the medications were taken separately.
Drug-supplement	A supplement or vitamin interferes with the way a drug acts or is absorbed.	Calcium supplements decrease the absorption of many medications, such as tetracycline. Potassium supplements reduce the effectiveness of the blood thinner warfarin.
Drug-food	The effects of a drug are changed when taken in combination with a particular food.	Grapefruit juice decreases the ability of statin drugs to be metabolized (broken down).
Drug-nutrient	A drug affects the way that the body absorbs, uses, or excretes a nutrient.	Diuretics, such as furosemide, increase the amount of potassium excreted in the urine.
Drug-laboratory	A drug alters the results of a laboratory test.	Corticosteroids, such as prednisone and dexamethasone, can elevate blood glucose levels.

Anticoagulants and Antiplatelets

Because blood thinners prevent blood clotting, their main side effect is bleeding. Combining multiple blood thinners increases bleeding risk and should be avoided. Patients should watch for stomach pain or black tarry stools, which indicate gastrointestinal bleeding. Signs and symptoms of a head bleed would be sudden headache, nausea, vomiting, blurred vision, weakness or numbness on one side of the body, or difficulty speaking. Patients taking blood thinners are also at a higher risk of having nosebleeds and excessive bleeding from minor scrapes and bruises.

Patients taking a blood thinner should avoid OTC aspirin and NSAIDs (ibuprofen, naproxen) because these medications can also thin the blood. The pharmacist should examine the patient's profile for any drug interactions that may put them at a higher risk for bleeding. Particular caution should be taken when dispensing warfarin because it is involved in many drug interactions that can increase the patient's risk of bleeding. Warfarin interacts with many antibiotics, antifungals, antiarrhythmics, statins, and antiepileptic medications. Patients taking warfarin should also avoid eating a lot of green leafy vegetables that are high in vitamin K.

Antiepileptic Medications

Common side effects of antiepileptic drugs include anxiety, suicidal thoughts, memory and concentration impairment, blurred vision, nausea, vomiting, dry mouth, skin rashes, headache, fatigue, drowsiness, and dizziness. Carbamazepine and oxcarbazepine can cause a rare but serious side effect called neutropenia, which hinders the body's ability to fight infection. Divalproex and valproic acid are teratogenic, meaning that if they are taken during pregnancy, they can cause birth defects. Some anticonvulsants, such as ezogabine, increase the risk of heart arrythmias. Gabapentin, pregabalin, and levetiracetam are associated with fewer adverse effects and fewer drug interactions.

Common drug interactions include diuretics, metformin, lithium, blood thinners, rifampin, digoxin, antidepressants, statins, and other antiepileptics. Carbamazepine, phenytoin, fosphenytoin, primidone, and phenobarbital tend to speed up the metabolism of other medications and reduce their effectiveness. This is of particular concern when used in combination with warfarin, lithium, digoxin, and other antiepileptic medications. Many seizure medications reduce the effectiveness of hormonal birth control, so a nonhormonal birth control method, such as an IUD, should be recommended instead.

Analgesics

Analgesics include acetaminophen, NSAIDs, and opioids.

- **Acetaminophen** is metabolized in the liver and therefore should be used judiciously in individuals with hepatic disease or a compromised liver.
- **NSAIDs** can thin the blood and increase bleeding risk. Therefore, they should not be administered to patients with stomach ulcers or patients taking other anticoagulants. NSAIDs can worsen asthma symptoms and should be avoided in asthmatic patients. They can also worsen renal failure and cause fluid retention, so patients with renal failure or heart failure should avoid NSAIDs. NSAIDs interact with diuretics, blood thinners, ACE inhibitors, methotrexate, and lithium.
- **Opioids** relax the bowel muscles and slow digestion. Therefore, they are contraindicated in patients with intestinal disorders or infection, including ulcerative colitis and *Clostridioides difficile*. Opioids work on the nervous system and cause central nervous system (CNS) depression. Therefore, they interact with other nervous system drugs, including antipsychotics and alcohol. If used in combination, adverse effects such as sedation and confusion can be made worse. Elderly patients should be more cautious because they are more prone to the sedative effects.

Cardiovascular Drugs

Drug interactions associated with common cardiovascular drugs include:

- **Beta-blockers** are contraindicated in patients with asthma because these drugs can cause airway constriction. They should also be avoided in diabetics because they can mask the symptoms of hypoglycemia. Beta-blockers should also be avoided during pregnancy. Drug interactions include verapamil, diltiazem, amiodarone, clonidine, and digoxin.
- **Angiotensin-converting enzyme (ACE) inhibitors** are contraindicated in pregnant women and patients with severe renal impairment. NSAIDs also cause renal impairment, so avoid using both drugs together. Because ACE inhibitors can raise potassium levels (hyperkalemia), they interact with other medications that raise potassium levels, including some diuretics.
- **Calcium channel blockers** should be avoided during pregnancy. They interact with digoxin, cyclosporine, and grapefruit juice. Verapamil and diltiazem should be avoided in heart failure, and they interact with beta-blockers and statins.
- **Diuretics** enhance the excretion of water and electrolytes in the urine. Therefore, they can cause electrolyte imbalances. They should be avoided in patients with gout. They interact with lithium, digoxin, NSAIDs, ACE inhibitors, and diabetes drugs. Triamterene interacts with methotrexate and phenytoin.
- **Nitrates**, such as nitroglycerin, interact with erectile dysfunction drugs, such as sildenafil (Viagra). Both medications lower blood pressure, so combined used can cause severe hypotension.

Statins

HMG CoA reductase inhibitors, more commonly known as statins, are used to treat high cholesterol. They should be avoided in pregnant women as well as in patients with liver failure because they are broken down in the liver.

Statins interact with warfarin, fibrates, HIV antivirals, cyclosporine, and macrolide antibiotics. Statin drugs can increase the effects of the anticoagulant warfarin and increase the risk of bleeding. More frequent warfarin monitoring and blood tests should be done when patients are taking both drugs together. Gemfibrozil and fenofibrate (fibrate drugs also used to treat high cholesterol) can increase the levels of statin drugs in the body and increase the risk of getting muscle symptoms (myopathy). HIV antivirals, cyclosporine, and macrolide antibiotics also increase statin levels and increase the risk of myopathy. Statin drugs should be withheld while completing a course of treatment with macrolide antibiotics because the risk outweighs the benefits. The statin can be resumed once the short course of antibiotics is completed.

Statins are also involved in a drug-food interaction with grapefruit juice that increases the risk of myopathy. Grapefruit juice should be avoided in patients taking statins.

ANTIBIOTICS

A thorough allergy history should be taken before dispensing antibiotics to a patient. If a patient has a penicillin allergy, they should avoid penicillin antibiotics as well as cephalosporins and carbapenem antibiotics due to a high risk of cross-reactivity.

Many antibiotics are contraindicated during pregnancy: vancomycin, tetracyclines, gentamicin, Bactrim, and metronidazole. Quinolone antibiotics (e.g., ciprofloxacin, levofloxacin) are contraindicated in epilepsy. Tetracyclines should not be given to children. Alcohol use should be avoided with any antibiotic, but it is particularly important to avoid alcohol when taking metronidazole to avoid a serious adverse effect.

Most antibiotics increase the effects of warfarin, so extra monitoring is required throughout the course of antibiotic use. Antibiotics can also reduce the effectiveness of contraceptives, so another birth control method should be used during antibiotic use. Some antibiotics, including tetracyclines and quinolones, cannot be taken with milk, antacids, or vitamins. Vancomycin and gentamicin interact with furosemide and cyclosporine. Macrolide antibiotics, such as erythromycin and clarithromycin, interact with statins. The statin drug should be withheld during antibiotic treatment. Bactrim should be avoided in patients taking methotrexate or phenytoin. The tuberculosis treatment rifampicin interacts with and reduces the effectiveness of many other drugs.

ANTIVIRALS AND ANTIFUNGALS

Most antiviral and antifungal drugs are metabolized in the liver, so they require dosage adjustments or avoidance in patients with liver impairment.

HIV antiviral drugs are involved in numerous significant drug interactions. Most antivirals increase the actions of other medications, making patients more prone to adverse effects. Some medications involved in this interaction include antihistamines, benzodiazepines, calcium channel blockers, antiepileptics, corticosteroids, statins, warfarin, and macrolide antibiotics. In contrast, protease antivirals (e.g., ritonavir) reduce the effectiveness of hormonal birth control, so women should be advised to use condoms or an IUD instead.

Antifungal drugs are also metabolized in the liver and are contraindicated in liver failure. Many antifungals increase the effects of other medications, making patients more prone to adverse effects. Ketoconazole should not be taken with antacids or alcohol. Amphotericin is a potent intravenous (IV) antifungal that can cause electrolyte imbalances, so caution should be taken when it is used in combination with diuretics, corticosteroids, or digoxin.

DIABETES MEDICATIONS

Diet has a huge impact on diabetes and blood glucose levels. Most diabetics are well trained on what foods to avoid and how to alter their insulin injections according to the carbohydrates they eat. Diabetics should also be counseled on the effects of alcohol on insulin. Alcohol increases the effects of insulin and lowers blood glucose levels, putting the patient at greater risk of hypoglycemia (blood sugar levels that are too low). Diabetics should avoid alcohol, but if they do drink, they should inject less insulin or eat more carbohydrates.

Insulin interacts with oral sulfonylurea antidiabetic drugs, so this combination should be avoided. The effects of insulin and oral antidiabetic drugs are reduced by corticosteroids and diuretics. Most oral antidiabetic medications should be avoided in pregnancy and severe hepatic impairment. The glitazones can worsen heart failure and should be avoided in patients with cardiac issues. Metformin should be avoided in renal impairment, and it interacts with other drugs that cause kidney impairment (e.g., NSAIDs).

Parkinson's Disease and Alzheimer's Disease Medications

Parkinson's disease (PD) is defined by low dopamine levels, so most treatment options aim to boost dopamine levels. Antipsychotic drugs do the opposite. They lower dopamine levels to prevent the symptoms of psychosis that are associated with high levels of dopamine. Therefore, antipsychotic medications should not be given to patients with PD. Anticholinergic medications, such as metoclopramide, should also be avoided in Parkinson's disease. Most PD drugs lower blood pressure, so they enhance the effects of antihypertensive medications. Caution should be used in patients with cardiac disease and elderly patients who are more prone to falls.

Alzheimer's disease (AD) drugs aim to increase acetylcholine levels. Therefore, they interact with anticholinergic medications that block acetylcholine. TCAs, antipsychotics, antiepileptics, irritable bowel syndrome drugs, and drugs used to treat urinary incontinence are anticholinergic and interact with AD treatments. If taken in combination, these medications can increase confusion, dizziness, fall risk, and the risk of cardiac symptoms.

Psychological Medications

All psychological drugs interact with alcohol, opioids, and antihistamines. Profound sedation occurs when these drugs are combined, and elderly patients are particularly sensitive to these interactions.

- **Antidepressants** increase the risk of seizure, so they should be avoided in epilepsy or with antiepileptic drugs. Additionally, antidepressants are contraindicated in cardiac disease because they can cause significant hypotension and increase the risk of arrhythmias. Antidepressants should be avoided in patients with bipolar disorder. Monoamine oxidase inhibitors are a class of antidepressant that are rarely used today because they are involved in a wide range of drug-drug and drug-food interactions.
- **Antipsychotics** should be avoided in patients with cardiac arrhythmias, liver impairment, epilepsy, PD, and hypotension. They interact with anti-Parkinson's drugs, antihypertensives, antiepileptics, antidepressants, and lithium.
- **Sedatives** include the benzodiazepines and Z-drugs used to treat anxiety and insomnia. Tolerance develops quickly with these schedule IV medications, and the potential for abuse is high. They should only be used short-term or for sporadic use.

Asthma and COPD Medications

Asthma and chronic obstructive pulmonary disease (COPD) are respiratory conditions in which the airway is inflamed, constricted, and blocked. Treatments for these conditions are similar and involve using inhalers and nebulizers to deliver drugs locally into the lungs. Drug classes used in inhaled treatments include bronchodilators (beta-agonists and antimuscarinics) to open the airway and corticosteroids to reduce inflammation. Although these drugs are delivered to the lungs, some systemic effects are possible.

Beta agonists stimulate the sympathetic immune system, so they can raise blood pressure, raise heart rate, and cause arrhythmias. Caution should be taken in patients with cardiac disease. Drug interactions include antihypertensives, antiarrhythmics, and sympathomimetics (e.g., pseudoephedrine).

Antimuscarinic bronchodilators have anticholinergic effects that can be enhanced when combined with other anticholinergic drugs, such as urinary incontinence drugs. In the treatment of respiratory disorders, the use of multiple antimuscarinic drugs should be avoided.

Asthmatic patients should avoid the use of NSAIDs (e.g., ibuprofen) because it can worsen asthma symptoms.

Medication Contraindications in Specific Populations

Elderly Patients

Elderly patients have a reduced ability to metabolize (break down) medications and are generally more susceptible to adverse effects. Many elderly patients have a reduced ability to excrete drugs via the kidneys, which can increase the risk of toxicity and kidney damage. Drugs that cause sedation can lead to delirium and confusion in elderly patients as well as increase their risk of falling and fracturing a bone.

The different types of medications that are contraindicated in elderly patients:

Drug Classification	Examples	Concern
Antihistamines	Benadryl, hydroxyzine, promethazine	Increased sedation can lead to delirium and falls.
Antispasmodics/ Anticholinergics	Dicyclomine, oxybutynin	
TCAs	Amitriptyline, nortriptyline, doxepin	
Muscle relaxants	Cyclobenzaprine, carisoprodol, methocarbamol	
Benzodiazepines	Alprazolam, lorazepam, diazepam	
Hypnotics (Z-drugs)	Zolpidem, zaleplon, zopiclone	
Antipsychotics	Haloperidol, olanzapine, quetiapine, risperidone	Increased risk of stroke.
Antihypertensives (alpha-blockers and centrally acting agents)	Doxazosin, prazosin, terazosin, clonidine	Increased risk of hypotension and orthostatic hypotension, which may lead to falls.
Cardiac glycosides	Digoxin	Increased risk of toxicity.
NSAIDs	Ibuprofen, naproxen, aspirin	Increased bleeding risk. Increased risk of kidney damage.

Pregnant Patients

Teratogenicity is the ability of a drug to be toxic to a fetus/embryo and lead to birth defects. Teratogenicity is an adverse effect of some medications that are contraindicated in pregnancy.

The following types of medications can be teratogenic: isotretinoin, thalidomide and its derivatives, ACE inhibitors, anticoagulants (e.g., warfarin), estrogens, androgens (e.g., testosterone), antiepileptics drugs (e.g., carbamazepine, phenytoin, phenobarbital, sodium valproate), medications used to treat hyperthyroidism (e.g., methimazole, carbimazole, radioactive iodine), lithium, NSAIDs, tetracycline antibiotics, sulfa antibiotics (e.g., Bactrim), ciprofloxacin, anticancer agents (e.g., cyclophosphamide, methotrexate), some oral antidiabetic drugs, vitamin A supplements, and alcohol.

Isotretinoin (Accutane) and thalidomide derivatives (Thalomid) have particularly profound birth defects when used during pregnancy. Because of their teratogenicity, these drugs are required by the FDA to participate in a Risk Evaluation and Mitigation Strategy (REMS) program. These REMS programs require documentation of at least two contraceptive methods and monthly pregnancy testing for women of childbearing potential.

Indications of Common Medications

An indication is a condition, disease state, or reason for using a medication, device, or medical treatment. The chart below denotes some of the common medications or medical treatments and their indications or reasons for use.

Treatment	Indication
Antihypertensive medications	Hypertension (high blood pressure)
Antidepressant medications	Clinical depression
Thyroidectomy (surgical removal of the thyroid gland)	Hyperthyroidism, thyroid cancer
Antacids	Heartburn (gastroesophageal reflux)
Antiemetic medications	Nausea/vomiting
Vasodilators/nitrate drugs	Angina (chest pain)
Anticoagulant medications	Blood clot, stroke, heart attack, prevention of blood clots following surgery
Diuretic medications	Edema (fluid buildup), hypertension
Inhaled corticosteroids	Asthma, COPD
Pseudoephedrine	Nasal/sinus congestion
Ibuprofen (Motrin)	Headache, joint pain, inflammation, swelling
Doxylamine (Unisom)	Insomnia (difficulty sleeping)
Anticonvulsant medications	Epilepsy/seizure disorders
Antipsychotic drugs	Psychosis, schizophrenia, bipolar disorder
Antibiotics	Bacterial infection
Insulin	Diabetes mellitus
Metformin	Diabetes mellitus
DMARDs	Rheumatoid arthritis
Bisphosphonates (e.g., alendronate)	Osteoporosis, fragile bones
Chemotherapy treatments	Cancer/malignancy
Dopamine agonists	Parkinson's Disease

Drug Stability

Drug stability is the ability of a drug to maintain its original physical and chemical properties. When a drug begins to degrade or change its properties and become unstable, it is adulterated and can no longer be used.

Changes in pH, exposure to light, and high temperatures are common culprits in drug instability. This is why some drugs must be stored in a refrigerator or in dark-colored packaging to prevent light exposure. The material that a drug is packaged in can also react with a medication and cause it to become unstable. If removing a drug from its original packaging, the drug must be compatible with the new packaging. This is particularly relevant when compounding or preparing IV medications because some medications cannot be packaged in polyvinyl chloride (PVC) IV bags. Additionally, some medications must be diluted prior to use (e.g., IV solutions, vaccines, antibiotic suspensions). Only diluents approved by the manufacturer should be used to prevent instability issues. Combining medications can also lead to instability, so it is best for nurses to check with a pharmacist before administering multiple medications in the same infusion.

Drug Instability

For tablets and capsules, signs of instability include discoloration (e.g., yellowing of white tablets) and changes in hardness. Ointments, creams, and gels also become discolored, but they can also go through changes in consistency (e.g., dryness, grittiness) and uniformity (liquid separates from solid). Liquid dosage forms can become discolored, acquire a foul odor, and undergo gas buildup (pressure upon opening the container). Unstable liquid dosage forms may also form precipitates (solid particles) and undergo phase separation. Phase separation occurs when the solid particles or oil droplets in a liquid mixture separate from the aqueous (watery) parts of a liquid, similar to expired milk becoming chunky. Emulsions and suspensions are particularly prone to phase separation because they contain solids or oils suspended in a watery liquid. Caking, creaming, and difficulty resuspending are signs of phase separation. Powder formulations (e.g., amoxicillin suspension) that are unstable can become discolored or smelly, and they can begin to cake or clump together.

Measurements

Common Conversions

Conversion factors are used to change from one unit of measure to another. For instance, if a drug is prescribed in milliliters and the patient wants to know their dose in teaspoons, you will have to use a conversion factor.

Conversion Factors	
1 kg	2.2 lb
1 tsp	5 mL
1 tbsp	3 tsp (15 mL)
1 fl oz	29.57 mL (often rounded to 30 mL)
1 cup	8 oz
1 L	33.8 oz
1 gr	64.8 mg

A gram (g) is the basic metric unit of mass or weight. All other metric units of mass are centered around the gram. Metric units of measure can be easily converted from one form to another by moving the decimal place. A kilogram (kg) is 10^3 or 1000 times larger than a gram. Therefore, to convert grams to kilograms, the decimal place must be moved to the left three places. Milligrams (mg) and micrograms (mcg) are smaller than a gram. A milligram is 10^{-3} or 1000 times smaller than a gram, whereas a microgram is 10^{-6} or 1,000,000 times smaller than a gram. To convert grams to milligrams, the decimal place must be moved to the right three places. To convert grams to micrograms, the decimal place must be moved to the right six places.

Unit of Measure	Kilogram	Gram	Milligram	Microgram
Conversion factor	10^3	1	10^{-3}	10^{-6}
Sample conversion	0.008	8	8000	8,000,000

Review Video: Measurement Conversions
Visit mometrix.com/academy and enter code: 316703

Fractions

In order to **add or subtract fractions**, you must first convert the fractions to an equivalent fraction so that both fractions have the same denominator (the number on the bottom of the fraction). An easy way of doing this is to multiply the two denominators together and multiply the numerators (the top number of the fraction) by the original denominator of the opposite fraction (cross-multiplication):

$$\frac{1}{4}+\frac{1}{6}=$$

Cross-multiply the numerators by the opposite denominator, and multiply the denominators to get a common denominator:

$$\frac{6}{24}+\frac{4}{24}=$$

Once the fractions are converted to have the same common denominator, the numerators (the numbers on the top of the fraction) can simply be added:

$$\frac{6}{24}+\frac{4}{24}=\frac{10}{24}$$

Reduce the fraction by converting it to its smallest possible form. Divide each part of the final fraction by a common whole number until the numbers cannot be divided any further:

$$\frac{10}{24}\div\frac{2}{2}=\frac{5}{12}$$

Review Video: Adding and Subtracting Fractions
Visit mometrix.com/academy and enter code: 378080

In order to **multiply fractions**, simply multiply the numerators (top numbers) and denominators (bottom numbers) separately. Then, reduce the final fraction to the smallest possible form by dividing the numerator and denominator by a common whole number until the numbers cannot be divided further.

Example:

$$\frac{1}{4}\times\frac{6}{8}=\frac{6}{32}$$

Reduce the fraction:

$$\frac{6}{32}\div\frac{2}{2}=\frac{3}{16}$$

In order to **divide fractions**, use the same process as multiplying fractions except flip the second fraction upside down. The mathematical term for a fraction that is flipped upside down is called the reciprocal. Then, reduce the fraction to its smallest possible form.

Example:

$$\frac{1}{4}\div\frac{6}{8}=$$

Flip the second fraction:

$$\frac{1}{4}\times\frac{8}{6}=\frac{8}{24}$$

Reduce the fraction:

$$\frac{8}{24}\div\frac{8}{8}=\frac{1}{3}$$

Review Video: Multiplying and Dividing Fractions
Visit mometrix.com/academy and enter code: 473632

Calculating Flow Rates

Flow rates can be expressed in mL/hour or mL/min depending upon what type of pump is being used to administer the IV:

$$\textbf{Flow rate} = \frac{\text{mL of IV solution}}{\text{hours or minutes}}$$

Sample problem: *An IV antibiotic was prescribed for a patient to be administered at a rate of 25 mL/hour. What volume (in mL) of IV solution would be needed to last 8 hours? What is the drip rate if the IV is running through at a rate of 10 gtts/mL?*

In this problem, the IV flow rate is given, and it is asking how many mL of solution are needed to run over an 8-hour time frame. In order to figure this out, the flow rate must be multiplied by the time period:

> Flow rate (mL/hour) × hours = total mL administered.
> 25 mL/hour × 8 hours = **200 mL** administered over 8 hours.

The drip rate is the number of drops of IV solution that are administered per minute.

$$\textbf{Drip rate} = \frac{\text{gtts of IV solution}}{\text{minute}}$$

In order to calculate the drip rate from the flow rate, the mL of solution must be converted into drops (gtts). A conversion factor will be given for this. In this problem, the rate is 10 gtts/mL. If the flow rate is given in hours, then the time must be converted into minutes to calculate the drip rate.

$$\text{Drip rate} = \frac{25\text{ mL}}{1\text{ hour}} \times \frac{10\text{ gtts}}{1\text{ mL}} \times \frac{1\text{ hour}}{60\text{ min}} = \frac{250\text{ gtts}}{60\text{ min}} = 4.2\frac{\text{gtts}}{\text{min}}$$

Review Video: Calculating IV Drip Rates
Visit mometrix.com/academy and enter code: 396112

Calculating Medication Doses

How many grams of glucose are there in a 500 mL bag of glucose 5% solution? How many grams are contained in a 500 mL bag of glucose 0.5% solution?

A concentration is the amount of substance in a volume of solution. Concentrations can be expressed as weight to volume (g/100 mL), volume to volume (mL/100 mL) or weight to weight (g/100 g).

A percentage is the quantity of substance in 100. Because concentrations are also expressed as an amount per 100, no conversion or decimal place movement is required to convert the percentage into a concentration. To solve this problem, multiply the concentration of the solution by the volume of the bag to find the total amount of glucose contained within the bag:

$$\text{Glucose 5\%} = \frac{5\text{ g}}{100\text{ mL}} \times \frac{500\text{ mL}}{\text{bag}} = \frac{(5 \times 500)}{100} = 25\text{ g}$$

$$\text{Glucose 0.5\%} = \frac{0.5\text{ g}}{100\text{ mL}} \times \frac{500\text{ mL}}{\text{bag}} = \frac{(0.5 \times 500)}{100} = 2.5\text{ g}$$

Ensure that these answers are reasonable and make sense. If there is 5% glucose in a solution (5 g/100 mL), then a 500 mL bag will have five times as much as a 100 mL bag. Because 5 × 5 = 25, our answer of 25 g makes sense. For the 0.5% solution, move the decimal place to the left one place to find the answer in comparison to the answer for a 5% solution. Therefore, 2.5 g is a reasonable answer.

Practice Test #1

Want to take this practice test in an online interactive format?
Check out the online resources page, which includes interactive practice questions and much more: **mometrix.com/resources719/mace**

1. Where should syringes and glass vials be disposed?

a. Trash can
b. Sharps container
c. Biohazard container
d. Autoclave bag

2. Which of the following is a beta-blocker used to treat hypertension?

a. Norvasc
b. Enalapril
c. Lopressor
d. Cardura

3. Which of the following drugs is NOT a narrow-therapeutic-index (NTI) drug?

a. Theophylline
b. Phenytoin
c. Digoxin
d. Phenelzine

4. What is the dose of gentamicin 2 mg/kg for a patient weighing 175 lb?

a. 120 mg
b. 160 mg
c. 180 mg
d. 200 mg

5. Januvia is indicated for the treatment of which of the following?

a. High cholesterol
b. Dementia
c. High blood pressure
d. Diabetes mellitus

6. What is one technique a medication aide can use to help a patient with aphasia?

a. Providing a time limit for the patient to respond
b. Speaking for the patient
c. Using a picture or letter board
d. Giving the patient a pen

7. What is the dosage form for nitroglycerin (Nitrostat)?

a. Intravenous (IV)
b. Extended-release capsule
c. Sublingual tablet
d. Oral suspension

8. What condition is required for a medication aide to carry out a delegated task?

a. If the task is within the aide's range of functions
b. If a nurse has delegated the task
c. If the task has been done by other medication aides
d. If the medication aide is familiar with the task

9. Which agency is responsible for ensuring that drugs are safe and effective?

a. Food and Drug Administration (FDA)
b. Drug Enforcement Agency (DEA)
c. Bureau of Alcohol, Tobacco, and Firearms (ATF)
d. National Institutes of Health (NIH)

10. A patient with hypothyroidism states that she takes Synthroid 0.112 mg daily, but the pharmacy has issued the drug labeled in micrograms. How many micrograms of Synthroid is equivalent to 0.112 mg?

a. 1.12 mcg
b. 11.2 mcg
c. 112 mcg
d. 1120 mcg

11. Which of the following is classified as a schedule IV controlled substance?

a. Phenergan with codeine (Phenergan)
b. Testosterone (Depo-Testosterone)
c. Pentobarbital (Nembutal)
d. Tramadol (Qdolo)

12. Which of the following prescription inscriptions has a higher probability of resulting in a medication error?

a. Synthroid 25 mcg
b. Lipitor 20 mg
c. Latanoprost 0.005%
d. Humalog 14 U @ HS

13. A medication aide has been assigned to care for a ventilated patient, which she has never done before. How should she handle the situation?

a. Notify the nurse manager that she is not sure how to care for the patient, and request additional instructions or training materials
b. Do the best she can while caring for the patient
c. Speak with the other medication aides to find out what additional care is needed for the patient
d. Request to switch patients with another medication aide

14. Which of the following antihypertensive drugs is a beta-blocker?

a. Verapamil
b. Bisoprolol
c. Losartan
d. Ramipril

15. Which of the following medications belongs to the same drug class as pantoprazole (Protonix)?

a. Esomeprazole (Nexium)
b. Cimetidine (Tagamet)
c. Famotidine (Pepcid)
d. Nizatidine (Axid)

16. All of the following medications must be stored in a refrigerator EXCEPT:

a. NovoLog
b. EpiPen
c. NuvaRing
d. Pneumovax 23

17. What classification of antibiotic do dicloxacillin, amoxicillin, ampicillin, and piperacillin belong to?

a. Bacteriostatic
b. Penicillins
c. Cephalosporins
d. Quinolones

18. How do diuretics work for treatment of hypertension?

a. Decreasing fluid volume in the blood
b. Blocking alpha stimulation
c. Dilating arterioles
d. Blocking arterial vasoconstriction

19. Which electronic communication to a friend is acceptable under the Health Insurance Portability and Accountability Act of 1996 for a medication aide working in home health care?

a. "Can you pick me up at my last patient's home at 2600 Roc Avenue?"
b. "Look at this picture of my patient and me!"
c. "My patient, Sally Brown, is my age."
d. "My last patient of the day lives near Pizza Palace, so I'll meet you there."

20. A medication aide has to ask a sensitive question to a patient who doesn't speak English. How should she ask the question?

a. Using the patient's family to translate
b. Calling the hospital's official translation service
c. Gesturing to the patient in the hope she will understand
d. Looking up relevant words on the internet before speaking with the patient

21. When a medication aide prioritizes doing good for her patient through compassion, advocacy, and empathy, what ethical principle is she displaying?

a. Nonmaleficence
b. Beneficence
c. Veracity
d. Confidentiality

22. A patient is prescribed Xalatan 0.005% ophthalmic solution. The order for the medication is to administer 1 gtt ou nightly. How many days will a 2.5 mL bottle last the patient? (Conversion factor: 20 drops/mL)

a. 50 days
b. 28 days
c. 25 days
d. 18 days

23. Which of the following statements about drug classifications is NOT true?

a. Amiodarone is an antiarrhythmic
b. Clopidogrel is an antiplatelet
c. Pioglitazone is an antibiotic
d. Duloxetine is an antidepressant

24. Tetracycline capsules should be taken on an empty stomach, at least 1 hour before or 2 hours after food. This is because certain foods, particularly dairy products, reduce its absorption. This is an example of a:

a. Drug-drug interaction
b. Drug-disease interaction
c. Drug-food interaction
d. Drug-laboratory interaction

25. What does it mean when a tablet is scored?

a. It is dissolvable in oil
b. It can be broken in half
c. It must be taken with food
d. It can be crushed

26. Which of the following medications is given orally to treat diabetes mellitus by lowering blood glucose levels?

a. Insulin glargine
b. Metformin
c. Exenatide
d. Glucagon

27. Which of the following is an antiviral drug used to treat HIV?

a. Tenofovir
b. Acyclovir
c. Ciprofloxacin
d. Vancomycin

28. Which of the following methods can be used to prevent needlestick injuries?

a. Use of retractable needle syringes
b. Recapping the needle after use
c. Removing needles from syringes after use
d. Disposing of needles in the hazardous waste bin

29. Which of the following products is NOT under strict FDA regulations?

a. Prescription medications
b. OTC medications
c. Dietary supplements
d. Medical devices

30. What is the most appropriate way to read the meniscus when measuring liquids?

a. Tap the volumetric vessel gently to try to flatten the meniscus before reading the measurement.
b. Use a medicine dropper to fill in the curve of the meniscus once the appropriate level is attained.
c. View the meniscus at eye level, and read the level that corresponds to the bottom of the meniscus.
d. View the meniscus at eye level, and read the level that corresponds to the top of the meniscus.

31. A patient's family asks how he is doing after his scheduled MRI. How should the medication aide respond?

a. He had an MRI today?
b. His MRI results are back. Everything is normal.
c. He seems to be in good spirits. Let me see if he's ready to visit with you and I'll find his nurse to talk to you about the results.
d. Good. He should be ready to go home soon.

32. Which of the following scenarios would be best described as a near-miss error?

a. Ampicillin was ordered for a patient allergic to penicillin. However, the pharmacist was alerted to the allergy during the computer order entry process, and the physician was called to review other treatment options.
b. A patient discovers that they were provided Seroquel 200 mg tablets instead of 300 mg tablets prior to taking a dose.
c. A medication aide administers potassium chloride 20 mEq instead of cefazolin 2 g due to the stark similarities between the two vials, resulting in a sentinel event.
d. The medication aide administers 10 mL from a Novolog vial instead of 10 mL from a Novolin vial, causing a patient to experience an adverse event.

33. Orally disintegrating/dissolving tablet dosage forms should be:

a. Placed on the gums under the upper lip or under the cheek and allowed to disintegrate/dissolve
b. Placed under the tongue and allowed to disintegrate/dissolve
c. Placed on the tongue and allowed to disintegrate/dissolve
d. Swished around in the mouth, then spit out after 30 seconds

34. A medication aide is stocking shelves outside a patient's room when the call bell rings. The medication aide is not responsible for the patient's care that day. How should the medication aide respond?

a. Ignoring the call bell until the patient's assigned aide responds
b. Getting the assigned aide to check on the patient
c. Checking on the patient right away to see what she needs
d. Checking on the patient after stocking the shelves

35. Which of the following foods would affect the way warfarin (Coumadin) might work in the body?

a. Kale
b. Eggplant
c. Bananas
d. Cucumbers

36. The physician had prescribed 10 mL of oral suspension twice daily for a child, but the mother is confused about the metric system and wants to know how many teaspoons of medication to give the child. How many teaspoons are equivalent to 10 mL of oral suspension?

a. 1 tsp
b. 2 tsp
c. 3 tsp
d. 5 tsp

37. A client is prescribed 0.25 mg terbutaline subcutaneously, but the medication is provided as 1 mg/mL. How much medication is needed to provide the correct dosage?

a. 0.25 mL
b. 0.5 mL
c. 2.5 mL
d. 1 mL

38. Hydromorphone is a controlled substance belonging to which schedule?

a. II
b. III
c. IV
d. V

39. All of the following are common side effects of antibiotics EXCEPT:

a. Allergic reaction
b. Skin rash
c. Constipation
d. Diarrhea

40. Which of the following drugs is considered a narrow therapeutic index (NTI) medication?

a. Metformin
b. Lithium
c. Eszopiclone
d. Dextromethorphan

41. Which organization provides guidelines and resources on medication safety, including a list of high-alert medications for different care facilities?

a. FDA
b. DEA
c. TJC
d. ISMP

42. If a patient refuses a treatment and the medication aide attempts to perform it anyway, what could the medication aide be charged with?

a. Assault
b. Battery
c. Either A or B
d. Neither A nor B

43. Which of the following is NOT an example of a medication that should not be crushed, split, or opened?

a. Remeron
b. Cardizem CD
c. Theo-24
d. Ambien CR

44. HIPAA guarantees a patient's right to which of the following?

a. Confidentiality
b. Informed consent
c. See their chart
d. Continuity of care

45. Based on your knowledge of common drug suffixes, which of the following medications would you expect to be a monoclonal antibody?

a. Apixaban
b. Tenofovir
c. Omalizumab
d. Dapagliflozin

46. Which of the following would be an example of a drug-disease interaction?

a. A patient who takes warfarin and aspirin is at an increased risk for bleeding.
b. Beta-blockers can cause airway constriction, so they are contraindicated in patients who have asthma or chronic obstructive pulmonary disease.
c. Patients who take simvastatin should not drink grapefruit juice because it can increase their risk of side effects.
d. A patient taking rifampicin has orange-colored urine.

47. Which of the following is considered a high-alert medication?

a. Methotrexate
b. Esomeprazole
c. Polyethylene glycol
d. Docusate

48. Which of the following drugs is classified as a diuretic?

a. Isosorbide mononitrate
b. Lisinopril
c. Thalitone
d. Amaryl

49. To whom should you report as a medication aide?

a. A licensed physician
b. The registered nurse or licensed practical nurse on your service
c. The administrative desk person at the facility
d. The professional assigning a particular task, which may be an RN, LPN, physical therapist, dietitian, etc.

50. What is the name of the agency that publishes a list of commonly confused look-alike, sound-alike drug names?

a. Centers for Medicare and Medicaid Services
b. Drug Enforcement Agency
c. Institute for Safe Medication Practices
d. Department of Health and Human Services

51. For which of the following adverse reactions events is it MOST important for a facility to report to the FDA's MedWatch program?

a. A patient experiences a rash after taking oral penicillin.
b. A patient fails to rinse their mouth after using their inhaler, resulting in oral thrush.
c. A patient taking ticagrelor (Brilinta) has a severe epidural hemorrhage that causes him to be hospitalized.
d. A patient on a daily aspirin regimen receives a mild bruise after hitting their hand on a corner of their desk.

52. Which of the following insulin products is long-acting and usually given once a day in the evening?

a. Insulin detemir
b. Insulin aspart
c. Insulin NPH
d. Insulin glulisine

53. A physician writes a prescription for a medication to be taken Q.I.D. How many times per day should the patient be administered this medication?

a. Once
b. Twice
c. Three times
d. Four times

54. What does the prefix *hypo-* mean?

a. Under
b. Above
c. Before
d. Both

55. Which of the following is an antidepressant that can also be used to treat neuropathic pain?

a. Lyrica
b. Amitriptyline
c. Meloxicam
d. Fluoxetine

56. Which of the following medications is used to treat hyperlipidemia (high cholesterol)?

a. Amlodipine
b. Enoxaparin
c. Zocor
d. Losartan

57. All of the following medications are indicated for epilepsy EXCEPT:

a. Keppra
b. Risperdal
c. Dilantin
d. Depakote

58. What type of information can a medication aide communicate to family members?

a. Lab results
b. The patient's prognosis
c. Information about procedures within his or her own scope of practice
d. Information about the overall care of the patient

59. If a medication aide begins to suspect that a patient is being abused by a family member, what should she do?

a. Report it to the charge nurse
b. Report it to the police
c. Ignore it because the nurse and doctor probably suspect it too
d. Confront the suspected abuser

60. Which of the following drugs has a potential to cause hypoglycemia?

a. Glipizide
b. Fluticasone
c. Simvastatin
d. Synthroid

Answer Key and Explanations for Test #1

1. B: The FDA recommends that used needles and other sharp waste be immediately placed in FDA-cleared sharps disposal containers. These containers must be rigid, leak resistant, impervious to moisture, puncture resistant, and safe to handle. Anything capable of cutting or penetrating skin or packaging material, such as needles, glass vials, microscope slides, and scalpels, should be disposed of in a sharps container. Autoclave bags are clear or orange polyethylene plastic bags used in an autoclave to decontaminate biological waste and sterilize medical instruments. Biohazard containers are used only for non-sharp biohazardous wastes (anything containing blood and other bodily fluids).

2. C: Knowing the common naming systems for different classifications of drugs will help you with these types of questions. Make sure you also know both the brand and generic names of the top 200 drugs listed on the PTCB website. Amlodipine (Norvasc) is a calcium channel blocker, of which most end with *-pine*. ACE inhibitors, including enalapril (Vasotec), end in *-pril*. Beta-blockers like metoprolol (Lopressor) end with the suffix *-olol*. Doxazosin (Cardura) is an alpha-1 blocker, most of which end in *-zosin*.

3. D: Although the list of narrow-therapeutic-index (NTI) drugs slightly varies between states as set forth by their boards of pharmacy, theophylline, phenytoin, and digoxin are all federally recognized NTI drugs. In addition to these, carbamazepine, levothyroxine, lithium, and warfarin are also on this list. Phenelzine (Nardil) is a monoamine oxidase inhibitor antidepressant.

4. B: First, one must convert pounds to kilograms. Divide 175 lb by 2.2 lb/kg to get 79.5 kg. Multiply the weight in kilograms by the dosage of 2 mg/kg for an answer of 160 mg.

5. D: Sitagliptin (Januvia) is a commonly prescribed antidiabetic drug. Other antidiabetic drugs on the top 200 drugs list include: metformin (Glumetza), glipizide (Glucotrol), glyburide (DiaBeta), canagliflozin (Invokana), and liraglutide (Victoza).

6. C: Aphasia is an acquired inability to understand language and express oneself through speech. Patients with aphasia have different levels of ability, and should be approached with patience. Setting a time limit and speaking for the patient are not productive or helpful in terms of helping the patient relearn these skills. A pen and paper may be helpful in some situations, but many patients aren't able to read or write as a result of their aphasia. A picture or letter board is a universal method of communication, and offers an easy way to communicate because it is so simple to use.

7. C: Nitroglycerin (Nitrostat) is a vasodilator indicated for the acute relief of an attack or acute prophylaxis of angina due to coronary artery disease. Nitrostat is supplied as white, round, flat-faced sublingual tablets in three strengths (0.3, 0.4, and 0.6 mg). Nitroglycerin can evaporate from tablets if strict precautions are not taken. Nitroglycerin should be kept in its original glass container and must be tightly capped after each use to prevent loss of tablet potency. Heat, moisture, and light will damage the tablets and result in the loss of tablet potency. Nitrostat should be dissolved under the tongue (sublingually) or in the buccal pouch (between the gums and cheek) at the first sign of an acute angina attack. The dose may be repeated approximately every 5 minutes until relief is obtained. If the pain persists after a total of three tablets in a 15-minute period, or if the pain is different than is typically experienced, the patient should seek prompt medical attention. Furthermore, Nitrostat may be used prophylactically 5–10 minutes prior to engaging in activities that might precipitate an acute attack. Administer Nitrostat at rest, preferably in the sitting position.

8. A: The medication aide may carry out a delegated task if it is within the aide's range of functions, and this range may vary somewhat from one state and one facility to another, so it's important that the medication aide understand the types of tasks that can be delegated to the aide. Even if a nurse delegates a task that the medication aide knows how to do, such as cutting toenails, the aide can only do it if it is a permitted task.

9. A: The Food and Drug Administration (FDA) is responsible for ensuring that drugs are safe, pure, and effective. The Drug Enforcement Agency (DEA) is responsible for enforcing the Controlled Substances Act. The Bureau of Alcohol, Tobacco, and Firearms (ATF) oversees the use and taxing of alcohol in institutions. The National Institutes of Health (NIH) is the national medical research agency and is part of the US Department of Health and Human Services. The NIH does not have any direct responsibilities to the management of drugs.

10. C: 112 micrograms: One milligram contains 1,000 micrograms, and 1 gram contains one million micrograms. Although the symbol µg is used to represent micrograms, the Food and Drug Administration (FDA) and the Institute for Safe Medication Practices (ISMP) recommend against using this symbol because it may easily be confused with the abbreviation for milligrams (mg). The abbreviation mcg is sometimes used.

Calculation: 0.112 mg × 1,000 = 112 micrograms.

11. D: Most drugs in the schedule IV classification are benzodiazepines: alprazolam (Xanax), chlordiazepoxide, clobazam, clonazepam (Klonopin), diazepam (Valium), flurazepam, loprazolam, lorazepam (Ativan), nitrazepam, oxazepam, temazepam, and triazolam. Z drugs used to treat insomnia are similar to benzodiazepines and are also schedule IV substances: zaleplon, zolpidem (Ambien), zopiclone (Imovane), and eszopiclone (Lunesta). Central nervous system stimulants used to aid in weight loss are schedule IV substances: phentermine (Adipex-P), diethylpropion, and mazindol. Modafinil (Provigil), a stimulant used to treat sleep disorders, is also a schedule IV substance. Some muscle relaxers are schedule IV controlled substances, including dextropropoxyphene and carisoprodol (Soma). The opioid pain medication tramadol (Qdolo) is also a schedule IV substance. The central nervous system depressant phenobarbital, which is used to treat seizure disorders, is also a schedule IV medication.

Phenergan with codeine (Phenergan) is a schedule V drug, and testosterone is a schedule III drug. Pentobarbital is similar in nature to phenobarbital, but it is more potent and is classified as a schedule II controlled substance.

12. D: The Joint Commission (TJC) is an organization responsible for accrediting and certifying more than 22,000 healthcare organizations and programs, including hospitals, ambulatory care clinics, office-based surgery suites, behavioral health facilities, laboratories, and long-term care centers. Any healthcare facility or program accredited by TJC must include a copy of TJC's "Do Not Use" list in their formulary. The purpose of this list is to reduce the risk of medication errors, especially with high-alert medications. Some items on the "Do Not Use" list include U (unit), IU (international unit), QD or QOD, trailing or leading zeros, MS, MSO_4, and $MgSO_4$.

13. A: The medication aide should never take on a patient or task that she does not feel sufficiently trained to handle or comfortable with. She should immediately speak privately with the nurse manager to request additional instructions or training. The medication aide should never "just do the best she can" because of the potential for serious complications. Colleagues may be an additional source of information, but the nurse manager should be immediately made aware of the situation, and should be the primary point of contact for the medication aide.

14. B: Beta-blockers end with the suffix *-olol*. They are commonly prescribed to treat high blood pressure, arrhythmias, and heart failure. Verapamil is a calcium channel blocker, losartan is an angiotensin receptor blocker, and ramipril is an angiotensin-converting enzyme inhibitor.

15. A: Pantoprazole (Protonix) belongs to the proton pump inhibitor (PPI) drug class. Although all of the drugs listed are used to treat gastroesophageal reflux disease, only esomeprazole (Nexium) is a PPI. Other drugs in the PPI category include omeprazole (Prilosec), lansoprazole (Prevacid), dexlansoprazole (Dexilant), and rabeprazole (Aciphex). Cimetidine (Tagamet), famotidine (Pepcid), and nizatidine (Axid) are histamine-2 receptor antagonists.

16. B: NovoLog is a type of insulin. All insulin products must be stored in a refrigerator. NuvaRing is a contraceptive formulated as a vaginal ring. It must be stored in a refrigerator. Pneumovax 23 is a pneumococcal vaccine. Most vaccines must be stored in a refrigerator. EpiPen is an injection used to treat severe, emergent allergic reactions that involve anaphylaxis. EpiPens should be stored at room temperature. The injection is sensitive to and should not be exposed to cold temperatures or heat.

17. B: Dicloxacillin, amoxicillin, ampicillin, and piperacillin are all generic forms of penicillin. The purpose of this type of drug is to inhibit bacteria from forming a cell wall. Penicillin-type drugs are commonly used to treat bacterial infections such as ear infections, respiratory infections, pneumonia, and abscesses. Common side effects that may be seen with penicillin-type products include diarrhea, rashes on the skin, and hives. Certain severe reactions may involve anaphylaxis. Penicillin is available in capsule and tablet forms as well as oral suspension and IV. It is important to note penicillin allergy information for patients to prevent an allergic reaction. The use of penicillin can make oral contraceptives less effective.

18. A: All of the choices describe actions that result in reduced blood pressure. Diuretics (e.g., furosemide and hydrochlorothiazide) decrease total peripheral resistance by reducing the amount of fluid volume in the blood. They enhance the excretion of water in the urine to reduce fluid volume in the blood. Alpha-blockers (e.g., doxazosin and prazosin) block alpha stimulation and cause vasodilation. Calcium channel blockers (e.g., amlodipine and diltiazem) dilate arterioles. Angiotensin-II receptor blockers (e.g., valsartan and losartan) block arterial vasoconstriction.

19. D: The electronic communication to a friend that is acceptable under the Health Insurance Portability and Accountability Act of 1996 for a medication aide working in home health care is "My last patient of the day lives near Pizza Palace, so I'll meet you there." The medication aide should not divulge any personally identifying information about a patient, such as the patient's name or address and should never take or post personal pictures of a patient on social media. In most cases, the medication aide should avoid any postings that refer to work or patients, even without identifying information.

20. B: When a sensitive topic is involved, the medication aide should utilize the hospital's translation system. This can help the patient feel more comfortable and answer the question more appropriately and accurately. Family members are a good source of assistance for routine tasks and matters that don't involve sensitive topics. Gesturing to the patient in the hope she will understand the question is not a great technique because it can easily lead to misunderstanding.

Looking up words on the internet can be helpful, but will not guarantee that either the patient or the medication aide will understand what the other is trying to say.

21. B: These are all ethical principles, which are standards of correct moral conduct. Beneficence (B) is the correct term for doing good for others. Nonmaleficence (A) refers to the ethical principle of providing care that does not cause harm. Veracity (C) means speaking truthfully at all times. Confidentiality (D) is the code of maintaining the privacy of the patient's information.

22. C: 1 gtt ou nightly means that the patient is to administer 1 drop into each eye every night. Therefore, the patient will be using 2 drops daily. There are 2.5 mL in each bottle. Multiply 2.5 mL by the conversion factor of 20 drops/mL to find out how many total drops are in the stock bottle. 2.5 mL × 20 drops/mL = 50 drops. Divide the total number of drops in the stock bottle (50 drops) by the number of drops that the patient is using daily (2 drops) to get the days' supply. Therefore, the correct answer is 25 days.

General formula to calculate days' supply:

Total # of units prescribed ÷ # of units per dose ÷ # of doses per day

23. C: Amiodarone is used for heart arrhythmias. Clopidogrel is used to help reduce the risk of heart attack and stroke by inhibiting the ability of platelets from forming clots. Duloxetine is used to treat depression and anxiety. Pioglitazone is an oral agent used to treat diabetes.

24. C: Drug-food interactions occur when the effects of a drug are changed when taken in combination with a particular food. Another example is how grapefruit juice decreases the ability of statin drugs to be metabolized (broken down). If the patient was taking a calcium supplement that reduced the absorption of tetracycline, then this would have been a drug-dietary supplement interaction. If the question said that tetracycline affected the way that calcium is absorbed or used in the body, resulting in reduced blood calcium levels, then this would have been a drug-nutrient interaction. This is not a true statement; it is merely being used as an example.

25. B: A scored tablet is one that can be split in half or quarters due to a demarcating line allowing for the split.

26. B: Metformin (Glumetza, Riomet) is a first-line treatment for diabetes mellitus type 2. Insulin glargine (Lantus) is a long-acting insulin. It cannot be administered orally and must be injected. Exenatide (Byetta) is a newer antidiabetic medication called an incretin mimetic. It cannot be administered orally and must be injected. Glucagon (GlucaGen) is an injectable medication used to increase blood glucose levels during a hypoglycemic emergency. A hypoglycemic emergency occurs when a patient's blood sugar falls too low due to a high dose of insulin or antidiabetic medications.

27. A: Most antiviral drugs end with "-vir". Examples of HIV antiretroviral drugs includes tenofovir, dolutegravir, abavacir, elvitegravir, darunavir, sofosbuvir, and ritonavir. However, there are a few HIV antiviral drugs that do not following the "-vir" naming rule. These include emtricitabine and lamivudine. Antiviral drugs used to treat herpes infections include acyclovir and valacyclovir. Oseltamivir (Tamiflu) is an antiviral drug used to treat influenza. Ciprofloxacin and vancomycin are antibiotics used to treat bacterial infections.

28. A: Use of needleless or retractable-needle devices is one of the best ways to prevent needlestick injuries. Once a needle is used, it should be placed in a sharps disposal container immediately. Sharps bins are usually plastic containers that have a one-way opening for the disposal of sharps and prevent the removal of objects from the container. Sharps bins should not be more than three-fourths of the way full or go above the fill line indicated on the container. Needles should not be recapped because the recapping process increases the risk of a needlestick injury. Additionally, capped needles may be mistaken for new needles and be used again. One should not attempt to remove the needle at the end of a syringe because this increases the risk of a needlestick injury. Discard any used sharps along with whatever they are attached to without trying to remove them. Chemotherapy sharps and other hazardous substances should be disposed of in a separate sharps bin labeled as hazardous. They should not be placed in the regular hazardous waste bin. If a patient does not have a sharps container, he or she should dispose of his or her sharps in a hard, sealable container, such as a laundry detergent bottle.

29. C: Per the Dietary Supplement Health and Education Act of 1994 (DSHEA), the FDA regulates dietary supplements under a much looser set of regulations than those of drug products (both prescription and OTC) and medical devices. Dietary supplement manufacturers are not required to present any clinical studies or safety data prior to approval. In fact, dietary supplements do not require FDA approval prior to marketing. However, under the DSHEA, manufacturers are prohibited from marketing dietary supplements that are adulterated or misbranded. The FDA is responsible for taking action against any adulterated or misbranded dietary supplement product after it reaches the market.

30. C: A meniscus is the curved surface that results when liquid is poured into a column. The column might be a graduated cylinder or other type of volumetric vessel. The vessel should be at eye level, whether it is placed on a flat surface or brought up to eye level by holding it in the nondominant hand. As the liquid is poured into the container, a medicine dropper or pipette should be used to add drops to reach the final volume. The correct way to read the meniscus is to read the level at the bottom of the curve. It is important for the container to be at eye level, however, to get the correct reading. The size of the meniscus will vary based on the circumference of the vessel; for example, a tall, thin vessel will produce a larger meniscus than a vessel with a wider circumference.

31. C: Unless the family member has a legal document stating that they are the patient's guardian or holds power of attorney, the patient has a right to privacy. Further, the medication aide should not give results to any patient or family member. It's fine to say that the patient seems to be feeling well and offer to get the nurse to discuss details about the test.

32. A: A near-miss event is a medication error that took place but was discovered before reaching the patient, as seen in Choice A. These types of events or situations are considered "close calls" because they are still a medication error, but one that did not reach the patient. A sentinel event is a medication error that results in death or serious injury to a patient.

33. C: Orally disintegrating/dissolving tablets should be placed on the tongue and allowed to disintegrate or dissolve. Buccal tablets should be placed on the gums under the upper lip or under the cheek and allowed to disintegrate. Some OTC medications use a dissolving film or oral drug strip that can be placed on the tongue and allowed to dissolve. Lidocaine viscous solution is unique in that it is intended to be swished around in the mouth until the patient's pain has resolved, and then it should be spit out. Orally disintegrating/dissolving tablets, buccal tablets, and dissolving films are not intended to be swallowed like typical tablets and capsules are.

34. C: Because of the potential for a patient emergency, it is never appropriate for a medication aide to ignore a call bell. She should respond to the bell and see if she is able to assist the patient. Stocking the shelves is not a priority, especially when it comes to patient care. It may be necessary for the medication aide to get the assigned aide to help with patient care, but she should verify that nothing urgent is needed first.

35. A: Recall that warfarin (Coumadin) is an anticoagulant drug used to prevent blood clots. It does this by inhibiting the synthesis of vitamin K-dependent clotting factors. Increasing vitamin K levels through diet or supplementation can promote clotting and reduce the effectiveness of warfarin. Foods that are high in vitamin K are typically leafy green vegetables, such as kale, spinach, collard greens, turnip greens, mustard greens, broccoli, etc., but they can also include things such as asparagus, avocado, dill pickles, green tea, and margarine. Patients are suggested to limit their consumption of foods containing high amounts of vitamin K, or at least maintain the same level, while they are taking warfarin.

36. B: Milliliters are metric measurements, and teaspoons are household measurements. Five milliliters is approximately equivalent to one teaspoon, so the child will require two teaspoons for 10 mL of oral suspension. Oral suspensions are often prescribed in household measurements to reduce the chance of medication errors for those unfamiliar with the metric system.

37. A: 0.25 mL. Calculation:

$$\begin{aligned} 1\ (\text{mg})/1\ (\text{mL}) &= 0.25\ (\text{mg})/x\ (\text{mL}) \\ 1 \times x &= 1x \\ 1 \times 0.25 &= 0.25 \\ 1x &= 0.25 \\ x &= 0.25\ \text{mL} \end{aligned}$$

38. A: Hydromorphone (Dilaudid) is a schedule II controlled substance, meaning that it has a high potential for abuse and prescribers must adhere to stricter prescription and storage requirements. Opioids, attention-deficit/hyperactivity disorder stimulants, and barbiturates are classified as schedule II substances. Other commonly prescribed schedule II substances are codeine, dihydrocodeine, hydrocodone, morphine (MS Contin), oxycodone (Oxycontin, Percocet), oxymorphone, fentanyl, methadone, meperidine (Demerol), amphetamine (Adderall), methylphenidate (Ritalin, Concerta), and pentobarbital.

39. C: Constipation is not a common side effect of antibiotics. Allergic reactions are common with antibiotics, particularly penicillins, cephalosporins, and sulfa drugs. Allergic reactions can vary from very severe anaphylaxis to minor skin rashes. Diarrhea, gas, and abdominal cramping are also common with antibiotics because they can disrupt the normal flora bacteria that live in the gut.

40. B: The FDA defines narrow therapeutic index (NTI) drugs as those drugs in which small differences in the dose or blood concentration may lead to dose and blood concentration dependencies, serious therapeutic failures, or adverse drug reactions. Lithium carbonate is considered an NTI drug. It is used to treat bipolar disorder. Lithium blood levels must be closely monitored during the initiation of treatment (twice a week until the patient's status and blood levels are stable). Any deviation out of the narrow range of optimal therapy can result in either poor therapeutic efficacy (<0.5 mEq/L) or lithium toxicity (>1.5 mEq/L). Metformin (antidiabetic agent), eszopiclone (insomnia medication), and dextromethorphan (antitussive) do not require tight monitoring of drug levels.

41. D: The Institute for Safe Medication Practices (ISMP) is an organization dedicated to preventing medication errors and is considered the gold standard for medication safety information. Although the FDA provides some guidelines on medication safety, it usually entails labeling and packaging requirements. The DEA only provides enforcement and oversight on controlled substances. The Joint Commission (TJC) provides accreditation regulations and standards for healthcare organizations.

42. C: A medication aide could be charged with assault if she threatens or tries to touch a patient (provide care) without the patient's consent. It does not matter if she actually touches the patient or provides the treatment; the patient just needs to be afraid that she will do it. Battery refers to the actual act of touching the patient in a threatening manner or in a way that the patient has not consented to. In the situation outlined in the question, the medication aide could be charged with both assault and battery, depending on the specific circumstances surrounding the incident.

43. A: The ISMP has established a list of oral medications that should not be crushed, commonly known as the "Do Not Crush" list. Medications belonging to the list should not be crushed primarily because of their special formulations and characteristics, such as dosage forms that are slow release, extended release, and enteric coated.

44. A: HIPAA guarantees a patient's confidentiality and privacy. It also requires healthcare providers to provide patients with a list of policies that have been designed to protect their privacy. Only providers who are directly caring for someone should have access to their medical chart.

45. C: Monoclonal antibodies end in "-mab." They are biologic drugs that are designed to attack specific antigens within the body. Monoclonal antibodies are a relatively new class of medications. They tend to be more expensive than other drugs and are usually only available in injectable form.

46. B: Drug-disease interactions occur when a drug interacts with or interferes with an existing medical condition. Another example would be that pseudoephedrine increases blood pressure and is not recommended in patients who have hypertension (high blood pressure). If the scenario had discussed how beta-blockers, such as propranolol, reduce the effectiveness of albuterol, an inhaled medication used to treat asthma, then this would be a drug-drug interaction.

47. A: High-alert medications have the potential to cause significant harm if an error is made. These include:

- IV adrenergic agonists (e.g., epinephrine)
- IV adrenergic antagonists (e.g., propranolol)
- Anesthetics (e.g., propofol)
- IV antiarrhythmics (e.g., amiodarone)
- Antithrombotic agents (e.g., warfarin, alteplase, apixaban)
- Chemotherapy agents (e.g., methotrexate)
- Dextrose solutions ≥20% (hypertonic dextrose)
- Dialysis solutions
- Epidural administration of any medication
- Oral hypoglycemic agents (e.g., glyburide, glimepiride, metformin)
- IV inotropic agents (e.g., digoxin)
- Insulin
- Intrathecal administration of any medication
- Liposomal formulations (e.g., liposomal amphotericin B)
- Narcotics/opioids (e.g., oxycodone, hydrocodone, hydromorphone)
- Neuromuscular blocking agents (e.g., succinylcholine, rocuronium, vecuronium)
- IV nitroprusside sodium
- Parenteral nutrition
- IV potassium chloride or potassium phosphate
- IV radiocontrast agents
- Sedation agents (e.g., chloral hydrate, midazolam, dexmedetomidine)

- Sterile water for injection, inhalation, and irrigation in containers of ≥100 mL
- IV sodium chloride >0.9% (hypertonic saline)
- IV vasopressin

48. C: Diuretics help patients remove excess fluid from their body. They reduce the amount of water and/or sodium retained by the kidneys, thereby allowing water to be excreted in the urine. Diuretics are commonly used to treat high blood pressure (hypertension) and heart failure. The following diuretics are in the top 200 drugs list: hydrochlorothiazide, furosemide (Lasix), spironolactone (Aldactone), triamterene and hydrochlorothiazide, chlorthalidone (Thalitone). Isosorbide mononitrate is a vasodilator used to treat angina (chest pain). Lisinopril (Zestril) is an ACE inhibitor used to treat hypertension. Glimepiride (Amaryl) is an oral antidiabetic drug used to treat type 2 diabetes mellitus.

49. B: A medication aide is assigned duties by either a registered nurse (RN) or licensed practical nurse (LPN) under the RN, and the aide should generally report to the nurse. There may be situations when a licensed physician (A) is in charge, but usually an RN is employed to carry out the medical plan. It is inappropriate to report to administrators (C) or other professionals (D).

50. C: The Institute for Safe Medication Practices (ISMP) publishes the List of Confused Drug Names. ISMP is a nonprofit agency with the singular mission of educating the public as well as the healthcare community about drug safety. The List of Confused Drug Names includes the names of medications that look the same and sound the same. It is published in its ISMP Medication Safety Alert! Acute Care newsletter to encourage healthcare providers to put safeguards in place to help prevent errors. The ISMP has partnered with the FDA to publish the list called Look-Alike Drug Names with Recommended Tall Man Letters. This list distinguishes look-alike names by capitalizing some of the letters. For example, cyclosporine and cycloserine are differentiated with "tall man" letters (capital letters) because the beginning letters are the same (i.e., cycloSPORINE and cycloSERINE). The ISMP has additional resources to help reduce the likelihood of medication errors.

51. C: The FDA's MedWatch program can be used to report adverse effects associated with any human drug (whether it is OTC or prescription-only), biologic (blood components, tissue-based products), medical device, vaccine, dietary supplement, infant formula, cosmetic, food, or beverage. MedWatch can even be used to report medication errors. Anyone can submit adverse drug reaction information to MedWatch, including pharmacists, pharmacy technicians, prescribers, or even patients. Although it is time-consuming, the FDA encourages use of the MedWatch reporting system, even if you are not certain of all the details of the event. Adverse event reporting through MedWatch is particularly encouraged for serious adverse reactions that involve hospitalization, a life-threatening reaction, result in disability or permanent damage, or result in death. The FDA also encourages the reporting of quality or safety concerns with a product, such as suspected contamination, suspected counterfeit products, defective products, inadequate packaging or labeling, or stability issues.

52. A: The following are types of insulin used to treat diabetes mellitus:

Generic Name	Brand Name	Duration of Action
	Rapid-Acting Insulins	
Insulin glulisine	Apidra	1–3 hours
Insulin aspart	NovoLog, NovoPen	3–5 hours
Insulin lispro	Humalog, HumaPen	3–4 hours
	Short-Acting Insulins	
Insulin regular	Novolin R, Humulin R	4–6 hours
	Intermediate-Acting Insulins	
Insulin NPH	Novolin N, Humulin N	10–18 hours
	Long-Acting Insulins	
Insulin glargine	Lantus	24 hours
Insulin detemir	Levemir	18–24 hours

53. D: There are many medical abbreviations for the indication of time. Q.I.D. indicates four times per day and is often confused with QD, which means every day. Other common abbreviations are listed in the table below.

Abbreviation	Meaning
a.c.	Before meals
p.c.	After meals
bid	Twice per day
tid	Three times per day
qid	Four times per day
qd	Every day
qod	Every other day
hs	At the hour of sleep, bedtime

As part of The Joint Commission's mission to improve patient safety, a list of abbreviations that should be avoided was developed. The abbreviations QD and QOD should be avoided because they can be easily mistaken for one another and the terms have different meanings. The word "daily" should be written for QD, and "every other day" should be written for QOD.

54. A: The prefix *hypo-* means *under,* as in hypodermic (under the skin). The prefix *epi-* means *above,* as in epidermis (outer layer of skin). The prefix *pro-* or *proto-* means *before,* as in prodrome (early sign of an attack or disease). The prefix *ambi-* means *both,* as in ambidextrous (equal use of both hands).

55. B: Tricyclic antidepressants are also commonly prescribed to treat neuropathic pain, which is a type of pain caused by damage to a nerve. Commonly prescribed tricyclic antidepressants include amitriptyline (Elavil), nortriptyline (Pamelor), and imipramine. Pregabalin (Lyrica) is an anticonvulsant drug that is also used to treat neuropathic pain. Fluoxetine (Prozac) is a selective serotonin reuptake inhibitor (SSRI) antidepressant. Meloxicam (Anjeso) is an NSAID used to treat inflammation.

56. C: Amlodipine (Norvasc) is a calcium channel blocker used to treat hypertension (high blood pressure). Enoxaparin (Lovenox) is a blood thinner. Losartan (Cozaar) is an angiotensin receptor blocker used to treat hypertension. Zocor (simvastatin) belongs to a category of drugs used to treat high cholesterol (antihyperlipidemics). They are commonly referred to as *statins* and include atorvastatin (Lipitor), pravastatin, rosuvastatin (Crestor), and lovastatin (Altoprev). Other common medications used to treat hyperlipidemia includes fenofibrate (Tricor), ezetimibe (Zetia), gemfibrozil (Lopid), and omega-3 acid (Lovaza).

57. B: Epilepsy is a medical diagnosis assigned to patients who have a seizure disorder. An indication is a diagnosis or disease state for which a medication is used. There are many antiepileptic drugs, and there are 8 in the top 200 drugs: gabapentin (Neurontin), lamotrigine (Lamictal), topiramate (Topamax), pregabalin (Lyrica), levetiracetam (Keppra), phenytoin (Dilantin), oxcarbazepine (Trileptal), and divalproex sodium (Depakote). Risperidone (Risperdal) is an antipsychotic drug that is used to treat schizophrenia and other psychoses. It is not indicated for epilepsy.

58. C: The medication aide should only discuss procedures that are within his or her own scope of practice, not any of the other choices. If family members have questions about the patient's overall care (D), they should be referred to the supervising nurse.

59. A: The medication aide should immediately report the suspected abuse to the charge nurse so she can determine how best to proceed. It is possible that the suspicions have already been addressed, which is why it is not appropriate to directly report the suspected abuse to the police or confront the potential abuser. The behavior should not be ignored, however, because of the potential for the patient being harmed.

60. A: Hypoglycemia means low blood sugar levels. Antidiabetic drugs are designed to lower blood glucose levels to treat diabetes mellitus. Therefore, many of the drugs in this class have the potential side effect of hypoglycemia. Insulins, particularly shorter-acting insulins, have a high risk of causing hypoglycemia. Of the oral antidiabetic drugs, sulfonylureas, such as glipizide (Glucotrol XL), are associated with the highest risk of hypoglycemia.

Practice Test #2

1. A product that is teratogenic should NOT be given in which of the following groups of patients?

a. Children under the age of 12
b. Patients with heart problems
c. Pregnant women
d. Patients with kidney impairment

2. All of the following are common side effects of opioids EXCEPT:

a. Nausea
b. Diarrhea
c. Respiratory depression
d. Dependence

3. What is the BEST way for a medication aide to assist during a code?

a. Administer emergency medications according to the physician's instructions
b. Document the events
c. Speak with the family and answer their questions about what is happening
d. Retrieve emergency equipment, including the code cart or intubation box, and carry out other assigned tasks that fall within a medication aide's scope of practice

4. Which of the following describes how transdermal medications should be administered?

a. By mouth, dissolved under the tongue
b. By inhalation
c. Applied onto the skin
d. By mouth, held on the inside of the cheek

5. Which of the following pairs of drugs would NOT likely be found on the ISMP's list of confused drug names?

a. Zyrtec and Zovirax
b. Mirapex and Miralax
c. Ditropan and Diprivan
d. Reminyl and Amaryl

6. Which of the following is a boundary violation?

a. The medication aide accepts a box of candy to be shared by the entire staff.
b. The medication aide helps a patient write a personal letter.
c. The medication aide listens while the patient tells the aide about family problems.
d. The medication aide accepts a plant that the patient gives the medication aide on discharge.

7. Dutasteride is a 5-alpha reductase inhibitor used to treat which of the following?

a. Prostate enlargement
b. Gouty arthritis
c. High cholesterol
d. Erectile dysfunction

8. Which of the following is a common side effect of most antibiotics?

a. Immunosuppression
b. Diarrhea
c. Cough
d. Muscle pain

9. Which of the following medication pairs would be considered a look-alike sound-alike medication?

a. Zyrtec - cetirizine
b. Norvasc - amlodipine
c. Duloxetine - fluoxetine
d. Fluticasone - hydrocortisone

10. When a patient fails to complete their full course of antibiotics, this can lead to:

a. Allergy
b. Increased side effects
c. Arrhythmias
d. Bacterial resistance

11. An opened vial of insulin detemir (Levemir) can be stored at room temperature for how many days?

a. 10 days
b. 14 days
c. 30 days
d. 42 days

12. Which of the following would be an appropriate temperature to store a medication that is required to be kept at room temperature?

a. 85 °F
b. 15 °C
c. 22 °C
d. 45 °F

13. What do the medical abbreviations IM, IV, O.D., O.S., O.U., P.O., P.R., SC, SL, and per neb refer to?

a. Form of medication
b. Measurement
c. Route of administration
d. Dosage information

14. Which of the following antibiotic suspensions needs to be refrigerated after reconstitution?

a. Cefdinir (Omnicef)
b. Clarithromycin (Biaxin)
c. Amoxicillin-clavulanate (Augmentin)
d. Nitrofurantoin (Macrobid)

15. What is the Patient's Bill of Rights?

a. A federal law listing rights of hospitalized patients
b. A federal act guaranteeing the privacy of patient health information
c. A document given to an admitted patient or resident listing his or her responsibilities while staying in the facility
d. A document given to an admitted patient or resident listing his or her rights while staying in the facility

16. Advair is commonly used to treat which of the following conditions?

a. Cystic fibrosis
b. Asthma
c. Psoriasis
d. Pulmonary hypertension

17. A newly trained medication aide has been delegated a task that the medication aide does not feel adequately prepared to do. What should the medication aide do?

a. Ask another medication aide for assistance
b. Ask a supervisor for assistance
c. Make an excuse for why the medication aide cannot do the task
d. Explain the concerns to the delegating nurse

18. A client was to receive 1 g of vancomycin intravenously in 200 mL of iso-osmotic solution over 60 minutes per infusion pump. However, the IV administration was discontinued after 45 minutes because the client developed nausea and chills. How many milligrams of vancomycin did the client receive?

a. 250 mg
b. 500 mg
c. 600 mg
d. 750 mg

19. The capacity to understand what a patient is feeling and respond appropriately is known as what?

a. Active listening
b. Empathy
c. Caring
d. Respect

20. Albuterol is a type of

a. Antidepressant
b. Insulin
c. Diuretic
d. Bronchodilator

21. If a patient asks the medication aide to explain the purpose of a new medical treatment, which of thc following would be the most appropriate response?

a. "I'll ask your nurse to come in and explain that to you."
b. "I can't give you that information."
c. "The purpose is to reduce your episodes of chest pain."
d. "I don't know what the purpose of the treatment is."

22. All of the following medication classes should be avoided in elderly patients EXCEPT:

a. Antihistamines
b. Tricyclic antidepressants
c. Benzodiazepines
d. Dihydropyridine calcium channel blockers

23. A patient's medication order instructs to administer one ounce of solution per dose. How many milliliters should the medication aide measure out for each dose?

a. 5 mL
b. 10 mL
c. 30 mL
d. 65 mL

24. Which of the following statements about corticosteroids is true?

a. They cause weight loss
b. They can be stopped abruptly
c. Creams and lotions should be applied liberally
d. They are used to treat inflammatory conditions

25. A patient has a few questions about the consent forms she signed for a scheduled invasive procedure. How should the medication aide respond?

a. Answer the questions to the best of her ability
b. Tell the patient that she will ask the nurse to contact the doctor
c. Tell the patient that she will have plenty of time to ask the doctor before the procedure
d. Remind the patient that she signed the consent and that the procedure has already been scheduled

26. This category of medications decreases the amount of fluid that a person has in their body compartments by promoting water loss in the urine:

a. Expectorants
b. Diuretics
c. Vasodilators
d. Corticosteroids

27. Which of the following medications has a narrow therapeutic index (NTI)?

a. Xarelto
b. Phenytoin
c. Fluoxetine
d. Lisinopril

28. Which of the following organizations publishes guidelines for the storage and handling of chemotherapy and hazardous substances?

a. Occupational Safety and Health Administration (OSHA)
b. Nuclear Regulatory Commission (NRC)
c. Food and Drug Administration (FDA)
d. World Health Organization (WHO)

29. Which of the following statements about MEDMARX is INCORRECT?

a. MEDMARX is overseen by the *United States Pharmacopeia* (USP).
b. MEDMARX is a voluntary reporting system that tracks adverse drug reactions and medication errors.
c. Information gathered through MEDMARX is used to determine the individual(s) responsible for the errors.
d. MEDMARX is designed for use by hospitals and health systems to collect, track, and analyze medication errors.

30. Which of the following medications prevents platelets from sticking together and forming blood clots?

a. Pradaxa
b. Clopidogrel
c. Warfarin
d. Pravachol

31. Most vaccinations must be stored in a refrigerator. However, there are a few vaccine products that must be kept in a freezer. Which of the following vaccine products must be stored in a freezer?

a. Flulaval (influenza vaccine)
b. Varivax (varicella vaccine)
c. Measles, mumps, and rubella vaccine
d. Adacel (tetanus, diphtheria, and pertussis vaccine)

32. Which drug reference is published annually by the FDA and provides a list of all prescriptions approved as safe and effective, along with therapeutic equivalence determinations using a two-letter therapeutic evaluation code?

a. Red Book database
b. *Orange Book*
c. *Physicians' Desk Reference*
d. *Drug Facts and Comparisons*

33. How does the right to informed consent impact nursing home residents?

a. Since they may be incapacitated, it must be obtained from any family member.
b. Informed consent must be obtained from the residents or their health care power of attorney prior to every test, treatment, or procedure.
c. It prevents them from changing or stopping treatments once a decision has been made.
d. Its applicability is broader than in other circumstances.

34. Which of the following is the most correct transcription of the prescription directions of "1 tab PO QD"?

a. Take one tablet by vagina two times daily.
b. Take one tablet by mouth four times daily.
c. Take one tablet by mouth daily.
d. Take one tablespoon by mouth daily.

35. Which of the following is administered by a metered-dose inhaler device?

a. Proventil HFA
b. Advair Diskus
c. Spiriva HandiHaler
d. Symbicort Turbuhaler

36. Which of the following vitamins should be avoided in patients who take warfarin?

a. Vitamin A
b. Vitamin D
c. Folic acid
d. Vitamin K

37. Which of the following is an antipsychotic medication that is commonly used to treat schizophrenia?

a. Risperidone
b. Prozac
c. Levetiracetam
d. Duloxetine

38. How many milligrams are in 1 grain?

a. 15 mg
b. 32.4 mg
c. 64.8 mg
d. 90 mg

39. Which of the following is an antibacterial agent?

a. Fluconazole
b. Nystatin
c. Doxycycline
d. Acyclovir

40. Which of the following adverse effects is associated with the use of lisinopril?

a. Headache
b. Constipation
c. Dry cough
d. Hypertension

41. Which of the following would be a common side effect of anticoagulants?

a. Skin rash
b. Excessive bruising or bleeding
c. Hair loss
d. Hypertension

42. Nephrotoxic drugs can cause damage to which of the following?

a. Liver
b. Kidney
c. Ear
d. Nerves

43. What is the meaning of the pharmaceutical abbreviation "*os*"?

a. Before meals
b. Left eye
c. Left ear
d. Right eye

44. Which of the following drug classes should be avoided in patients with hypertension?

a. Beta-blockers
b. Decongestants
c. ACE inhibitors
d. Calcium channel blockers

45. If a nurse delegates a routine nursing task to a medication aide, the person who is legally accountable for the patient's safety is which of the following?

a. Delegating nurse
b. Medication aide
c. Supervisor
d. Director of nursing

46. A medication aide is caring for a patient who is becoming agitated. How should the medication aide speak to the patient?

a. In an assertive and confident manner
b. Not at all; the patient's family members or other staff should interact with the patient
c. The medication aide should not acknowledge the inappropriate behavior and carry on as normal
d. Calmly and clearly, while attempting to determine why the patient is agitated

47. If a medication aide observes the nursing supervisor acting in a negligent way, what should be done?

a. Speak with the doctor in charge of the patient
b. Follow the institution's chain of command to determine who to report the behavior to
c. Go to the institution's president of nursing to report the behavior
d. Confront the nursing supervisor directly

48. Which of the following drug classes is NOT used to treat hypertension?

a. Beta-blockers
b. Thiazolidinediones
c. Diuretics
d. ACE inhibitors

49. Through which route of administration is insulin glulisine (Apidra) commonly administered?

a. Oral
b. Subcutaneous
c. Topical
d. Inhalation

50. Which of the following drugs is NOT indicated for hypertension?

a. Lisinopril
b. Norvasc
c. Enoxaparin
d. Diovan

51. A patient has rung the call bell for the sixth time during the first two hours of a medication aide's shift. How should the aide respond?

a. Ignore the bell
b. Call the nurse manager
c. Remove the bell from the patient's reach
d. Reassure the patient she will be checked on frequently

52. Which of the following abbreviations should NOT be used due to a high potential for confusion and error?

a. qod
b. po
c. hs
d. sol

53. An SDS contains information about:

a. Therapeutic equivalency of drugs
b. Sterile compounding requirements
c. Hazardous chemicals
d. Air flow monitoring

54. Nitroglycerin tablets are stored in brown bottles, and nitroglycerin IV solutions are stored in either brown or foil bags. The reason for this is that nitroglycerin is:

a. Sensitive to moisture in the air
b. Sensitive to changes in temperature
c. Incompatible with certain plastics
d. Sensitive to light

55. Which of the following drugs is commonly used to treat depression?

a. Levothyroxine
b. Metoprolol
c. Alprazolam
d. Citalopram

56. Which of the following is a selective serotonin reuptake inhibitor?

a. Sumatriptan
b. Amitriptyline
c. Citalopram
d. Effexor

57. Which of the following items must be disposed of in a sharps container?

a. Glucose test strips
b. Lancets
c. Metered-dose inhalers
d. Oral syringes

58. Which of the following is an example of a brand name of a medication?

a. Amlodipine
b. Bisoprolol
c. Lasix
d. Fluticasone

59. What is the institution responsible for overseeing the certification of, qualification of, and complaints against nurse aides?

a. National Council State Board of Nursing
b. American Association of Nurse Aides
c. Nurse Aide Registry
d. National League for Nursing

60. Which of the following is NOT a medication error reporting system?

a. MedWatch
b. FAERS
c. VAERS
d. ISMP MERP

Answer Key and Explanations for Test #2

1. C: Teratogenicity is the ability of a drug to be toxic to a fetus/embryo and lead to birth defects. Therefore, teratogenic medications are contraindicated (not recommended) in pregnancy.

The following types of medications can be teratogenic: isotretinoin, thalidomide and derivatives, ACE inhibitors, anticoagulants (e.g., warfarin), estrogens, androgens (e.g., testosterone), antiepileptics drugs (e.g., carbamazepine, phenytoin, phenobarbital, sodium valproate), medications used to treat hyperthyroidism (e.g., methimazole, carbimazole, radioactive iodine), lithium, NSAIDs, tetracycline antibiotics, sulfa antibiotics (e.g., Bactrim), ciprofloxacin, anticancer agents (e.g., cyclophosphamide, methotrexate), some oral antidiabetic drugs, vitamin A supplements, alcohol.

2. B: Opioids are central nervous system depressants used to treat pain. Common side effects of opioids include dependence, addiction, nausea, vomiting, respiratory depression (slow respiratory rate), and slowing of the digestive system. Opioids slow down the movement of the digestive tract and can lead to reduced bowel movements. Therefore, they commonly cause constipation, NOT diarrhea.

3. D: During a code, the medication aide should promptly retrieve emergency equipment or other supplies according to the needs of the physicians and nurses. That may include blood from the blood bank, needles, syringes, etc. Documenting the events and administering medications is the responsibility of the nurse during emergency situations. The medication aide should not answer medical questions from the family, but may be able to provide comfort or support if necessary.

4. C: Transdermal medications are formulated as patches and patients are to apply the patch onto their skin. Sublingual tablets are administered by mouth and allowed to dissolve under the tongue. Buccal tablets are also administered orally, held on the inside of the cheek and allowed to dissolve slowly. Inhalations are formulated as inhalers of nebulizer solutions that are to be inhaled into the lungs.

5. A: The Institute for Safe Medication Practices (ISMP) provides guidelines and resources on black box warnings, error-prone abbreviations, confused drug name lists, "do not crush" lists, and high-alert medication lists, just to name a few. Their list of confused drug names is updated regularly and contains common look-alike/sound-alike (LASA) drug name pairs. LASA drug name pairs are drugs with similar-looking and similar-sounding names. However, even though the names are similar, their mechanisms of action are very different and could have potentially harmful effects if inadvertently interchanged. The only similarity between Zyrtec and Zovirax is the first letter. Although this creates a similarity, it is not enough to create confusion, unlike the other pairs listed.

6. D: It is a boundary violation to accept a personal gift, such as a plant, from a patient even though the gift may seem quite insignificant. The medication aide should thank the patient and explain the facility's policy against accepting any gifts. At most facilities, it is acceptable to accept a gift of candy if it is intended for the entire staff and not just an individual, but each facility should have clear policies in place about the appropriateness of accepting such gifts.

7. A: Benign prostatic hyperplasia (prostate enlargement) can be treated with 5-alpha reductase inhibitors, alpha-1 blockers (which treat hypertension), and anticholinergic drugs (which treat urinary frequency). The two commonly prescribed 5-alpha reductase inhibitors are dutasteride

(Avodart) and finasteride (Proscar). Commonly prescribed alpha-1 blockers include terazosin, doxazosin (Cardura), and alfuzosin (Uroxatral).

8. B: Antibiotics are used to treat bacterial or microbial infections. All antibiotics have the potential to cause nausea, vomiting, diarrhea, stomach upset, and abdominal pain. Antibiotics can also kill the normal flora (good bacteria) in the body and lead to secondary infections, such as thrush or intestinal infection (colitis, *Clostridioides difficile*). This is more common with broad-spectrum (less-specific) antibiotics and longer courses of treatment. Patients can take a probiotic to help prevent this side effect. Penicillin (e.g., amoxicillin, penicillin) allergies occur in 1–10% of patients, with about 10% of those patients also being allergic to cephalosporins (e.g., cephalexin). Tetracyclines (e.g., tetracycline, doxycycline) cause sensitivity to sunlight and staining of the teeth, so they should be avoided in children. Quinolones (e.g., ciprofloxacin, levofloxacin) can cause tendon rupture and increase the risk of seizures in at-risk patients.

9. C: Duloxetine and fluoxetine look and sound alike, making them easier to confuse and increasing the risk for dispensing errors. Zyrtec is the brand name for cetirizine. Norvasc is the brand name for amlodipine. Fluticasone and hydrocortisone are both corticosteroids.

10. D: When patients do not complete their full course of antibiotics, bacteria can develop resistance to the antibiotic so that it will be less effective in the future. Up to 10% of patients are allergic to penicillin antibiotics, but failing to finish the course will not increase the likelihood of allergy. Failing to finish the course will not lead to side effects of arrhythmias either. In fact, many patients stop taking their antibiotic due to side effects. It is common to get nausea, vomiting, diarrhea, and abdominal pain with antibiotics.

11. D: Insulin detemir (Levemir) is a long-acting insulin used once or twice daily through subcutaneous injection for the treatment of diabetes. Both the pen (Levemir FlexTouch) and vials can be stored at room temperature (below 86 °F [30 °C]) for 42 days, regardless of whether the product has been opened. Unopened pens and vials can be stored in the refrigerator until the expiration date assigned by the manufacturer.

12. C: Most medications can be stored at room temperature, which is defined as 20-25 °C (59-77 °F). This includes most tablets, capsules, liquid solutions, creams, inhalers, and patches.

13. C: These terms refer to the route of administration. The route of administration is the method by which the medication will enter the body. IM indicates intramuscularly. IV indicates intravenously. O.D. and O.S. refer to right eye and left eye, respectively, and O.U. refers to both eyes. P.O. means by mouth or orally. P.R. refers to a medication given rectally. SC refers to subcutaneous administration such as with insulin administration. SL is sublingual, or under the tongue, such as with nitroglycerin. Per neb means administered via nebulizer, which is typically a medication related to breathing. It is always important to verify the route of administration.

14. C: Amoxicillin-clavulanate (Augmentin) reconstituted oral suspension must be stored under refrigeration and discarded after 10 days. The clavulanic acid in Augmentin is unstable to heat and can deteriorate quickly, making it less effective in killing bacteria. Clarithromycin (Biaxin) dry granules and reconstituted suspension should not be stored in the refrigerator. Cefdinir (Omnicef) and nitrofurantoin (Macrobid) do not require refrigeration and can be safely kept at room temperature.

15. D: A Patient's Bill of Rights is a listing of his or her rights while in the facility; it is specific to the facility but generally covers rights such as privacy, confidentiality, respectful care, etc. Patients generally get a list of responsibilities (C) when admitted but that is a different issue. There is a federal act governing privacy of healthcare information (B) called HIPAA or Health Insurance Portability and Accountability Act.

16. B: Advair is an inhaler that contains a combination of two medications, salmeterol (a bronchodilator) and fluticasone (a corticosteroid). Bronchodilators dilate, or open, the airways to make it easier for patients to breathe. They are used to treat respiratory diseases, such as asthma and chronic obstructive pulmonary disease, but they can also be used short term during a respiratory illness to help relieve shortness of breath. Corticosteroids are anti-inflammatory medications that are used to treat a wide range of diseases, including respiratory illnesses such as asthma. Other similar medications that are commonly prescribed include Symbicort (budesonide, formoterol), another combination of a bronchodilator and a corticosteroid used to treat asthma. Albuterol (Ventolin, ProAir, Proventil) is a quick-acting bronchodilator used to treat acute asthma attacks. Tiotropium (Spiriva) is a long-acting bronchodilator used to treat chronic obstructive pulmonary disease.

17. D: If a newly trained medication aide has been delegated a task that the medication aide does not feel adequately prepared to do, the aide should explain the concerns to the delegating nurse. Because it's the nurse's responsibility to supervise the medication aide, the nurse should be willing to assist and help the aide to complete the task. With experience, the medication aide will increase in confidence and skills.

18. D: The simplest solution to the problem is to convert 1 g to 1000 mg and then, since the infusion was set for 60 minutes and three-fourths of the time elapsed, simply multiply 1000 × 0.75 = 750 mg. If using an algebraic formula:

$$\begin{aligned} 1000/60 &= x/45 \\ 60x &= 45{,}000 \\ 6x &= 4500 \\ 6x/6 &= 4500/6 \\ x &= 750 \text{ mg} \end{aligned}$$

19. B: This is the definition of empathy. All of the responses, however, are good tools for communicating with a patient. Active listening (A) is listening attentively while conversing, caring (C) is having genuine regard for the patient's safety and welfare, and respect (D) is showing consideration and regard for the patient's values.

20. D: Albuterol is a generic type of bronchodilator. Bronchodilators work to relax the respiratory muscles to make breathing easier such as in patients with asthma, chronic obstructive pulmonary disease, or chronic bronchitis. Albuterol is a short-acting bronchodilator that will provide quick relief to patients experiencing breathing difficulties. Other types of short-acting bronchodilators include metaproterenol, albuterol, and ipratropium. Albuterol is available in tablet form or as a syrup. It is also available as an inhaler or for use in a nebulizer. It can be used for exercise-induced bronchospasm and should be taken 15 minutes prior to exercise. Albuterol should never be taken with other types of stimulant medications because of the potential for causing chest pains in individuals with heart disease.

21. A: If a patient asks the medication aide to explain the purpose of a new medical treatment, the most appropriate response is, "I'll ask your nurse to come in and explain that to you." Explaining medical treatments is within the scope of practice of the nurse and not within the range of functions of the medication aide, so even when the aide knows the purpose, the explanation should be left to the nurse who should be better prepared to answer questions about the treatment.

22. D: Elderly patients have a reduced ability to metabolize (break down) and excrete medications, and they are generally more susceptible to adverse effects. Sedating drugs can lead to delirium and confusion in elderly patients as well as increase their risk of falling. Classes of medications that should be used with caution in elderly patients include antihistamines, tricyclic antidepressants, muscle relaxers, benzodiazepines, hypnotics (sleeping pills), antipsychotics, antihypertensives, cardiac glycosides (digoxin), and nonsteroidal anti-inflammatory drugs.

23. C: A fluid ounce is equivalent to 30 mL of fluid. A teaspoon is equivalent to 5 mL of fluid. A tablespoon is equivalent to 15 mL of fluid. Answer D may have been confused with the conversion for grains; there are approximately 65 mg in one grain.

24. D: Corticosteroid are anti-inflammatory medications that are used to treat a wide range of diseases, including eczema and asthma. When taken orally, they are associated with many side effects, including weight gain, fluid retention, hyperglycemia (high blood glucose), and increased risk of infection. For this reason, the lowest possible dose should be used for the shortest possible time period. Creams and lotions should be applied sparingly once or twice a day for a short period of time. When taken orally, they should not be stopped abruptly. Instead, patients will be prescribed a dose that tapers down over a period of time.

25. B: A medication aide should not discuss procedures or what was in the consent forms the patient signed. Only a physician can review and inform a patient of the risks and benefits of having a procedure or treatment. A patient can always withdraw their consent, even if they're about to go into the procedure room. The nurse should notify the physician that the patient has questions so he can arrange to see the patient and discuss her concerns.

26. B: Diuretics, such as furosemide and hydrochlorothiazide, treat edema (swelling) and high blood pressure (hypertension) by promoting the excretion of water in the urine. Expectorants, such as guaifenesin, help thin the mucus that builds up during a cold or respiratory illness so that it can be expelled more easily. Vasodilators increase the diameter of blood vessels in order to lower blood pressure or treat chest pains (angina). Corticosteroids are anti-inflammatory medications that are used to treat a wide variety of diseases. They promote fluid retention, NOT fluid excretion.

27. B: The following medications have a narrow therapeutic index: lithium (Lithobid), warfarin (Coumadin), digoxin (Lanoxin), phenytoin (Dilantin), theophylline (Theo-24), cyclosporine (Sandimmune), tacrolimus (Prograf), and many chemotherapy agents. This means that there is a narrow range of safe dosages and even minor changes in the dose can cause serious side effects in the patient. Rivaroxaban (Xarelto), fluoxetine (Prozac), and lisinopril (Prinvil) do not have a narrow therapeutic index.

28. A: The Occupational Safety and Health Administration (OSHA) is a federal agency that enforces health and safety legislation. OSHA publishes guidelines for the storage and handling of chemotherapy and hazardous substances. The Nuclear Regulatory Commission (NRC) publishes guidelines for the storage and handling of radiopharmaceuticals. The Food and Drug Administration (FDA) is a federal agency that assures safety, security, and efficacy of drugs, biologics, medical devices, cosmetics, dietary supplements, and food. The World Health Organization (WHO) is the authority on global health matters.

29. C: Like most error reporting systems, MEDMARX is anonymous. The purpose of all of these medical product and vaccine safety reporting programs is to determine the causes of the errors in hopes of not repeating them again. Healthcare professionals and consumers are encouraged to report any concerns or errors without fear of punishment. MEDMARX is overseen by the USP and is designed for use by hospitals and health systems to collect, analyze, and report adverse drug reactions and medication errors.

Recall: MedWatch and FAERS are both overseen by the FDA. VAERS is cosponsored by the FDA and CDC. MERP, the Medication Errors Reporting Program, and C-MERP (consumer) are overseen by the ISMP. All of these systems collect information anonymously with the goal of preventing future errors.

30. B: Blood thinners are administered to patients who have arrhythmias, heart disease, pulmonary embolisms, strokes, or deep vein thrombosis, or who have undergone recent surgeries to prevent the formation of blood clots. There are two types of blood thinners, antiplatelets and anticoagulants. Antiplatelets prevent platelets from sticking to each other, whereas anticoagulants prevent the activation of clotting factors in the blood. Commonly prescribed antiplatelets include clopidogrel (Plavix), prasugrel (Effient), ticagrelor (Brilinta), and aspirin (Bayer). Commonly prescribed anticoagulants include heparin, warfarin (Coumadin), enoxaparin (Lovenox), rivaroxaban (Xarelto), apixaban (Eliquis), and dabigatran (Pradaxa).

31. B: There are two vaccines that must be stored in a freezer: Varivax (varicella vaccine), which protects against chicken pox, and Zostavax (herpes zoster vaccine), which protects against shingles but is no longer available in the US. All other vaccines available on the market require refrigeration. This includes a newer version of the vaccine used to protect against shingles called Shingrix. Other commonly used vaccines that require refrigeration are influenza vaccines (Fluad, Flulaval, Fluzone), tetanus, diphtheria, and pertussis vaccines (Daptacel, Adacel, Boostrix), hepatitis B vaccines (Engerix-B, Recombivax HB), hepatitis A vaccines (Havrix, Vaqta), *Haemophilus influenzae* type B vaccine (ActHIB, PedvaxHIB), meningococcal vaccines (Menactra, Menveo), measles, mumps, and rubella vaccination, human papillomavirus vaccination (Gardasil), and pneumococcal vaccines (Pneumovax 23, Prevnar 13).

32. B: The *Orange Book*, also known as *Approved Drug Products with Therapeutic Equivalence Evaluations*, is used to determine whether one drug is therapeutically equivalent to another. The *Orange Book* serves as a guide for identifying suitable generic alternatives for branded products. This drug reference is nicknamed the *Orange Book* after its distinct bright-orange cover. The Red Book database provides information on drug pricing and product information on prescription and over-the-counter (OTC) drug products. The *Physicians' Desk Reference* and *Drug Facts and Comparisons* are the most commonly used drug reference books for clinical pharmacology information. They include information on more than 22,000 prescription and 6,000 OTC products.

33. B: Just as with other types of patients, the right of informed consent applies and means that prior to performance of any test, treatment, or procedure, the patient or his or her representative must be informed of the risks and benefits so that he or she may consent or decline. That negates responses A and D. However, under the right of freedom of choice, the patient can later change or stop treatments (C).

34. C: The abbreviation "tab" stands for tablet, "PO" stands for by mouth or per oral, and "QD" stands for daily. According to the Institute for Safe Medication Practices (ISMP), the abbreviation "QD" should never be used in communicating information to other healthcare professionals. Abbreviations should be avoided in all prescription writing and medical communications. Abbreviations have led to many serious medication errors. QD has been mistaken for QID, and fourfold dosing errors have occurred as a result. In addition, numerals should be spelled out.

35. A: Metered-dose inhalers (MDIs) contain a drug solution within a canister. When the patient presses down on the canister, a propellant (e.g., HFA) helps spray a set amount of a drug solution into the patient's mouth to be inhaled. Examples of MDIs include albuterol sulfate (ProAir HFA, Ventolin HFA, Proventil HFA), fluticasone propionate (Flovent HFA), ipratropium bromide (Atrovent HFA), fluticasone propionate-salmeterol (Advair HFA), and beclomethasone dipropionate HFA (Qvar). Dry powder inhalers (DPIs) contain drugs within small granules of powder. Before inhaling, the patient must prep the device. Then, the patient must inhale deeply to draw the powder into their lungs. Examples of DPIs include fluticasone propionate-salmeterol (Advair Diskus), tiotropium bromide (Spiriva HandiHaler), and budesonide-formoterol (Symbicort Turbuhaler).

36. D: Vitamin K is a warfarin K antagonist that interferes with blood clotting. Therefore, vitamin K should be avoided because it reduces the effectiveness of warfarin. Patients should be instructed to avoid vitamin K supplements and vitamin K-rich foods, such as spinach and green, leafy vegetables. In fact, vitamin K (menadiol, phytomenadione) is an antidote or reversal agent used to treat warfarin overdoses. Vitamin D (ergocalciferol) is used to promote bone health and treat osteoporosis and renal failure. Vitamin B_{12} (hydroxocobalamin) is used to prevent or treat deficiencies in patients with gastrointestinal disorders. Folic acid (folate) is used to prevent neural tube defects in pregnant women; it is also used alongside methotrexate therapy in order to reduce side effects.

37. A: Risperidone (Risperdal), quetiapine (Seroquel), and aripiprazole (Abilify) are antipsychotic medications used to treat schizophrenia. Fluoxetine (Prozac), sertraline (Zoloft), citalopram (Celexa), escitalopram (Lexapro), duloxetine (Cymbalta), venlafaxine (Effexor), paroxetine (Paxil), and mirtazapine (Remeron) are antidepressants. Levetiracetam (Keppra), lamotrigine (Lamictal), topiramate (Topamax), phenytoin (Dilantin), and oxcarbazepine (Trileptal) are commonly used to treat epilepsy or seizure disorders.

38. C: The grain (gr) is a measurement used in pharmacy. It is part of a historical system of measurement called the apothecaries' system, although it is still used occasionally in modern pharmacy. There is 64.8 mg per grain.

39. C: Fluconazole and nystatin are antifungal agents. Acyclovir is an antiviral agent. Doxycycline is an antibacterial agent.

40. C: Recall that lisinopril (Zestril) is an ACE inhibitor and is commonly used to treat hypertension. ACE inhibitors are associated with a dry, persistent cough in 5–35% of patients who take them, with the cough usually occurring within the first few months of treatment. Other common side effects include hypotension, dizziness, and increased serum creatinine. Patients experiencing an ACE inhibitor-induced cough often can be prescribed an angiotensin receptor blocker (ARB) for hypertension without the risk for cough. (Hint: The generic names of ACE inhibitors end in -pril. The generic names of ARBs end in -sartan.)

41. B: Anticoagulants are also known as blood thinners because they prevent the blood from forming clots. The most common complaint with anticoagulant use is bruising or bleeding easily. Patients should watch for stomach pain or black, tarry stool, which indicates gastrointestinal bleeding. Signs and symptoms of a head bleed would be sudden headache, nausea, vomiting, blurred vision, weakness or numbness on one side of the body, or difficulty speaking.

42. B: The prefix "nephro-" means kidney. The prefix meaning liver would be "hepat/o-," so drugs that cause damage to the liver are referred to as hepatotoxic. The prefix for ear is "oto-," so drugs that damage the ear are called ototoxic. The prefix for nerve is "neuro-," so drugs damaging nerves would be referred to as neurotoxic.

43. B: The abbreviation "os" means left eye, "od" means right eye, and "ou" means both eyes. The abbreviation "as" means left ear, "ad" means right ear, and "au" means both ears. The abbreviation "ac" means before meals and "pc" means after meals.

44. B: Patients with cardiovascular conditions such as hypertension (high blood pressure) and heart disease should avoid the use of decongestants because they have been shown to cause adverse cardiovascular effects. Palpitations, tachycardia, arrhythmia, exacerbated hypertension, reflex bradycardia, coronary occlusion, cerebral vasculitis, myocardial infarction, cardiac arrest, and death have been reported. Patients with cerebrovascular insufficiency (stroke, transient ischemic attack, etc.) and hyperthyroidism are also warned to avoid or limit the use of decongestants. ACE inhibitors, beta-blockers, and calcium channel blockers are all drug classes that are used to treat hypertension.

45. A: If a nurse delegates a routine nursing task to a medication aide, the person who is legally accountable for the patient's safety is the delegating nurse. The nurse determines whether the task is within the range of functions of the medication aide in their state and whether the task can be safely delegated. The nurse must consider the needs of the patient, the extent of the task, and the medication aide's abilities.

46. D: Patients may become agitated for any number of reasons. They might be in pain or be uncomfortable. They could be hungry, thirsty, have to go to the bathroom, or even be bored or scared. Understanding what is causing someone's agitation is the best way to relieve it. The medication aide should continue to interact with the patient in a calm, clear, and professional manner. She may need to set boundaries as necessary, especially if the behavior persists.

47. B: The medication aide should follow the chain of command when determining who to report the behavior to. It is inappropriate to contact the physician in charge of the patient's care because he does not have any authority to deal with this type of nursing situation. It is inappropriate to go directly to the nursing supervisor or president of nursing without following the guidelines set in place by the institution.

48. B: Recall that "hypertension" means high blood pressure, which is commonly treated using angiotensin-converting enzyme (ACE) inhibitors, angiotensin II receptor blockers, alpha-blockers, beta-blockers, calcium channel blockers, and/or diuretics, to name a few. These medications work to reduce blood pressure. Thiazolidinediones are a class of oral hypoglycemic medications that may be used to treat type 2 diabetes.

49. B: Insulin glulisine (Apidra) is a rapid-acting insulin used in the treatment of type 1 or 2 diabetes in adults and type 1 diabetes in children older than the age of 4. All insulin products are commonly injected into subcutaneous (subcut) tissue at a 90-degree angle using a 4–5 mm needle. Common injection sites include the abdomen, thigh, and upper arm. Injection sites should be rotated within the same region (abdomen, thigh, or upper arm) from one injection to the next to reduce the risk of lipodystrophy. Apidra is used to improve blood glucose control in patients and should be administered at mealtime (within 15 minutes before a meal or within 20 minutes after starting a meal). Apidra should be used in a regimen with an intermediate- or long-acting insulin. All insulin products can possibly cause hypokalemia and should be used cautiously in patients who may be at risk for hypokalemia.

(Note: In the past, "subcutaneous" has been abbreviated "SC," "SQ," or "subQ." However, these abbreviations are on the Institute for Safe Medication Practices' (ISMP) list of error-prone abbreviations, symbols, and dose designations and should be avoided. For patient safety purposes, the subcutaneous route of administration can be safely abbreviated "subcut" or written out as "subcutaneously.")

50. C: Hypertension, also known as high blood pressure, is a very common disorder for which there are many drug treatments available. Many antihypertensive drugs are in the top 200 list of drugs, so you will be expected to know both the generic and brand name for these medications: lisinopril (Zestril), hydrochlorothiazide (APO-Hydro), lisinopril/hydrochlorothiazide (Zestoretic), metoprolol (Lopressor/Toprol), amlodipine (Norvasc), atenolol (Tenormin), carvedilol (Coreg), losartan (Cozaar), losartan/hydrochlorothiazide (Hyzaar), triamterene/hydrochlorothiazide (Maxzide), valsartan (Diovan), valsartan/hydrochlorothiazide (Diovan HCT), enalapril (Vasotec), amlodipine/benazepril (Lotrel), benazepril (Lotensin), clonidine (Catapres-TTS-1), ramipril (Altace), hydralazine (Apresoline), nifedipine (Procardia XL), olmesartan (Benicar), nebivolol (Bystolic), doxazosin (Cardura), irbesartan (Avapro), terazosin (APO-Terazosin). Enoxaparin (Lovenox) is a blood thinner used to treat/prevent blood clots.

51. D: The medication aide should never ignore a patient's call bell because it could potentially alert the staff to a dangerous situation. That doesn't mean, however, that the patient has a right to abuse the staff and call bell system. The medication aide should establish clear boundaries and expectations about when it is okay to use the call bell. She should also understand that it is quite likely that the patient is anxious or lonely, and should agree to check on her at established intervals. This may help alleviate some of the anxiety. The nurse manager may need to get involved if the above interventions aren't successful.

52. A: The following abbreviations should NOT be used: U (unit), IU (international unit), qd (daily), qod (every other day), chemical abbreviations of drugs (e.g., $MgSO_4$, NaCl, KCl), and drug name abbreviations (e.g., MS, HCTZ, NS). Trailing zeros (e.g., 5.0 mg) and leading decimal points (e.g., .5mg) should be avoided for numbers. Therefore, answer A is the correct answer. The other three answer choices are approved abbreviations: po (by mouth), hs (at bedtime), and sol (solution).

53. C: SDS stands for Safety Data Sheet. The SDS contains information about hazardous chemicals, including flammability, volatility, storage requirements, exposure prevention, and what to do following a spill or exposure. All workplaces are required by the Occupational Safety and Health Administration (OSHA) to keep an MSDS binder for all of the hazardous chemicals that employees may work with. The FDA's Orange Book contains information about therapeutic equivalency of drugs (e.g., generic substitutions). USP 797 contains standards for sterile compounding, including air flow monitoring requirements.

54. D: Medications that are stored in brown bottles or bags or in foil are often required to be protected from light in order to preserve their shelf life. Although nitroglycerin must also be protected from moisture, high temperatures, and certain plastics, the brown packaging will not help with this. The reason for the brown or foil packaging is because nitroglycerin is particularly sensitive to light.

55. D: Citalopram (Celexa) is an SSRI antidepressant medication used to treat depression. Other agents in this drug class include escitalopram (Lexapro), fluoxetine (Prozac), fluvoxamine (Luvox), paroxetine (Paxil), and sertraline (Zoloft). Levothyroxine (Euthyrox, Levoxyl, Synthroid, Tirosint, and Unithroid) is used to treat hypothyroidism. Metoprolol (Lopressor and Toprol XL) is a beta-blocker that is used to treat angina, hypertension, and heart failure with reduced ejection fraction.

Alprazolam (Xanax) is a benzodiazepine that is used to treat anxiety disorders, panic disorder, and preoperative anxiety.

56. C: Selective serotonin reuptake inhibitors (SSRIs) are a class of antidepressants. Commonly prescribed SSRIs include citalopram (Celexa), escitalopram (Lexapro), paroxetine (Paxil), fluoxetine (Prozac), sertraline (Zoloft), and fluvoxamine (Luvox). You may have noticed that there is no standard naming system for this class of drugs.

57. B: Lancets, needles, and parenteral syringes must be disposed of in a sharps container. Glucose test strips, metered-dose inhalers, and oral syringes do not contain any sharp or pointy components that would require them to be disposed of in a sharps container.

58. C: Lasix is the brand name for furosemide. The other three medications listed are generic names. Amlodipine is the generic name for Norvasc, bisoprolol is the generic for SANDOZ, and fluticasone is the generic name for Flovent.

59. C: A Nurse Aide Registry is maintained by all 50 states and the District of Columbia, and each has individuals or departments assigned to investigate complaints about nurse aides. Long-term care facilities are required to verify that an individual applying for a position as a nurse aide is certified and has met competency requirements prior to employment. The registry provides information about the individual regarding education, work experience, and any substantiated findings of abuse, neglect, or misappropriation of property (these findings preclude an individual from employment). Copies of disciplinary actions may be available. While state laws may vary somewhat, generally nurse aides must report employment in order to maintain current status. Nurse aides who have been unemployed for extended periods (typically 24 months) may need to take a competency test before certification renewal and listing on the Registry.

60. C: Although still an adverse event reporting system, the Vaccines Adverse Event Reporting System (VAERS) is used to report adverse events associated with vaccines, not medications. VAERS is a collaboration between the FDA and CDC. Similar to the FDA Adverse Event Reporting System (FAERS), VAERS collects and analyzes postmarketing safety information from reports of adverse events following the administration of vaccines. MedWatch is the FDA's medical product safety reporting program for health professionals, patients, and consumers. MedWatch collects, analyzes, and publishes safety reports for FDA-regulated products, such as prescription and OTC medicines, biologics, medical devices, combination products, nutritional products (supplements, medical food, and infant formula), cosmetics, and foods. The ISMP established a voluntary error-reporting program called Medication Error Reporting and Prevention (MERP) in which information is collected anonymously to learn about and analyze medication errors.

How to Overcome Test Anxiety

Just the thought of taking a test is enough to make most people a little nervous. A test is an important event that can have a long-term impact on your future, so it's important to take it seriously and it's natural to feel anxious about performing well. But just because anxiety is normal, that doesn't mean that it's helpful in test taking, or that you should simply accept it as part of your life. Anxiety can have a variety of effects. These effects can be mild, like making you feel slightly nervous, or severe, like blocking your ability to focus or remember even a simple detail.

If you experience test anxiety—whether severe or mild—it's important to know how to beat it. To discover this, first you need to understand what causes test anxiety.

Causes of Test Anxiety

While we often think of anxiety as an uncontrollable emotional state, it can actually be caused by simple, practical things. One of the most common causes of test anxiety is that a person does not feel adequately prepared for their test. This feeling can be the result of many different issues such as poor study habits or lack of organization, but the most common culprit is time management. Starting to study too late, failing to organize your study time to cover all of the material, or being distracted while you study will mean that you're not well prepared for the test. This may lead to cramming the night before, which will cause you to be physically and mentally exhausted for the test. Poor time management also contributes to feelings of stress, fear, and hopelessness as you realize you are not well prepared but don't know what to do about it.

Other times, test anxiety is not related to your preparation for the test but comes from unresolved fear. This may be a past failure on a test, or poor performance on tests in general. It may come from comparing yourself to others who seem to be performing better or from the stress of living up to expectations. Anxiety may be driven by fears of the future—how failure on this test would affect your educational and career goals. These fears are often completely irrational, but they can still negatively impact your test performance.

Elements of Test Anxiety

As mentioned earlier, test anxiety is considered to be an emotional state, but it has physical and mental components as well. Sometimes you may not even realize that you are suffering from test anxiety until you notice the physical symptoms. These can include trembling hands, rapid heartbeat, sweating, nausea, and tense muscles. Extreme anxiety may lead to fainting or vomiting. Obviously, any of these symptoms can have a negative impact on testing. It is important to recognize them as soon as they begin to occur so that you can address the problem before it damages your performance.

The mental components of test anxiety include trouble focusing and inability to remember learned information. During a test, your mind is on high alert, which can help you recall information and stay focused for an extended period of time. However, anxiety interferes with your mind's natural processes, causing you to blank out, even on the questions you know well. The strain of testing during anxiety makes it difficult to stay focused, especially on a test that may take several hours. Extreme anxiety can take a huge mental toll, making it difficult not only to recall test information but even to understand the test questions or pull your thoughts together.

Effects of Test Anxiety

Test anxiety is like a disease—if left untreated, it will get progressively worse. Anxiety leads to poor performance, and this reinforces the feelings of fear and failure, which in turn lead to poor performances on subsequent tests. It can grow from a mild nervousness to a crippling condition. If allowed to progress, test anxiety can have a big impact on your schooling, and consequently on your future.

Test anxiety can spread to other parts of your life. Anxiety on tests can become anxiety in any stressful situation, and blanking on a test can turn into panicking in a job situation. But fortunately, you don't have to let anxiety rule your testing and determine your grades. There are a number of relatively simple steps you can take to move past anxiety and function normally on a test and in the rest of life.

Physical Steps for Beating Test Anxiety

While test anxiety is a serious problem, the good news is that it can be overcome. It doesn't have to control your ability to think and remember information. While it may take time, you can begin taking steps today to beat anxiety.

Just as your first hint that you may be struggling with anxiety comes from the physical symptoms, the first step to treating it is also physical. Rest is crucial for having a clear, strong mind. If you are tired, it is much easier to give in to anxiety. But if you establish good sleep habits, your body and mind will be ready to perform optimally, without the strain of exhaustion. Additionally, sleeping well helps you to retain information better, so you're more likely to recall the answers when you see the test questions.

Getting good sleep means more than going to bed on time. It's important to allow your brain time to relax. Take study breaks from time to time so it doesn't get overworked, and don't study right before bed. Take time to rest your mind before trying to rest your body, or you may find it difficult to fall asleep.

Along with sleep, other aspects of physical health are important in preparing for a test. Good nutrition is vital for good brain function. Sugary foods and drinks may give a burst of energy but this burst is followed by a crash, both physically and emotionally. Instead, fuel your body with protein and vitamin-rich foods.

Also, drink plenty of water. Dehydration can lead to headaches and exhaustion, especially if your brain is already under stress from the rigors of the test. Particularly if your test is a long one, drink water during the breaks. And if possible, take an energy-boosting snack to eat between sections.

Along with sleep and diet, a third important part of physical health is exercise. Maintaining a steady workout schedule is helpful, but even taking 5-minute study breaks to walk can help get your blood pumping faster and clear your head. Exercise also releases endorphins, which contribute to a positive feeling and can help combat test anxiety.

When you nurture your physical health, you are also contributing to your mental health. If your body is healthy, your mind is much more likely to be healthy as well. So take time to rest, nourish your body with healthy food and water, and get moving as much as possible. Taking these physical steps will make you stronger and more able to take the mental steps necessary to overcome test anxiety.

Mental Steps for Beating Test Anxiety

Working on the mental side of test anxiety can be more challenging, but as with the physical side, there are clear steps you can take to overcome it. As mentioned earlier, test anxiety often stems from lack of preparation, so the obvious solution is to prepare for the test. Effective studying may be the most important weapon you have for beating test anxiety, but you can and should employ several other mental tools to combat fear.

First, boost your confidence by reminding yourself of past success—tests or projects that you aced. If you're putting as much effort into preparing for this test as you did for those, there's no reason you should expect to fail here. Work hard to prepare; then trust your preparation.

Second, surround yourself with encouraging people. It can be helpful to find a study group, but be sure that the people you're around will encourage a positive attitude. If you spend time with others who are anxious or cynical, this will only contribute to your own anxiety. Look for others who are motivated to study hard from a desire to succeed, not from a fear of failure.

Third, reward yourself. A test is physically and mentally tiring, even without anxiety, and it can be helpful to have something to look forward to. Plan an activity following the test, regardless of the outcome, such as going to a movie or getting ice cream.

When you are taking the test, if you find yourself beginning to feel anxious, remind yourself that you know the material. Visualize successfully completing the test. Then take a few deep, relaxing breaths and return to it. Work through the questions carefully but with confidence, knowing that you are capable of succeeding.

Developing a healthy mental approach to test taking will also aid in other areas of life. Test anxiety affects more than just the actual test—it can be damaging to your mental health and even contribute to depression. It's important to beat test anxiety before it becomes a problem for more than testing.

Study Strategy

Being prepared for the test is necessary to combat anxiety, but what does being prepared look like? You may study for hours on end and still not feel prepared. What you need is a strategy for test prep. The next few pages outline our recommended steps to help you plan out and conquer the challenge of preparation.

Step 1: Scope Out the Test

Learn everything you can about the format (multiple choice, essay, etc.) and what will be on the test. Gather any study materials, course outlines, or sample exams that may be available. Not only will this help you to prepare, but knowing what to expect can help to alleviate test anxiety.

Step 2: Map Out the Material

Look through the textbook or study guide and make note of how many chapters or sections it has. Then divide these over the time you have. For example, if a book has 15 chapters and you have five days to study, you need to cover three chapters each day. Even better, if you have the time, leave an extra day at the end for overall review after you have gone through the material in depth.

If time is limited, you may need to prioritize the material. Look through it and make note of which sections you think you already have a good grasp on, and which need review. While you are studying, skim quickly through the familiar sections and take more time on the challenging parts.

Write out your plan so you don't get lost as you go. Having a written plan also helps you feel more in control of the study, so anxiety is less likely to arise from feeling overwhelmed at the amount to cover.

Step 3: Gather Your Tools

Decide what study method works best for you. Do you prefer to highlight in the book as you study and then go back over the highlighted portions? Or do you type out notes of the important information? Or is it helpful to make flashcards that you can carry with you? Assemble the pens, index cards, highlighters, post-it notes, and any other materials you may need so you won't be distracted by getting up to find things while you study.

If you're having a hard time retaining the information or organizing your notes, experiment with different methods. For example, try color-coding by subject with colored pens, highlighters, or post-it notes. If you learn better by hearing, try recording yourself reading your notes so you can listen while in the car, working out, or simply sitting at your desk. Ask a friend to quiz you from your flashcards, or try teaching someone the material to solidify it in your mind.

Step 4: Create Your Environment

It's important to avoid distractions while you study. This includes both the obvious distractions like visitors and the subtle distractions like an uncomfortable chair (or a too-comfortable couch that makes you want to fall asleep). Set up the best study environment possible: good lighting and a comfortable work area. If background music helps you focus, you may want to turn it on, but otherwise keep the room quiet. If you are using a computer to take notes, be sure you don't have any other windows open, especially applications like social media, games, or anything else that could distract you. Silence your phone and turn off notifications. Be sure to keep water close by so you stay hydrated while you study (but avoid unhealthy drinks and snacks).

Also, take into account the best time of day to study. Are you freshest first thing in the morning? Try to set aside some time then to work through the material. Is your mind clearer in the afternoon or evening? Schedule your study session then. Another method is to study at the same time of day that you will take the test, so that your brain gets used to working on the material at that time and will be ready to focus at test time.

Step 5: Study!

Once you have done all the study preparation, it's time to settle into the actual studying. Sit down, take a few moments to settle your mind so you can focus, and begin to follow your study plan. Don't give in to distractions or let yourself procrastinate. This is your time to prepare so you'll be ready to fearlessly approach the test. Make the most of the time and stay focused.

Of course, you don't want to burn out. If you study too long you may find that you're not retaining the information very well. Take regular study breaks. For example, taking five minutes out of every hour to walk briskly, breathing deeply and swinging your arms, can help your mind stay fresh.

As you get to the end of each chapter or section, it's a good idea to do a quick review. Remind yourself of what you learned and work on any difficult parts. When you feel that you've mastered the material, move on to the next part. At the end of your study session, briefly skim through your notes again.

But while review is helpful, cramming last minute is NOT. If at all possible, work ahead so that you won't need to fit all your study into the last day. Cramming overloads your brain with more information than it can process and retain, and your tired mind may struggle to recall even previously learned information when it is overwhelmed with last-minute study. Also, the urgent nature of cramming and the stress placed on your brain contribute to anxiety. You'll be more likely to go to the test feeling unprepared and having trouble thinking clearly.

So don't cram, and don't stay up late before the test, even just to review your notes at a leisurely pace. Your brain needs rest more than it needs to go over the information again. In fact, plan to finish your studies by noon or early afternoon the day before the test. Give your brain the rest of the day to relax or focus on other things, and get a good night's sleep. Then you will be fresh for the test and better able to recall what you've studied.

Step 6: Take a Practice Test

Many courses offer sample tests, either online or in the study materials. This is an excellent resource to check whether you have mastered the material, as well as to prepare for the test format and environment.

Check the test format ahead of time: the number of questions, the type (multiple choice, free response, etc.), and the time limit. Then create a plan for working through them. For example, if you have 30 minutes to take a 60-question test, your limit is 30 seconds per question. Spend less time on the questions you know well so that you can take more time on the difficult ones.

If you have time to take several practice tests, take the first one open book, with no time limit. Work through the questions at your own pace and make sure you fully understand them. Gradually work up to taking a test under test conditions: sit at a desk with all study materials put away and set a timer. Pace yourself to make sure you finish the test with time to spare and go back to check your answers if you have time.

After each test, check your answers. On the questions you missed, be sure you understand why you missed them. Did you misread the question (tests can use tricky wording)? Did you forget the information? Or was it something you hadn't learned? Go back and study any shaky areas that the practice tests reveal.

Taking these tests not only helps with your grade, but also aids in combating test anxiety. If you're already used to the test conditions, you're less likely to worry about it, and working through tests until you're scoring well gives you a confidence boost. Go through the practice tests until you feel comfortable, and then you can go into the test knowing that you're ready for it.

Test Tips

On test day, you should be confident, knowing that you've prepared well and are ready to answer the questions. But aside from preparation, there are several test day strategies you can employ to maximize your performance.

First, as stated before, get a good night's sleep the night before the test (and for several nights before that, if possible). Go into the test with a fresh, alert mind rather than staying up late to study.

Try not to change too much about your normal routine on the day of the test. It's important to eat a nutritious breakfast, but if you normally don't eat breakfast at all, consider eating just a protein bar. If you're a coffee drinker, go ahead and have your normal coffee. Just make sure you time it so that the caffeine doesn't wear off right in the middle of your test. Avoid sugary beverages, and drink enough water to stay hydrated but not so much that you need a restroom break 10 minutes into the test. If your test isn't first thing in the morning, consider going for a walk or doing a light workout before the test to get your blood flowing.

Allow yourself enough time to get ready, and leave for the test with plenty of time to spare so you won't have the anxiety of scrambling to arrive in time. Another reason to be early is to select a good seat. It's helpful to sit away from doors and windows, which can be distracting. Find a good seat, get out your supplies, and settle your mind before the test begins.

When the test begins, start by going over the instructions carefully, even if you already know what to expect. Make sure you avoid any careless mistakes by following the directions.

Then begin working through the questions, pacing yourself as you've practiced. If you're not sure on an answer, don't spend too much time on it, and don't let it shake your confidence. Either skip it and come back later, or eliminate as many wrong answers as possible and guess among the remaining ones. Don't dwell on these questions as you continue—put them out of your mind and focus on what lies ahead.

Be sure to read all of the answer choices, even if you're sure the first one is the right answer. Sometimes you'll find a better one if you keep reading. But don't second-guess yourself if you do immediately know the answer. Your gut instinct is usually right. Don't let test anxiety rob you of the information you know.

If you have time at the end of the test (and if the test format allows), go back and review your answers. Be cautious about changing any, since your first instinct tends to be correct, but make sure you didn't misread any of the questions or accidentally mark the wrong answer choice. Look over any you skipped and make an educated guess.

At the end, leave the test feeling confident. You've done your best, so don't waste time worrying about your performance or wishing you could change anything. Instead, celebrate the successful completion of this test. And finally, use this test to learn how to deal with anxiety even better next time.

Review Video: Test Anxiety
Visit mometrix.com/academy and enter code: 100340

Important Qualification

Not all anxiety is created equal. If your test anxiety is causing major issues in your life beyond the classroom or testing center, or if you are experiencing troubling physical symptoms related to your anxiety, it may be a sign of a serious physiological or psychological condition. If this sounds like your situation, we strongly encourage you to seek professional help.

Online Resources

Due to our efforts to try to keep this book to a manageable length, we've created a link that will give you access to all of your online resources:

mometrix.com/resources719/mace

It's Your Moment, Let's Celebrate It!

Share your story @mometrixtestpreparation